Advanced Automotive Fault Diagnosis

003

03

13

Advanced Automotive Fault Diagnosis

Tom Denton *BA, AMSAE, AMITRE, Cert.Ed.*

Senior Lecturer in Motor Vehicle Engineering, Colchester Institute, and Associate Lecturer, Open University, UK

ARNOLD

A member of the Hodder Headline Group
LONDON

First published in Great Britain in 2000 by
Arnold, a member of the Hodder Headline Group,
338 Euston Road, London NW1 3BH

http://www.arnoldpublishers.com

British Library Cataloging in Publication Data
A catalogue record for this book is available from the British Library

Library of Congress Cataloging-in-Publication Data
A catalog record for this book is available from the Library of Congress

ISBN 0 340 74123 6

1 2 3 4 5 6 7 8 9 10

Production Editor: Rada Radojicic
Production Controller: Priya Gohil
Cover Design: Terry Griffiths

Typeset by J&L Composition Ltd, Filey, North Yorkshire
Printed and bound in Great Britain by The Bath Press, Bath

What do you think about this book? Or any other Arnold title?
Please send your comments to feedback.arnold@hodder.co.uk

Contents

Preface

The aspect I enjoy most about working on vehicles is being able to diagnose a fault that has beaten others! This skill takes a few years to develop but it is worth the effort. Diagnostic work is much like that of a detective solving a difficult case; all the clues are usually there – if you know where to look.

To help you learn 'where to look', this book combines some aspects of automotive technology covered in my other books. However, it goes much further with a new approach to the art of diagnostics as a science. On and off-board diagnostics are included as is a section on what equipment you will need.

The skills needed to be a good diagnostic technician are many and varied. For one job you may need to listen to a rumbling noise as the car corners, for another you may need to interpret an oscilloscope waveform!

As vehicles continue to become more complicated, particularly in the area of electronics, there will be a greater need for technicians with good diagnostic skills. This could be you and you should be paid well!

Look on the bright side of having more complicated technology on vehicles – fewer 'home mechanics' and more work for you and me!

Tom Denton
2000

P.S. Comments, questions and contributions are always welcome at my web site: http://www.automotive-technology.co.uk. You will also find lots of useful information, updates and news about new books as well as automotive software and web links.

Acknowledgements

I am grateful to the following companies who have supplied information and/or permission to reproduce photographs and/or diagrams. Figure numbers are as listed:

AA Photo Library 4.2, 4.4, 4.7, 4.14, 4.23
Autodata Ltd. 2.14, 2.15, 2.16
Autologic Data Systems Ltd. 2.11, 2.12, 2.13, 4.3, 7.37
Eberspaecher GmbH 4.10, 4.11
Emitec GmbH 7.25
Ford Motor Company Ltd. 4.17, 4.18, 4.19, 4.20, 4.24, 4.34, 4.35, 4.36, 4.37, 4.41, 4.44, 8.20
GenRad Ltd. 3.8, 3.14, 3.15
Hella UK Ltd. 6.27, 6.28
Institute of Road Transport Engineers
Jaguar Cars Ltd. 6.32
Kavlico Corp. 5.5, 5.15
Lucas Ltd. 3.3, 3.12, 4.8, 5.9, 5.29, 6.44, 7.4, 7.24
LucasVarity Ltd. 5.24, 5.34, 6.2, 6.3, 6.5, 6.8, 7.33
Mazda Cars UK Ltd. 6.24
NGK Spark Plugs UK Ltd. 7.11, 7.13
Pioneer Radio Ltd. 6.45
Renault UK Ltd. 8.19

Robert Bosch GmbH 4.29, 6.1, 6.9, 6.12, 7.3, 7.40
Robert Bosch UK Ltd. 7.10, 8.10
Robert Bosch Press Photos 3.1, 5.10, 5.18, 5.19, 6.15, 7.8, 7.27, 7.28, 7.30, 7.31, 7.32, 7.38, 7.39, 7.41, 7.44, 8.4, 8.8, 8.13
Rover Cars Ltd. 4.26, 4.27, 4.28, 4.32, 4.42, 5.3, 6.26, 6.55, 6.59, 6.65, 7.7
Saab Cars UK Ltd.
Scandmec UK Ltd. 6.72
Snap-on Tools Inc. 3.9, 3.10, 4.6, 4.9, 4.39, 7.12
Sun Electric UK Ltd. 4.30, 7.34
Sykes-Pickavant Ltd. 3.11, 4.13, 4.15, 7.35
Valeo UK Ltd. 4.16, 5.28, 6.11, 6.34, 6.63, 6.67, 6.71
ZF Servomatic Ltd. 4.22, 4.33

Many if not all the companies here have good web pages. You will find a link to them from my site. Thanks again to the listed companies. If I have used any information or mentioned a company name that is not noted here, please accept my apologies and acknowledgments.

Last but by no means least, thank you once again to my family: Vanda, Malcolm and Beth.

1

Introduction

1.1 'If it ain't broke, don't fix it!'

1.1.1 What is needed to find faults?

Finding the problem when complex automotive systems go wrong is easy, if you have the necessary knowledge. This knowledge is in two parts:

- understanding of the system in which the problem exists;
- the ability to apply a logical diagnostic routine.

It is also important to be clear about two definitions:

- **symptom(s)** what the user/operator/repairer of the system (vehicle or whatever) notices;
- **fault** the error in the system that causes the symptom(s).

'If it is not broken then do not go to the trouble of repairing it,' is the translation of this main section heading! It's a fair comment but if a system is not operating to its optimum then it should be repaired. This is where the skills come in to play. It is necessary to recognise that something is not operating correctly by applying your knowledge of the system, and then by applying this knowledge further and combining it with the skills of diagnostics, to be able to find out why.

Each main chapter of this book includes a basic explanation of the vehicle system followed by diagnostic techniques that are particularly appropriate for that area. Examples of faultfinding charts are also included. In the main, references will be to generic systems rather than to specific vehicles or marques. For specific details about a particular vehicle or system the manufacturer's information is the main source. Alternatively 'Autodata' produce a fine range of books; visit www.autodata.com for more details. 'Autologic' produce a 'workshop manual on a CD'; visit www.autologicdatasystems.co.uk for more details.

The knowledge requirement and the necessity for diagnostic skills are further illustrated in the next chapter.

Figure 1.1 shows a diagnostic procedure in action!

Figure 1.1 Diagnostics in action

1.1.2 Heavy or light vehicles?

An important note about diagnostics is that the general principles or techniques can be applied to *any* system, physical or otherwise. As far as heavy or light vehicles are concerned then this is definitely the case. As discussed earlier, there is a need for knowledge of the particular system, but diagnostic skills are transferable.

1.2 Safe working practices

1.2.1 Introduction

Safe working practices in relation to diagnostic procedures and indeed any work on a vehicle are essential – for your safety as well as that of others. You only have to follow two rules to be safe:

● use your common sense – don't fool about;
● if in doubt – seek help.

Further, always wear appropriate personal protective equipment (PPE) when working on vehicles.

The following section lists some particular risks when working with electricity or electrical systems, together with suggestions for reducing them. This is known as risk assessment.

1.2.2 Risk assessment and reduction

The following table notes some identified risks involved with working on vehicles. It is by no means exhaustive but serves as a good guide.

Identified risk	Reducing the risk
Battery acid	Sulphuric acid is corrosive so always use good PPE – in this case overalls and if necessary rubber gloves. A rubber apron is ideal, as are goggles if working with batteries a lot
Electric shock	Ignition HT (high tension, which simply means high voltage) is the most likely place to suffer a shock, up to 25 000 V is quite normal. Use insulated tools if it is necessary to work on HT circuits with the engine running. Note that high voltages are also present on circuits containing windings due to back emf (electromotive force) as they are switched off; a few hundred volts is common. Mains supplied power tools and their leads should be in good condition and using an earth leakage trip is highly recommended
Exhaust gases	Suitable extraction must be used if the

engine is running indoors. Remember it is not just the carbon monoxide (CO) that might make you ill or even kill you, other exhaust components could cause asthma or even cancer

Fire	Do not smoke when working on a vehicle. Fuel leaks must be attended to immediately. Remember the triangle of fire – (heat/fuel/oxygen) – don't let the three sides come together
Moving loads	Only lift what is comfortable for you; ask for help if necessary and/or use lifting equipment. As a general guide, do not lift on your own if it feels too heavy!
Raising or lifting vehicles	Apply brakes and/or chock the wheels and when raising a vehicle on a jack or drive on lift. Only jack under substantial chassis and suspension structures. Use axle stands in case the jack fails
Running engines	Do not wear loose clothing; good overalls are ideal. Keep the keys in your possession when working on an engine to prevent others starting it. Take extra care if working near running drive belts
Short circuits	Use a jump lead with an in-line fuse to prevent damage due to a short when testing. Disconnect the battery (earth lead off first and back on last) if any danger of a short exists. A very high current can flow from a vehicle battery, it will burn you as well as the vehicle
Skin problems	Use a good barrier cream and/or latex gloves. Wash skin and clothes regularly

1.3 Terminology

1.3.1 Introduction

The terminology included in the following tables is provided to ensure that we are talking the same language. These tables are provided just as a simple reference source.

1.3.2 Diagnostic terminology

Symptom	The effect of a fault noticed by the driver, user or technician
Fault	The root cause of a symptom/problem
Diagnostics	The process of tracing a fault by means of its symptoms, applying knowledge and analysing test results
Knowledge	The understanding of a system that is required to diagnose faults
Logical procedure	A step by step method used to ensure nothing is missed
Report	A standard format for the presentation of results

1.3.3 General terminology

System	A collection of components that carry out a function
Efficiency	This is a simple measure of any system. It can be scientific for example if the power out of a system is less then the power put in, its percentage efficiency can be determined ($P_{out}/P_{in} \times 100\%$). This could, for example, be given as 80%. In a less scientific example, a vehicle using more fuel than normal is said to be inefficient
Noise	Emanation of sound from a system that is either simply unwanted or is not the normal sound that should be produced
Active	Any system that is in operation all the time (steering for example)
Passive	A system that waits for an event before it is activated (an air bag is a good example)
Short circuit	An electrical conductor is touching something that it should not be (usually another conductor or the chassis)
Open circuit	A circuit that is broken (a switched off switch is an open circuit)
High resistance	In relation to electricity, this is part of a circuit that has become more difficult for the electricity to get through. In a mechanical system a partially blocked pipe would have a resistance to the flow of fluid
Worn	This word works better with further additions such as: worn to excess, worn out of tolerance, or even, worn, but still within tolerance!
Quote	To make an estimate of or give exact information on the price of a part or service. A quotation may often be considered to be legally binding
Estimate	A statement of the expected cost of a certain job (e.g. a service or repairs) An estimate is normally a best guess and is not legally binding
Dodgy, knackered or @#%&*!	Words often used to describe a system or component, but they mean nothing! Get used to describing things so that misunderstandings are eliminated

1.4 Report writing

1.4.1 Introduction

As technicians you may be called on to produce a report for a customer. Also, if you are involved in research of some kind it is important to be able to present results in a professional way. The following sections describe the main headings that a report will often need to contain together with an example report based on the performance testing of a vehicle alternator.

Laying out results in a standard format is the best way to ensure that all the important and required aspects of the test have been covered. Keep in mind that the report should convey clearly to another person what has been done. Further, a 'qualified' person should be able to extract enough information to be able to repeat the test – and check your findings! Use clear simple language remembering that in some cases the intended audience may not be as technically competent as you are.

1.4.2 Main headings of a report

The following suggestions for the headings of a professional report will cover most requirements but can of course be added to or subtracted from if necessary. After each heading I have included brief notes on what should be included.

Contents

If the report is more than about five pages, a list of contents with page numbers will help the reader find his/her way through it.

Introduction

Explain the purpose of what has been done and set the general scene.

Test criteria

Define the limits within which the test was carried out. For example, temperature range or speed settings.

Facilities/resources

State or describe what equipment was used. For example: 'A "*Revitup*" engine dynamometer, model number *C3PO* was used for the consumption test'.

Test procedures

Explain here exactly what was done to gain the results. In this part of the report it is very important not to leave out any details.

Measured results

Present the results in a way that is easy to interpret. A simple table of figures may be appropriate. If the trend of the results or a comparison is important, a graph may be better. Pictures of results or oscilloscope waveforms may be needed. If necessary a very complex table of results from which you draw out a few key figures, could be presented as an appendix. You should also note the accuracy of any figures presented (± 0.5% for example).

Analysis of results

This is the part where you should comment on the results obtained. For example, if say a fuel consumption test was carried out on two vehicles, a graph comparing one result to the other may be appropriate. Comments should be added if necessary, such as any anomaly that could have affected the results (change of wind direction for example).

Conclusions/comments/observations

Note here any further tests that may be necessary. Conclude that device X does perform better than device Y – if it did! If appropriate, add observations such as how device Y performed better under the set conditions, but under other circumstances the results could have been different. Comment on the method used if necessary.

Forecast

If necessary comment on how the 'item' tested will continue to perform based on the existing data.

Appendices

Detailed pages of results that would 'clog up' the main report or background material such as leaflets relating to the test equipment.

1.4.3 Example report

An example report is presented here relating to a simple alternator test where its actual output is to be compared to the rated output. Minimal details are included so as to illustrate the main points.

Introduction

A '*Rotato*' 12 V alternator was tested under normal operating conditions to check its maximum output. The manufacturer's specifications stated that the alternator, when hot, should produce 95 A at 6000 rev/min.

Test criteria

- Start at room temperature.

- Run alternator at 3000 rev/min, 30 A output for 10 minutes.
- Run alternator at 6000 rev/min, maximum output. Check reading every 30 seconds for 10 minutes.
- Run alternator at 6000 rev/min, maximum output for a further 20 minutes to ensure that output reading is stable.

Facilities/resources

A '*Krypton*' test bench model *R2D2* was used to drive the alternator. The test bench revcounter was used and a '*Flake*' digital meter fitted with a 200 A shunt was used to measure the output. A variable resistance load was employed.

Test procedures

The alternator was run for 10 minutes at 3000 rev/min and the load adjusted to cause an output of 30 A. This was to ensure that it was at a nominal operating temperature. The normal fan was kept in place during the test.

Speed was then increased to 6000 rev/min and the load adjusted to achieve the maximum possible output. The load was further adjusted as required to keep the maximum possible output in case the load resistance changed due to temperature. Measurements were taken every 30 seconds for a period of 10 minutes.

Measured results

Speed held constant at 6000 (± 200) rev/min.
Room temperature (18°C).

Time (±1 s)	0	30	60	90	120	150	180	210	240	270
Output (± 0.2 A)	101	100	99	99	98	98	98	98	98	98

Time (±1 s)	300	330	360	390	420	450	480	510	540	570	600
Output (± 0.2 A)	97	97	96	96	96	96	96	96	96	96	96

To ensure that the alternator output had stabilised it was kept running for a further 20 minutes at full output. It continued to hold at 96 A.

Analysis of results

Figure 1.2 shows the results in graphical format.

Conclusions

The manufacturer's claims were validated. The device exceeded the rated output by 6% at the start of the test and under continuous operation at full load, continued to exceed the rated output by 1%.

Figure 1.2 Results presented in graphical format

The maximum duration of this test was 20 minutes. It is possible, however, that the device would increase in temperature and the output may fall further after prolonged operation. Fur-

ther tests are necessary to check this. Overall the device performed in excess of its rated output. (Sign and date the report)
Tom Denton, Saturday, 1st Jan 2000

2

Diagnostic techniques

2.1 Introduction

2.1.1 Logic

Diagnostics or faultfinding is a fundamental part of an automotive technician's work. The subject of diagnostics does not relate to individual areas of the vehicle. If your knowledge of a vehicle system is at a suitable level, then you will use the same logical process for diagnosing the fault, whatever the system.

2.1.2 Information

Information and data are available for carrying out many forms of diagnostic work. The data may come as a book or on CD. This information is vital and will ensure that you find the fault – particularly if you have developed the diagnostic skills to go with it. Faultfinding charts and specific examples are presented in later chapters.

The general type of information available is as follows:

- engine diagnostics, testing and tuning;
- servicing, repairs and times;
- fuel and ignition systems and carburettor;
- auto electrics;
- ABS diagnostics;
- component location;
- body repairs, tracking and tyres.

2.1.3 Where to stop?

This is one of the most difficult skills to learn. It is also one of the most important. The secret is twofold:

- know your own limitations – it is not possible to be good at everything;
- leave systems alone where you could cause more damage or even injury – for example air bag circuits.

Often with the best of intentions, a person new to diagnostics will not only fail to find the fault but introduce more faults into the system in the process.

I would suggest you learn your own strengths and weaknesses; you may be confident and good at dealing with mechanical system problems but less so when electronics is involved. Of course you may be just the opposite of this.

Remember that diagnostic skill is in two parts – the knowledge of the system and the ability to apply diagnostics. If you do not yet fully understand a system – leave it alone!

2.2 Diagnostic process

2.2.1 Six-stage process

A key check list – the six stages of fault diagnosis – is given in Table 2.1.

Here is a very simple example to illustrate the diagnostic process. The reported fault is excessive use of engine oil.

1. Question the customer to find out how much oil is being used (is it excessive?).
2. Examine the vehicle for oil leaks and blue smoke from the exhaust.
3. If leaks are found the engine could still be burning oil but leaks would be a likely cause.
4. A compression test, if the results were acceptable, would indicate the leak to be the most likely fault. Clean down the engine and run for a while. The leak will show up better.
5. Change a gasket or seal, etc.
6. Run through an inspection of the vehicle systems particularly associated with the engine.

Table 2.1

1. Verify the fault
2. Collect further information
3. Evaluate the evidence
4. Carry out further tests in a logical sequence
5. Rectify the problem
6. Check all systems

Double check the fault has been rectified and that you have not caused any further problems.

The stages of faultfinding will be used extensively to illustrate how a logical process can be applied to any situation.

2.2.2 The art of diagnostics

The knowledge needed for accurate diagnostics is in two parts:

1. understanding of the system in which the problem exists;
2. having the ability to apply a logical diagnostic routine.

The knowledge requirement and use of diagnostic skills can now be illustrated with a very simple example. After connecting a hose pipe and turning on the tap, no water comes out of the end! Your knowledge of this system tells you that water should come out providing the tap is on, because the pressure from a tap pushes water through the pipe, and so on. This is where your diagnostic skills become essential. The following stages are now required.

1. Confirm that no water is coming out by looking down the end of the pipe!
2. Does water come out of the other taps, or did it come out of this tap before you connected the hose?
3. Consider what this information tells you; for example, if the answer is '*Yes*' the hose must be blocked or kinked.
4. Walk the length of the pipe looking for a kink.
5. Straighten out the hose.
6. Check that water now comes out and that no other problems have been created.

Much simplified I accept, but the procedure you have just followed made the hose work and it is also guaranteed to find a fault in *any* system. It is easy to see how it works in connection with a hose pipe and I'm sure anybody could have found that fault (well most people anyway)! The higher skill is to be able to apply the same logical routine to more complex situations. The routine (Table 2.1) is represented by Figure 2.1. The loop will continue until the fault is located. I will now explain each of these steps further in relation to a more realistic automotive workshop situation – not that getting the hose to work is not important!

Often electrical faults are considered to be the

most difficult to diagnose – but this is not true. I will use a vehicle cooling system fault as an example here, but electrical systems will be covered in detail in later chapters. Remember that the diagnostic procedure can be applied to any problem, mechanical, electrical or even personal!

However, let's assume that the reported fault with the vehicle is overheating. As is quite common in many workshop situations that's all the information we have to start with. Now work through the six stages.

- **Stage 1** Take a quick look to check for obvious problems such as leaks, broken drive belts or lack of coolant. Run the vehicle and confirm that the fault exists. It could be the temperature gauge for example.
- **Stage 2** Is the driver available to give more information? For example, does the engine overheat all the time or just when working hard? Check records, if available, of previous work done to the vehicle.
- **Stage 3** Consider what you now know. Does this allow you to narrow down what the cause of the fault could be? For example, if the vehicle overheats all the time and it had recently had a new cylinder head gasket fitted, would you be suspicious about this? Don't let two and two make five, but do let it act as a pointer. Remember that in the science of *logical* diagnostics, two and two always makes four! However, until you know this for certain then play the best odds to narrow down the fault.
- **Stage 4** The further tests carried out would now be directed by your thinking at stage three. You don't yet know if the fault is a leaking head gasket, the thermostat stuck closed or some other problem. Playing the odds, a cooling system pressure test would probably be the next test. If the pressure increases when the engine is running then it is likely to be a head gasket or similar problem. If no pressure increase then move on to the next test and so on. After each test go back to stage 3 and evaluate what you know, *not* what you don't know!
- **Stage 5** Let's assume the problem was a thermostat stuck closed – replace it and top up the coolant, etc.
- **Stage 6** Check that the system is now working. Also check that you have not caused any further problems such as leaks or loose wires. This example is simplified a little, but like the

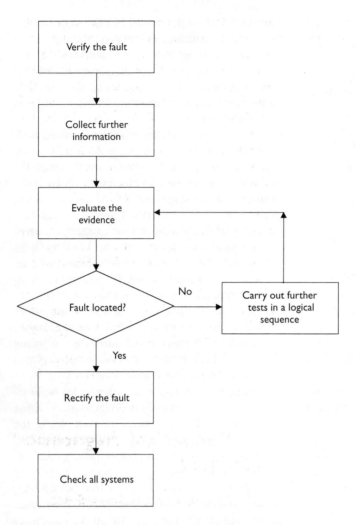

Figure 2.1 Diagnostic routine

hose pipe problem it is the sequence that matters, particularly the '*stop and think*' at stage 3. It is often possible to go directly to the cause of the fault at this stage, providing that you have an adequate knowledge of how the system works.

2.2.3 Summary

I have introduced the six-stage process of diagnostics, not so it should necessarily be used as a checklist but to illustrate the process that must be followed. Much more detail is required still, particular in relation to stages 3 and 4. The purpose of this set process is to ensure that 'we' work in a particular, logical way.

I would like to stress the need for a logical process again – with a quotation! '*Logic is the*

beginning of wisdom not the end.' (Spock to Valeris, Star Trek II)

2.3 Diagnostics on paper

2.3.1 Introduction

This section is again a way of changing the way you approach problems on a vehicle. The key message is that if you stop and think before 'pulling the car to pieces', it will often save a great deal of time. In other words, some of the diagnostic work can be done 'on paper' before we start on the vehicle. To illustrate this, the next section lists symptoms for three separate faults on a car and for each of these symptoms, three possible faults. All the faults are possible but in each case choose the 'most likely' option.

2.3.2 Examples

Symptoms	Possible faults
A The brake/stop lights are reported not operating. On checking it is confirmed that neither of the two bulbs or the row of high-mounted LEDs is operating as the pedal is pressed. All other systems work correctly	1. Two bulbs and 12 LEDs blown 2. Auxiliary systems relay open circuit 3. Brake light switch not closing
B An engine fitted with full management system tends to stall when running slowly. It runs well under all other conditions and the reported symptom is found to be intermittent	1. Fuel pump output pressure low 2. Idle control valve sticking 3. Engine speed sensor wire loose
C The off side dip beam headlight not operating. This is confirmed on examination and also noted is that the off side tail light does not work	1. Two bulbs blown 2. Main lighting fusible link blown 3. Short circuit between off side tail and dip beam lights

The most likely fault for example A, is number 3. It is possible that all the lights have blown but unlikely. It could not be the auxiliary relay because this would affect other systems.

For example B, the best answer would be number 2. It is possible that the pump pressure is low but this would be more likely to affect operation under other conditions. A loose wire on the engine speed sensor could cause the engine to stall but it would almost certainly cause misfire under other conditions.

The symptoms in C would suggest answer 1. The short circuit suggested as answer 3 would be more likely to cause lights and others to stay on rather that not work, equally the chance of a short between these two circuits is remote if not impossible. If the lighting fusible link were blown then none of the lights would operate.

The technique suggested here relates to stages 1 to 3 of the 'the six stages of fault diagnosis' process. By applying a little thought before even taking a screwdriver to the car, a lot of time can be saved. If the problems suggested in the previous table were real we would at least now be able to start looking in the right area for the fault.

2.3.3 How long is a piece of string?

Yes I know, twice the distance from the middle to one end! What I am really getting at here though is the issue about what is a valid reading/measurement and what is not – when com-pared to data. For example if the 'data book' says the resistance of the component should be between 60 and 90 Ω, what do you do when the measured value is 55 Ω? If the measured value was 0 Ω or 1000 Ω then the answer is easy – the component is faulty! However, when the value is very close you have to make a decision. In this case (55 Ω) it is very likely that the component is serviceable.

The decision over this type of issue is difficult and must in many cases be based on experience. As a general guide however, I would suggest that if the reading is in the right 'order of magnitude', then the component has a good chance of being OK. By this I mean that if the value falls within the correct range of 1s, 10s, 100s or 1000s, etc. then it is probably good.

Do notice that I have ensured that words or phrases such as 'probably', 'good chance' and 'very likely' have been used here! This is not just to make sure I have a get out clause; it is also to illustrate that diagnostic work can involve 'playing the best odds' – as long as this is within a logical process.

2.4 Mechanical diagnostic techniques

2.4.1 Check the obvious first!

Start *all* hands on diagnostic routines with 'hand and eye checks'. In other words look over the vehicle for obvious faults. For example, if automatic transmission fluid is leaking on to the floor then put this right before carrying out complicated stall tests. Here are some further suggestions that will at some point save you a lot of time.

● If the engine is blowing blue smoke out of the exhaust – consider the worth of tracing the cause of a tapping noise in the engine!
● When an engine will not start – check that there is fuel in the tank!

2.4.2 Noise, vibration and harshness

Noise, vibration and harshness (NVH) concerns have become more important as drivers have become more sensitive to these issues. Drivers have higher expectations of comfort levels. Noise, vibration and harshness issues are more noticeable due to reduced engine noise and better insulation in general. The main areas of the vehicle that produce NVH are:

- tyres;
- engine accessories;
- suspension;
- driveline.

It is necessary to isolate the NVH into its specific area(s) to allow more detailed diagnosis. A road test as outlined later is often the best method.

The five most common sources of non-axle noise are exhaust, tyres, roof racks, trim and mouldings, and transmission. Ensure that none of the following conditions is the cause of the noise before proceeding with a driveline strip down and diagnosis.

1. In certain conditions, the pitch of the exhaust may sound like gear noise or under other conditions like a wheel bearing rumble.
2. Tyres can produce a high pitched tread whine or roar, similar to gear noise. This is particularly the case for non-standard tyres.
3. Trim and mouldings can cause whistling or whining noises.
   Clunk may occur when the throttle is applied or released due to backlash somewhere in the driveline.
   Bearing rumble sounds like marbles being tumbled.

2.4.3 Noise conditions

Noise is very difficult to describe. However, the following are useful terms and are accompanied by suggestions as to when they are most likely to occur.

- Gear noise is typically a howling or whining due to gear damage or incorrect bearing pre-load. It can occur at various speeds and driving conditions, or it can be continuous.
- 'Chuckle' is a rattling noise that sounds like a stick held against the spokes of a spinning bicycle wheel. It usually occurs while decelerating.
- Knock is very similar to chuckle though it may be louder and occurs on acceleration or deceleration.

Check and rule out tyres, exhaust and trim items before any disassembly to diagnose and correct gear noise.

2.4.4 Vibration conditions

Clicking, popping or grinding noises may be noticeable at low speeds and be caused by the following:

- inner or outer CV joints worn (often due to lack of lubrication so check for split gaiters);
- loose drive shaft;
- another component contacting a drive shaft;
- damaged or incorrectly installed wheel bearing, brake or suspension component.

The following may cause vibration at normal road speeds:

- out-of-balance wheels;
- out-of-round tyres.

The following may cause shudder or vibration during acceleration:

- damaged power train/drive train mounts;
- excessively worn or damaged out-board or inboard CV joints.

The cause of noise can often be traced by first looking for leaks. A dry bearing or joint will produce significant noise.

1. Inspect the CV joint gaiters (boots) for cracks, tears or splits.
2. Inspect the underbody for any indication of grease splatter near the front wheel half shaft joint boots.
3. Inspect the in-board CV joint stub shaft bearing housing seal for leakage at the bearing housing.
4. Check the torque on the front axle wheel hub retainer.

2.4.5 Road test

A vehicle will produce a certain amount of noise! Some noise is acceptable and may be audible at certain speeds or under various driving conditions such as on a new road.

Carry out a thorough visual inspection of the vehicle before carrying out the road test. Keep in mind anything that is unusual. A key point is to *not* repair or adjust anything until the road test is carried out. Of course this does not apply if the condition could be dangerous or the vehicle will not start!

Establish a route that will be used for all diagnosis road tests. This allows you to get to know what is normal and what is not! The roads selected should have sections that are reasonably smooth, level and free of undulations as well as lesser quality sections needed to diagnose faults that only occur under particular conditions. A road that allows driving over a range of speeds is best. Gravel, dirt or bumpy roads are unsuitable because of the additional noise they produce.

If a customer complains of a noise or vibration on a particular road and only on a particular road, the source of the concern may be the road surface. Test the vehicle on the same type of road.

Make a visual inspection as part of the preliminary diagnosis routine prior to the road test; note anything that does not look right.

1. Tyre pressures, but do not adjust them yet.
2. Leaking fluids.
3. Loose nuts and bolts.
4. Bright spots where components may be rubbing against each other.
5. Check the luggage compartment for unusual loads.

Road test the vehicle and define the condition by reproducing it several times during the road test. During the road test recreate the following conditions.

1. **Normal driving speeds of 20 to 80 km/h (15 to 50 mph)** with light acceleration, a moaning noise may be heard and possibly a vibration is felt in the front floor pan. It may get worse at a certain engine speed or load.
2. **Acceleration/deceleration** with slow acceleration and deceleration, a shake is sometimes noticed through the steering wheel seats, front floor pan, front door trim panels, etc.
3. **High speed** a vibration may felt in the front floor pan or seats with no visible shake, but with an accompanying sound or rumble, buzz, hum, drone or booming noise. Coast with the clutch pedal down or gear lever in neutral and engine idling. If vibration is still evident, it may be related to wheels, tyres, front brake discs, wheel hubs or wheel bearings.
4. **Engine rev/min sensitive** a vibration may be felt whenever the engine reaches a particular speed. It may disappear in neutral coasts. Operating the engine at the problem speed while the vehicle is stationary can duplicate the vibration. It can be caused by any component, from the accessory drive belt to the clutch or torque converter, which turns at engine speed when the vehicle is stopped.
5. **Noise and vibration while turning** clicking, popping or grinding noises may be due to the following: damaged CV joint; loose front

wheel half shaft joint boot clamps; another component contacting the half shaft; worn, damaged or incorrectly installed wheel bearing; damaged power train/drive train mounts.

After a road test, it is often useful to do a similar test on a lift. When carrying out the shake and vibration diagnosis or engine accessory vibration diagnosis on a lift, observe the following precautions.

- If only one drive wheel is allowed to rotate, speed must be limited to 55 km/h (35 mph) indicated on the speedometer. This is because the actual wheel speed will be twice that indicated on the speedometer.
- The suspension should not be allowed to hang free. If a CV joint were run at a high angle, extra vibration as well as damage to the seals and joints could occur.

Support the front suspension lower arm as far out-board as possible. This will ensure that the vehicle is at its correct ride height. The procedure is outlined by the following steps.

1. Raise and support the vehicle.
2. Explore the speed range of interest using the road test checks as previously discussed.
3. Carry out a coast down (overrun) in neutral. If the vehicle is free of vibration when operating at a steady indicated speed and behaves very differently in drive and coast, a transmission concern is likely.

Note, however, that a test on the lift may produce different vibrations and noises than a road test because of the effect of the lift. It is not unusual to find a vibration on the lift that was not noticed during the road test. If the condition found on the road can be duplicated on the lift, carrying out experiments on the lift may save a great deal of time.

2.4.6 Engine noises

How do you tell a constant tapping from a rattle? Worse still, how do you describe a noise in a book? I'll do my best! Try the following table as a non-definitive guide to the source or cause of engine or engine ancillary noises.

Noise description	Possible source
Tap	Valve clearances out of adjustment, cam followers or cam lobes worn
Rattle	A loose component, broken piston ring or component

Light knock	Small end bearings worn, cam or cam follower	
Deep knock or thud	Big end bearings worn	
Rumble	Main bearings worn	
Slap	Worn pistons or bores	
Vibration	Loose or out of balance components	
Clatter	Broken rocker shaft or broken piston rings	
Hiss	Leak from inlet or exhaust manifolds or connections	
Roar	Air intake noise, air filter missing, exhaust blowing or a seized viscous fan drive	
Clunk	Loose flywheel, worm thrust bearings or a loose front pulley/damper	
Whine	Power steering pump or alternator bearing	
Shriek	Dry bearing in an ancillary component	
Squeal	Slipping drive belt	

2.4.7 Sources of engine noise

The following table is a further guide to engine noise. Possible causes are listed together with the necessary repair or further diagnosis action as appropriate.

Sources of engine noise	Possible cause	Required action
Misfiring/backfiring	Fuel in tank has wrong octane/cetane number, or is wrong type of fuel	Determine which type of fuel was last put in the tank
	Ignition system faulty	Check the ignition system
	Engine temperature too high	Check the engine cooling system
	Carbon deposits in the combustion chamber start to glow and cause misfiring	Remove the carbon deposits by using fuel additives and driving the vehicle carefully
	Timing incorrect, which causes misfiring in the intake/exhaust system.	Check the timing
Valve train faulty	Valve clearance too large due to faulty bucket tappets or incorrect adjustment of valve clearance	Adjust valve clearance if possible and renew faulty bucket tappets – check cam condition
	Valve timing incorrectly adjusted, valves and pistons are touching	Check the valve timing and adjust if necessary
	Timing belt broken or damaged	Check timing belt and check pistons and valves for damage – renew any faulty parts

Engine components faulty	Pistons Piston rings Cylinder head gasket Big end and/or main bearing journals	Disassemble the engine and check components
Ancillary components	Engine components or ancillary components loose or broken	Check that all components are secure, tighten/ adjust as required. Renew if broken

2.5 Electrical diagnostic techniques

2.5.1 Check the obvious first!

Start *all* hands on diagnostic routines with 'hand and eye checks'. In other words look over the vehicle for obvious faults. For example, if the battery terminals are loose or corroded then put this right before carrying out complicated voltage readings. Here are some further suggestions that will at some point save you a lot of time.

- A misfire may be caused by a loose plug lead – it is easier to look for this than interpret the ignition waveforms on a scope.
- If the ABS warning light stays on – look to see if the wheel speed sensor(s) are covered in mud or oil.

2.5.2 Test lights and analogue meters – warning!

A test lamp is ideal for tracing faults in say a lighting circuit because it will cause a current to flow which tests out high resistance connections. However, it is this same property that will damage delicate electronic circuits – so don't use it for any circuit that contains an electronic control unit (ECU). Even an analogue voltmeter can cause enough current to flow to at best give you a false reading and at worst damage an ECU – so don't use it!

A digital multimeter is ideal for all forms of testing. Most have an internal resistance in excess of 10 MΩ. This means that the current they draw is almost insignificant. An LED test lamp or a logic probe is also acceptable.

2.5.3 Generic electrical testing procedure

The following procedure is very generic but with a little adaptation can be applied to any electrical system. Refer to manufacturer's recommendations if in any doubt. The process of checking any system circuit is broadly as follows.

1. Hand and eye checks (loose wires, loose switches and other obvious faults) – all connections clean and tight.
2. Check battery (see Chapter 6) – must be 70% charged.
3. Check motor/solenoid/linkage/bulbs/unit – visual check.
4. Fuse continuity – (do not trust your eyes) voltage at both sides with a meter or a test lamp.
5. If used does the relay click (if yes, jump to stage 8) – this means the relay has operated; it is not necessarily making contact.
6. Supply to the switch – battery volts.
7. Supply from the switch – battery volts.
8. Supplies to the relay – battery volts.
9. Feed out of the relay – battery volts.
10. Voltage supply to the motor – within 0.5 V of the battery.
11. Earth circuit (continuity or voltage) – 0 Ω or 0 V.

2.5.4 Volt drop testing

Volt drop is a term used to describe the difference between two points in a circuit. In this way we can talk about a voltage drop across a battery (normally about 12.6 V) or the voltage drop across a closed switch (ideally 0 V but may be 0.1 or 0.2 V).

The first secret to volt drop testing is to remember a basic rule about a series electrical circuit: *The sum of all volt drops around a circuit always adds up to the supply*.

The second secret is to ensure that the circuit is switched on and operating – or at least the circuit should be 'trying to operate'!

In Figure 2.2 this means that $V_1 + V_2 + V_3 = V_s$. When electrical testing, therefore, and if the battery voltage measured as say 12 V, a reading of less than 12 V at V_2 would indicate a volt drop between the terminals of V_1 and/or V_3. Likewise the correct operation of the switch, that is it closes and makes a good connection, would be confirmed by a very low reading on V_1.

What is often described as a 'bad earth' (when what is meant is a high resistance to earth), could equally be determined by the reading on V_3.

To further narrow the cause of a volt drop down a bit, simply measure across a smaller area. The voltmeter V_4, for example, would only assess the condition of the switch contacts.

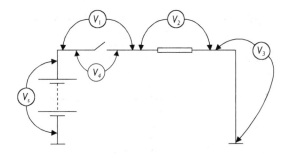

Figure 2.2 Volt drop testing

2.5.5 Testing for short circuits to earth

This fault will normally blow a fuse – or burn out the wiring completely! To trace a short circuit is very different from looking for a high resistance connection or an open circuit. The volt drop testing above will trace an open circuit or a high resistance connection.

My preferred method of tracing a short, after looking for the obvious signs of trapped wires, is to connect a bulb or test lamp across the blown fuse and switch on the circuit. The bulb will light because on one side it is connected to the supply for the fuse and on the other side it is connected to earth via the fault. Now disconnect small sections of the circuit one at a time until the test lamp goes out. This will indicate the particular circuit section that has shorted out.

2.5.6 On and off load tests

On load means that a circuit is drawing a current. Off load means it is not! One example where this may be an issue is when testing a starter circuit. Battery voltage may be 12 V off load but only 9 V when on load.

A second example is the supply voltage to the positive terminal of an ignition coil via a high resistance connection (corroded switch terminal for example). With the ignition on and the vehicle not running, the reading will almost certainly be battery voltage because the ignition ECU switches off the primary circuit and no volt drop will show up. However, if the circuit were switched on (with a fused jumper lead if necessary) a lower reading would result showing up the fault.

2.5.7 Black box technique

The technique that will be covered here is known as 'black box faultfinding'. This is an excellent technique and can be applied to many vehicle systems from engine management and ABS to cruise control and instrumentation.

As most systems now revolve around an ECU, the ECU is considered to be a 'black box', in other words we know what it should do but how it does it is irrelevant! Any colour, so long as it's black. [Henry Ford (1920s)]. I doubt that he was referring to ECUs though . . .

Figure 2.3 shows a block diagram that could be used to represent any number of automobile electrical or electronic systems. In reality the arrows from the 'inputs' to the ECU and from the ECU to the 'outputs' are wires. Treating the ECU as a 'black box' allows us to ignore its complexity. The theory is that if all the sensors and associated wiring to the 'black box' are OK, all the output actuators and their wiring are OK and the supply/earth connections are OK, then the fault must be the 'black box'. Most ECUs are very reliable, however, and it is far more likely that the fault will be found in the inputs or outputs.

Normal faultfinding or testing techniques can be applied to the sensors and actuators. For example, if an ABS system uses four inductive type wheel speed sensors, then an easy test is to measure their resistance. Even if the correct value were not known, it would be very unlikely for all four to be wrong at the same time so a comparison can be made. If the same resistance reading is obtained on the end of the sensor wires at the ECU then almost all of the 'inputs' have been tested with just a few ohmmeter readings.

The same technique will often work with 'outputs'. If the resistance of all the operating windings in say a hydraulic modulator were the same, then it would be reasonable to assume the figure was correct.

Sometimes, however, it is almost an advantage *not* to know the manufacturer's recommended readings. If the 'book' says the value should be between 800 and 900 Ω, what do you do when your ohmmeter reads 905 Ω? Answers on a postcard please . . . (or see Section 2.3.3).

Finally, don't forget that no matter how complex the electronics in an ECU, they will not work without a good power supply and an earth!

2.5.8 Sensor to ECU method

This technique is simple but very useful. Figure 2.4 shows a resistance test being carried out on a component. Ω_1 is a direct measure of its resistance whereas Ω_2 includes the condition of the circuit. If the second reading is the same as the first then the circuit must be in good order.

Warning
The circuit supply must always be off when carrying out ohmmeter tests.

2.5.9 Flight recorder tests

It is said that the best place to sit in an aeroplane is on the black box flight recorder! Well, apart from the black box usually being painted bright orange so it can be found after a crash, my reason for mentioning it is to illustrate how the flight recorder principle can be applied to automotive diagnostics.

Most hand-held scopes now have flight record facilities. This means that they will save the signal from any probe connection in memory for later play back. The time duration will vary depending on the available memory and the sample speed but this is a very useful feature.

Figure 2.3 System block diagram

Figure 2.4 Ohmmeter tests

As an example, consider an engine with an intermittent misfire that occurs only under load. If a connection is made to the suspected component (coil HT output for example), and the vehicle is road tested, the waveforms produced can be examined afterwards.

Many engine (and other system) ECUs have built in flight recorders in the form of self-diagnostic circuits. If a wire breaks loose causing a misfire but then reconnects the faulty circuit will be 'remembered' by the ECU.

2.5.10 Faultfinding by luck!

Or is it logic? If four electric windows stopped working at the same time, it would be very unlikely that all four motors had burned out. On the other hand if just one electric window stopped working, then it may be reasonable to suspect the motor. It is this type of reasoning that is necessary when faultfinding. However, be warned it is theoretically possible for four motors to apparently burn out all at the same time!

Using this 'playing the odds' technique can save time when tracing a fault in a vehicle system. For example, if both stop lights do not work and everything else on the vehicle is OK, I would suspect the switch (stages 1 to 3 of the normal process). At this stage though, the fault could be anywhere – even two or three blown bulbs. None-the-less a quick test at the switch with a voltmeter would prove the point. Now, let's assume the switch is OK and it produces an output when the brake pedal is pushed down. Testing the length of wire from the front to the back of the vehicle further illustrates how 'luck' comes into play.

Figure 2.5 represents the main supply wire from the brake switch to the point where the wire 'divides' to each individual stop light (the odds say the fault must be in this wire). For the purpose of this illustration we will assume the open circuit is just before point 'I'. The procedure continues in one of the two following ways. Either:

- guess that the fault is in the first half and test at point F;
- we were wrong! Guess that the fault is in the first half of the second half and test at point I;
- we were right! Check at H and we have the fault . . . on test number THREE;

or:

- test from A to K in a logical sequence of tests;
- we would find the fault . . . On test number NINE!

You may choose which method you prefer!

2.5.11 Colour codes and terminal numbers

This section is really more to be used as a reference source. It is useful, however, to become familiar with a few key wire colours and terminal numbers when diagnosing electrical faults. As seems to be the case for any standardisation a number of colour code systems are in operation! For reference purposes I will just mention two.

Firstly, the British Standard system (BS AU 7a: 1983): this system uses 12 colours to determine the main purpose of the cable and tracer colours to further refine its use. The main colour uses and some further examples are given in the following table.

Colour	Symbol	Destination/use
Brown	N	Main battery feed
Blue	U	Headlight switch to dip switch
Blue/White	UW	Headlight main beam
Blue/Red	UR	Headlight dip beam
Red	R	Side light main feed
Red/Black	RB	Left hand side lights and no. plate
Red/Orange	RO	Right hand side lights
Purple	P	Constant fused supply

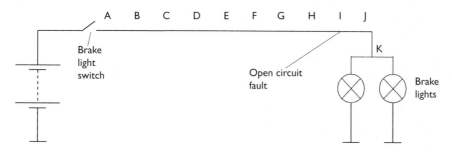

Figure 2.5 Faultfinding by luck!

Green	G	Ignition controlled fused supply
Green/Red	GR	Left side indicators
Green/White	GW	Right side indicators
Light Green	LG	Instruments
White	W	Ignition to ballast resistor
White/Black	WB	Coil negative
Yellow	Y	Overdrive and fuel injection
Black	B	All earth connections
Slate	S	Electric windows
Orange	O	Wiper circuits (fused)
Pink/White	KW	Ballast resistor wire
Green/Brown	GN	Reverse
Green/Purple	GP	Stop lights
Blue/Yellow	UY	Rear fog light

Secondly there is a 'European' system used by a number of manufacturers and based broadly on the following table. Please note there is no correlation between the 'Euro' system and the British Standard colour codes. In particular note the use of the colour brown in each system! After some practice with the use of colour code systems the job of the technician is made a lot easier when faultfinding an electrical circuit.

Colour	Symbol	Destination/use
Red	Rt	Main battery feed
White/Black	Ws/Sw	Headlight switch to dip switch
White	Ws	Headlight main beam
Yellow	Ge	Headlight dip beam
Grey	Gr	Side light main feed
Grey/Black	Gr/Sw	Left hand side lights
Grey/Red	Gr/Rt	Right hand side lights
Black/Yellow	Sw/Ge	Fuel injection
Black/Green	Sw/Gn	Ignition controlled supply
Black/White/Green	Sw/Ws/Gn	Indicator switch
Black/White	Sw/Ws	Left side indicators
Black/Green	Sw/Gn	Right side indicators
Light Green	LGn	Coil negative
Brown	Br	Earth
Brown/White	Br/Ws	Earth connections
Black	Sw	Reverse
Black/Red	Sw/Rt	Stop lights
Green/Black	Gn/Sw	Rear fog light

A system now in use almost universally is the terminal designation system in accordance with DIN 72 552. This system is to enable easy and correct connections to be made on the vehicle, particularly in after sales repairs. Note that the designations are not to identify individual wires but to define the terminals of a device. Listed below are some of the most popular numbers.

1	Ignition coil negative
4	Ignition coil high tension
15	Switched positive (ignition switch output)
30	Input from battery positive

31	Earth connection
49	Input to flasher unit
49a	Output from flasher unit
50	Starter control (solenoid terminal)
53	Wiper motor input
54	Stop lamps
55	Fog lamps
56	Headlamps
56a	Main beam
56b	Dip beam
58L	Left side lights
58R	Right side lights
61	Charge warning light
85	Relay winding out
86	Relay winding input
87	Relay contact input (change over relay)
87a	Relay contact output (break)
87b	Relay contact output (make)
L	Left side indicators
R	Right side indicators
C	Indicator warning light (vehicle)

The Ford motor company now uses a circuit numbering and wire identification system. This is in use worldwide and is known as Function, System-Connection (FSC). The system was developed to assist in vehicle development and production processes. However, it is also very useful in helping the technician with faultfinding. Many of the function codes are based on the DIN system. Note that earth wires are now black! The system works as follows.

$$31S\text{-}AC3A \parallel 1.5 \; BK/RD$$

Function:

> 31 = ground/earth
> S = additionally switched circuit

System:

> AC = headlamp levelling

Connection:

> 3 = switch connection
> A = branch

Size:

> $1.5 = 1.5 \; mm^2$

Colour:

> BK = black (determined by function 31)
> RD = red stripe

The new Ford colour codes table is as follows:

Code	Colour
BK	Black
BN	Brown
BU	Blue

GN	Green
GY	Grey
LG	Light-green
OG	Orange
PK	Pink
RD	Red
SR	Silver
VT	Violet
WH	White
YE	Yellow

Ford system codes are as follows.

Letter	Main system	Examples
D	Distribution systems	DE = earth
A	Actuated systems	AK = wiper/washer
B	Basic systems	BA = charging
		BB = starting
C	Control systems	CE = power steering
G	Gauge systems	GA = level/pressure/ temperature
H	Heated systems	HC = heated seats
L	Lighting systems	LE = headlights
M	Miscellaneous systems	MA = air bags
P	Power train control systems	PA = engine control
W	Indicator systems ('indications' not turn signals)	WC = bulb failure
X	Temporary for future features	XS = too much!

As a final point to this section it must be noted that the colour codes and terminal designations given are for illustration only. Further reference should be made for specific details to the manufacturer's information.

2.5.12 Back probing connectors

Just a quick warning! If you are testing for a supply (for example) at an ECU, then use the probes of your digital meter with care. Connect to the back of the terminals; this will not damage the connecting surfaces as long as you do not apply excessive force. Sometimes a pin clamped in the test lead's crocodile/alligator clip is ideal for connecting 'through' the insulation of a wire without having to disconnect it. Figure 2.6 shows the 'back probing' technique.

2.6 Fault codes

2.6.1 Fast and slow

Most modern vehicle management systems carry out self-diagnostic checks on the sensors and actuators that connect to the vehicle ECU(s). A fault in one of the components or its

Figure 2.6 Test the voltage at a connection with care

associated circuit causes a code to be stored in the ECU memory.

The codes may be described as 'fast' or 'slow'. Some ECUs produce both types. An LED, dash warning light, scope or even an analogue voltmeter can be used to read slow codes. Normally, slow codes are output as a series of flashes that must then be interpreted by looking up the code in a fault code table. The slow codes are normally initiated by shorting two connections on the diagnostic plug and then switching the ignition on. Refer to detailed data before shorting any pins out!

Fast codes can only be read by using a fault code reader or scanner. Future ECUs will use fast codes. In the same way as we accept that a good digital multimeter is an essential piece of test equipment, it is now necessary to consider a fault code reader in the same way.

If a code reader is attached to the serial port on the vehicle harness, fast and slow codes can be read out from the vehicle computer. These are either displayed in the form of a two, three or four digit output code or in text format if software is used.

2.6.2 Fault code examples

A number of codes and descriptions are reproduced below as an example of the detailed information that is available from a self-diagnosis system. The data relates to the Bosch Motronic 1.7 and 3.1. Fault code lists are available in publications such as those by 'Autodata' and 'Autologic'.

FCR	Description code
000	No faults found in the ECU
001	Fuel pump relay or fuel pump relay circuit
001	Crank angle sensor (CAS) or circuit (alternative code)
002	Idle speed control valve circuit
003	Injector number 1 or group one circuit
004	Injector number 3 or circuit
005	Injector number 2 or circuit
006	Injectors or injector circuit
012	Throttle position switch or circuit
016	CAS or circuit
018	Amplifier to ECU amplifier circuit
019	ECU
023	Ignition amplifier number 2 cylinder or circuit
024	Ignition amplifier number 3 cylinder or circuit
025	Ignition amplifier number 1 cylinder or circuit
026	ECU supply
029	Idle speed control valve (ISCV) or circuit
031	Injector number 5 or circuit
032	Injector number 6 or injector group two circuit
033	Injector number 4 or circuit
036	Carbon filter solenoid valve (CFSV) or circuit
037	Oxygen sensor (OS) or circuit
041	Mass airflow (MAF) sensor or circuit
046	ECU
048	Air conditioning (AC) compressor or circuit
050	ignition amplifier cylinder number 4 or circuit
051	Ignition amplifier cylinder number 6 or circuit
054	ECU
055	Ignition amplifier or circuit
062	Electronic throttle control or circuit
064	Ignition timing (electronic)
067	Vehicle speed sensor (VSS) or circuit
067	CAS or circuit
070	OS or circuit
073	Vehicle speed sensor (VSS) or circuit
076	CO potentiometer (non-cat)
077	Intake air temperature sensor (ATS) or circuit
078	Engine coolant temperature sensor (CTS) or circuit
081	Alarm system or circuit
082	Traction control or circuit
083	Suspension control or circuit
085	AC compressor or circuit
100	ECU
200	ECU
201	OS control or circuit
202	ECU
203	Ignition primary or circuit
204	Electronic throttle control signal or circuit
300	Engine

2.6.3 Clearing

Fault codes can be cleared from the ECU memory in two ways:

- using the facilities of a fault code reader (scanner) to clear the memory;
- disconnecting the battery earth lead for about two minutes.

The first method is clearly recommended because disconnecting the battery will also 'reset' many other functions such as the radio code, the clock and even the learnt or adaptive functions in the ECUs.

2.7   Systems

2.7.1 What is a system

System is a word used to describe a collection of related components which interact as a whole. A motorway system, the education system or computer systems are three varied examples. A large system is often made up of many smaller systems which in turn can each be made up of smaller systems and so on. Figure 2.7 shows how this can be represented in a visual form.

One further definition: *A group of devices serving a common purpose.*

Figure 2.7 Vehicle systems representation

Using the systems approach helps to split extremely complex technical entities into more manageable parts. It is important to note, however, that the links between the smaller parts and the boundaries around them are also very important. System boundaries will overlap in many cases.

The modern motor vehicle is a complex system and in itself forms just a small part of a larger transport system. It is the capacity for the motor vehicle to be split into systems on many levels which aids in both its design and construction. The systems approach helps in particular with understanding how something works and, further, how to go about repairing it when it doesn't!

2.7.2 Vehicle systems

Splitting the vehicle into systems is not an easy task because it can be done in many different ways. A split between mechanical systems and electrical systems would seem a good start. However, this division can cause as many problems as it solves. For example, in which half do we put anti-lock brakes, mechanical or electrical. The answer is of course both! None-the-less, it is still easier if we just consider one area of the vehicle and do not try to comprehend the whole.

Once a complex set of interacting parts such as a motor vehicle has been 'systemised', the function or performance of each part can be examined in more detail. In other words, knowing what each part of the system should do in turn helps in determining how each part actually works. It is again important to stress that the links and interactions between various sub-systems are a very important consideration. Examples of this would be how the power demands of the vehicle lighting system will have an effect on the charging system operation, or in the case of a fault, how an air leak from a brake servo could cause a weak air/fuel ratio.

To further analyse a system, whatever way it has been sub-divided from the whole, consideration should be given to the inputs and the outputs. Many of the complex electronic systems on a vehicle lend themselves to this form of analysis. Considering the ECU of the system as the control element and looking at its inputs and outputs is the recommended approach.

2.7.3 Open loop systems

An open loop system is designed to give the required output whenever a given input is applied. A good example of an open loop vehicle system would be the headlights. With the given input of the switch being operated the output required is that the headlights will be illuminated. This can be taken further by saying that an input is also required from the battery and a further input of say the dip switch. The feature which determines that a system is open loop is that no feedback is required for it to operate. Figure 2.8 shows this example in block diagram form.

2.7.4 Closed loop systems

A closed loop system is identified by a feedback loop. It can be described as a system where there is a possibility of applying corrective measures if the output is not quite what is wanted. A good example of this in a vehicle is an automatic temperature control system. The interior temperature of the vehicle is determined by the output from the heater which is switched on or off in response to a signal from a temperature sensor inside the cabin. The feedback loop is the fact that the output from the system, temperature, is also an input to the system. This is represented by Figure 2.9.

The feedback loop in any closed loop system can be in many forms. The driver of a car with a conventional heating system can form a feedback loop by turning the heater down when he/she is too hot and turning it back up when cold. The feedback to a voltage regulator in an alternator is an electrical signal using a simple wire.

2.7.5 Block diagrams

Another secret to good diagnostics is the 'block diagram' approach. Most systems can be considered as consisting of 'inputs to a control which has outputs'. This technique means that

Figure 2.8 Open loop system

Figure 2.9 Closed loop system

Figure 2.10 Block diagram

complex systems can be considered in manageable 'chunks'.

Many complex vehicle electronic systems can be represented as block diagrams. In this way several inputs can be shown supplying information to an ECU that in turn controls the system outputs. As an example of this, consider the operation of a vehicle alarm system (Figure 2.10). In its simplest form the inputs are the 'sensors' (such as door switches) and the 'outputs' are the actuators (such as the siren). The 'control' section is the alarm ECU.

The diagnostic approach is that if all the sensors are providing the correct information to the control and the actuators respond when tested, then the fault must be the control unit. If a sensor does not produce the required information then the fault is equally evident.

2.8　On- and off-board diagnostics

2.8.1　On-board diagnostics

On-board diagnostics refers to the systems on the vehicle carrying out some form of self-monitoring. The more complex automobiles become, the greater the number of electronic systems and the more difficult it is to register the actual condition in case of a defect.

Many connecting cables and adapters are required to achieve this. Data about the different systems and their working together is needed to allow a system specific diagnosis. Modern electronics with self-diagnosis supports the technician by registering actual values, comparing them with the nominal values, and diagnosing faults that are stored for repair purposes.

Internal to an ECU, a checksum of the program memory is calculated. Then a read and

write test of the random access memory (RAM) is performed. Other elements such as A/D (analogue/digital) converters are also checked within this test cycle.

During the operating time of the vehicle, the ECUs are constantly checking the sensors they are connected to. The ECUs are then able to determine whether a sensor has a short circuit to ground or battery voltage, or if a cable to the sensor is open circuit. By comparing the measured values and the stored data, an ECU is able to determine whether the measured values exceed or are still within the tolerance required. Combining information provided by other sensors allows the ECU to monitor for plausibility of the sensor signals.

Measuring the current normally taken by their circuits is used to carry out a check on actuators. Powering the actuator and observing the reaction of the system can test the function of an actuator in some cases.

If discrepancies to the nominal values are diagnosed, the information is stored in an internal fault memory together with other parameters, such as engine temperature or speed. In this way, defects that appear intermittent or only under certain conditions can be diagnosed. If a fault occurs only once during a set period of time, it is deleted. The fault memory can be read later in the workshop and provides valuable information for the technician.

When a defective sensor is detected, the measured values are replaced by a nominal value, or an alternative value is calculated using the information from other sensors to provide a limp-home function. With the help of an appropriate code reader or scanner, a technician can communicate with the ECUs, read the fault memory and the measured values, and send signals to the actuators.

Another task of self-diagnosis is to indicate a defect to the driver. A warning light on the dashboard is the most common method used to do this. Regulations concerning exhaust emissions mean an extension of self-diagnosis is desirable. The control units will soon have to be able to control all exhaust gas functions and components and to clearly indicate a defective function or the exceeding of the permissible exhaust limits.

2.8.2　Off-board diagnostics

The continual increase in the use of electronics within vehicles represents a major challenge for customer service and workshop operations.

Modern diagnosis and information systems must cope with this challenge and manufacturers of test equipment must provide instruments that are flexible and easy to handle. Quick and reliable fault diagnosis in modern vehicles requires extensive technical knowledge, detailed vehicle information, up-to-date testing systems and the skill to be able to apply all of these.

The test equipment on the market can be subdivided into two main categories:

- hand-held or portable instruments;
- stationary equipment.

Hand-held instruments are commonly used for the control of engine functions like ignition or fuel injection and the request of error codes from the ECUs.

Stationary test equipment may be able to cover the whole range of function and performance checks of the engine, gear, brakes, chassis, and exhaust monitoring. Most of the common testers are used for diagnosing engine faults.

For repair, service, and maintenance, many different manuals and microfiches are used in workshops. It is difficult to collect all the necessary information, especially when vehicles of different makes have to be repaired. It is, however, becoming common to supply material on CD-ROMs. Workshops equipped with appropriate data systems will be able to receive updates via telephone line or by periodic receipt of updated CDs. A committee of the Society of Automotive Engineers (SAE) has prepared rules for the standardisation of manuals.

2.9 Examples of available data

2.9.1 Autologic CD-ROM

This system, which can be used on any 'normal' specification computer with a CD drive, currently has the following very useful features:

Figure 2.11 'Autologic' fuel and ignition circuit diagram

Ford Fiesta 1.6 XR2i   **1992–1992**

Component location

ECU		K4/ J15
relay	automatic gearbox	J4 / J15
relay	headlamp dip	J4 / J15
relay	ABS	J4 / J15
relay	electronic fuel injection	J4 / J15 K14/ J15
relay	fog light	J4 / J15
relay	front wiper	J4 / J15
relay	fuel pump	J4 / J15
relay	heated rear window	J4 / J15
relay	headlamp washers	J4 / J15
relay	heated windscreen	J4 / J15
relay	horn	J4 / J15
relay	idle	J4 / J15
relay	ignition	J4 / J15
relay	inertia	J4 / J15
relay	power	J4 / J15
fuse box		J4 / J15
flasher/hazard warning lights		J4 / J15

Figure 2.12 'Autologic' component location information

- fuel and ignition diagnostics;
- fuel and ignition circuit diagrams (Figure 2.11 shows an example of a circuit diagram);
- ABS diagnostics;
- adjustment data;
- timing belts;
- component location (Figure 2.12 shows an example of the component location screen);
- mechanical repair times;
- service schedules.

The service schedule example shown as Figure 2.13 is a useful reminder that the best way of preventing complicated diagnostics is to prevent the fault developing in the first place!

2.9.2 Autodata books

This range of books is well known and well respected. Very comprehensive manuals are available ranging from the standard 'Data book' to full vehicle circuit diagrams and engine management diagnostic tests data.

Figure 2.14 shows an example sheet from the Data book. Figure 2.15 shows a typical sheet from an engine management book. These sheets include test data as well as test procedures related to specific vehicles or specific systems. Figure 2.16 shows the range of books available.

Ford Mondeo 1.8i 16 valve

1993–1998

Service at 40 000 miles
Carried out on 30/06/99

Customer Name	*Tom Denton*
Vehicle Registration:	*N884 CEV*
Current Mileage:	*38996*

The items checked on this inspection are shown below. Where inspection has indicated the need for further attention in the interests of safety and maintenance of your vehicle value, we recommend that corrective action is taken as soon as possible.

OK ✓

Requires further attention **X**

Service details:

- Service interval system: reset
- Lights / indicators / controls / warning lamps: check
- Windscreen wiper / wash: check fluid level / antifreeze content
- Battery: distilled water top-up
- Clutch: cable stroke check / adjust
- **** for the above see Special Notes (10) ****
- Cooling system: pressure test
- **** for the above see Special Notes (2) ****
- Brake fluid level: check
- Brake fluid: replace
- **** for the above see Special Notes (3) ****
- **** for the above see Special Notes (10) ****
- Cooling system: check for level / specific gravity
- Steering servo: fluid level check
- Inlet manifold: tighten bolts / nuts
- Air conditioning belt: check / adjust / replace
- V-belt(s): check / adjust / replace
- PAS belt: check / adjust / renew
- Spark plugs: replace / adjust
- **** for the above see Special Notes (8) ****
- Timing belt(s): replace
- **** for the above see Special Notes (4) ****
- Automatic transmission: check fluid level
- CVT: operating cable check / adjust
- Engine oil: change
- Oil filter: replace
- Automatic transmission: lubricate selector mechanism
- Drive shaft gaiters: check for splits and leaks
- Steering: check for leaks, wear, secure fixings, etc.
- Suspension: check for leaks / wear / damage etc.
- Tyres including spare: check condition / pressure / tread depth
- Brake system: inspect for damage and leaks
- **** for the above see Special Notes (1) ****
- Brake pads front: clean / check / replace
- Brake pads rear: clean / check / replace
- Linings rear: clean / check / replace
- Check for brake fluid leaks and condition of seals

- **** for the above see Special Notes (3) ****
- Wheel bolts / nuts: check tightness
- Locks / hinges / door catches: lubricate
- Steering wheel / locks / handles: clean

Special Notes

1. 2.9 V6 only except 24v
2. every 4 years
3. every 3 years
4. at 80 000 miles
5. A4LD only
6. CTX only
7. 4x4 only – not Cosworth
8. not Duratec-Ve engines
9. Duratec-Ve engines only
10. where applicable

I confirm that all the appropriate checks and adjustments have been made correctly.

Technician: .... Workshop Supervisor: ....

Figure 2.13 'Autologic' service data example

PORSCHE		Technical Data			*Autodata*
		1	**2**	**3**	**4**	**5**

			1	2	3	4	5
1	Vehicle Identification	Ref. No.	1064	2811	2810	2812	1073
2	Model		944S	944 Turbo	944 S2	928 GT	928 S4
3							
4							
5	Engine specially tuned for			R-Cat	R-Cat	R-Cat	R-Cat
6	Year		1986-89	1989-93	1989-93	1989-92	1989-94
7	Engine	Code	M44/40	M44/52	M44/41	M28/47	M28/41/42
8	No. of cylinders / Type		4/OHC	4/OHC	4/OHC	8/OHC	8/OHC
9	Capacity	cm³	2479	2479	2990	4957	4957
10	Output	kW (DIN hp) rpm	140 (190) 6000	184 (250) 6000	155 (211) 5800	243 (330) 6200	235 (320) 6000
11	Minimum octane rating	RON	95	95	95	95	95
12	Ignition system	Description	Map-h	Map-h	Map-h	Map-i	Map-i
13		Trigger location	Crankshaft	Crankshaft	Crankshaft	Crankshaft	Crankshaft
14	Fuel system	Make	Bosch	Bosch	Bosch	Bosch	Bosch
15		Type	Motronic	Motronic	Motronic	LH-Jetronic	LH-Jetronic
16		Description	MFI-i	MFI-i	MFI-i	MFI-i	MFI-i
17	Air metering	Type	Flow	Flow	Flow	Mass	Mass
18	Combined ignition and fuel ECU		Yes	Yes	Yes	No	No
19	Diagnostic socket		Yes	Yes	Yes	Yes	Yes
20	**Tuning and emissions**				**2**		**1**
21	Ignition coil supply voltage	V	12.0	12.0	12.0	11.0	12.0
22	Primary resistance	Ω	0.4–0.6	0.4–0.6	0.4–0.6	0.4–0.6	0.4–0.6
23	Secondary resistance	Ω	5000–7200	5000–7200	5000–7200	5000–7000	5000–7200
24	Firing order		1-3-4-2	1-3-4-2	1-3-4-2	1-3-7-2-6-5-4-8	1-3-7-2-6-5-4-8
25	Ignition distributor (ECU)	No.	(0 261 200 080)	(0 261 200 088)	(0 261 200 195)	(0 227 400 164)	(0 227 400 034)
26	Ignition timing BTDC	°Engine / rpm	10±3/840	5±3/840	10±3/840	10±2/775	10±2/675
27	alternative	°Engine / rpm	–	–	–	–	–
28	o without + with vacuum		o	–	–	–	o
29	Ignition advance checks	°Engine / rpm	ECU controlled	ECU controlled	ECU controlled	ECU controlled	ECU controlled
30	a = without vacuum and basic timing b = without vacuum, with basic timing	°Engine / rpm	–	–	–	–	–
31	c = with vacuum and basic timing	°Engine / rpm	–	–	–	–	–
32	Vacuum advance range	°Engine	–	–	–	–	–
33	Idle speed	rpm	840±40	840±40	840±40	775±25	675±25
34	alternative	rpm	–	–	–	–	–
35	Oil temperature for CO test	°C	90	90	90	90	90
36	CO content at idle - tail pipe	Vol.%	1.0±0.5	0.5 Max	0.5 Max	0.5 Max	0.5 Max
37	- sample pipe	Vol.%	–	0.4–0.8	0.4–0.8	0.4–1.2	0.4–1.2
38	CO_2 / O_2 content at idle speed	Vol.%	13–16/0.5–2.0	14.5–16/0.1–0.5	14.5–16/0.1–0.5	14.5–16/0.1–0.5	14.5–16/0.1–0.5
39	HC content at idle speed	ppm	300	100	100	100	100
40	Increased idle speed for CO test	rpm	–	2500–2800	2500–2800	2500–2800	2500–2800
41	CO content at increased idle speed	Vol.%	–	0.3	0.3	0.3	0.3
42	Lambda at increased idle speed	λ	–	0.97–1.03	0.97–1.03	0.97–1.03	0.97–1.03
43	**Service checks and adjustments**						
44	Spark plugs	Make	Bosch	Bosch	Bosch	Bosch	Bosch
45	(also see Spark Plugs list)	Type	WR5DC	WR7DC	WR5DC	WR7DC	WR7DC
46	Electrode gap	mm	0.7	0.7	0.7 ·	0.7	0.6-0.8
47	Valve clearance - inlet	mm	Hydraulic	Hydraulic	Hydraulic	Hydraulic	Hydraulic
48	- exhaust	mm	Hydraulic	Hydraulic	Hydraulic	Hydraulic	Hydraulic
49	Compression pressure	bar	–	–	–	–	–
50	Oil pressure	bar / rpm	3.5/6000	3.5/6000	3.5/6000	5/4000	5/5000
51	**Lubricants and capacities**						
52	Engine oil grade	SAE (API)	15W/40 (SF)	15W/40 (SF)	15W/40 (SF)	15W/40 (SF)	15W/40 (SF)
53	Engine with filter	litres	6.5	7.0	7.0	7.5	7.5
54	Gearbox oil grade	SAE	75W/90	75W/90	75W/90	75W/90	75W/90
55	4/5 speed	litres	2.0	2.0	2.0	4.5	4.5
56	Automatic transmission fluid	Type	Dexron II D	–	–	–	Dexron II D
57	refill	litres	6.0	–	–	–	7.3
58	Differential oil grade	SAE	90W	–	–	–	90W
59	front / rear	litres	1.0 (AT)	–	–	–	3.0 (AT)

POR 3	■ = refer to **Technical Information** at end of this manufacturer	△ = setting not adjustable

Figure 2.14 'Autodata' data book example

TOYOTA

☐ Carina E 2,0 GLi   1992-

2.7 Injector valves

Technical Data
Resistance between
terminals   13,4–14,2 Ω (approx.)

Injector spray pattern and leak rate — refer to General Test Procedures.

Resistance - 12

● Ensure ignition switched OFF.
● Disconnect injector valve multi-plug.
● Connect ohmmeter across injector valve terminals.
● Compare resistance indicated with that specified.

2.8 Lambda sensor

Self-diagnosis code: 21

Technical Data
Heater resistance at 20°C   5100–6300 Ω

Checking sensor - 13

● Bridge terminals TE1 and E1 of diagnostic socket.
● Run engine at 2500 rev/min for two minutes to heat up Lambda sensor.
● Connect voltmeter between terminals VF1 and E1 of diagnostic socket.
● Hold engine speed at 2500 rev/min
● Check that voltmeter needle fluctuates more than 6 times in 10 seconds.
● If less than 6 times, disconnect bridge between terminals TE1 and E1.
● Engine at 2500 rev/min, check voltage between terminals VF1 and E1.
● If more than 0 V, replace sensor.

Checking sensor heater - 14

● Ensure ignition switched OFF.
● Disconnect sensor multi-plug.
● Connect ohmmeter across terminals +B and HT of sensor connector.
● Compare resistance indicated with that specified.

2.9 Fuel pump relay

Checking - 15

● Ensure ignition switched OFF.
● Remove relay located in LH fascia.
● Check for continuity with ohmmeter between terminals STA and E1 and +B and FC.
● Check for open circuit with ohmmeter connected between terminals +B and FP.
● Connect battery voltage between terminals STA and E1.
● Check for continuity between terminals +B and FP.
● Connect battery voltage between terminals +B and FC and check for continuity between terminals +B and FP.

Figure 2.15 'Autodata' fuel injection testing example

Figure 2.16 Data books are an excellent source of information

3
Tools and equipment

3.1 Basic equipment

3.1.1 Introduction

As the complexity of the modern vehicle continues to increase, developments in suitable test equipment must follow. Many mechanical and electronic systems now have ECUs, that contain self-diagnosis circuits. This is represented by Figure 3.1. Activating the blink code output can access the information held in the ECU memory. This is done in some cases by connecting two wires and then switching on the ignition. A further refinement is to read the information via a serial link, which requires suitable test equipment.

Diagnostic techniques are very much linked to the use of test equipment. In other words you must be able to interpret the results of tests. In most cases this involves comparing the result of a test to the reading given in a data book or other source of information. By way of an introduction, the following table lists some of the basic words and descriptions relating to tools and equipment.

Hand tools	Spanners and hammers and screwdrivers and all the other basic bits!
Special tools	A collective term for items not held as part of a normal tool kit. Or items required for just one specific job
Test equipment	In general, this means measuring equipment. Most tests involve measuring something and comparing the result of that measurement to data. The devices can range from a simple ruler to an engine analyser
Dedicated test equipment	Some equipment will only test one specific type of system. The large manufacturers supply equipment

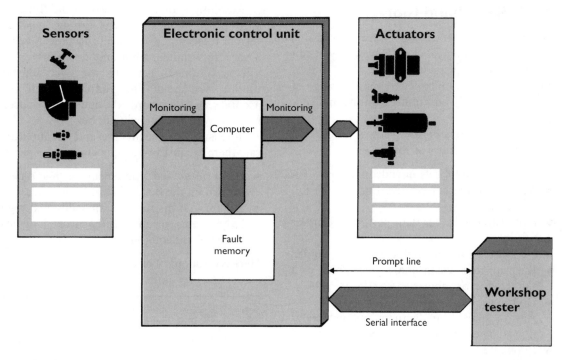

Figure 3.1 Engine control with self-diagnosis

dedicated to their vehicles. For example, a diagnostic device which plugs in to a certain type of fuel injection ECU

Accuracy	Careful and exact, free from mistakes or errors and adhering closely to a standard
Calibration	Checking the accuracy of a measuring instrument
Serial port	A connection to an ECU, a diagnostic tester or computer for example. Serial means the information is passed in a 'digital' string like pushing black and white balls through a pipe in a certain order
Code reader or scanner	This device reads the 'black and white balls' mentioned above, or the on-off electrical signals, and converts them to language we can understand
Combined diagnostic and information system	Usually now PC based, these systems can be used to carry out tests on vehicle systems and they also contain an electronic workshop manual. Test sequences guided by the computer can also be carried out
Oscilloscope	The main part of 'scope' is the display, which is like a TV or computer screen. A scope is a voltmeter but instead of readings in numbers it shows the voltage levels by a trace or mark on the screen. The marks on the screen can move and change very fast allowing us to see the way voltages change

3.1.2 Basic hand tools

You cannot learn to use tools from a book; it is clearly a very practical skill. However, you can follow the recommendations made here and of course by the manufacturers. Even the range of basic hand tools is now quite daunting and very expensive.

It is worth repeating the general advice and instructions for the use of hand tools.

- Only use a tool for its intended purpose.
- Always use the correct size tool for the job you are doing.
- Pull a wrench rather than pushing whenever possible.
- Do not use a file or similar, without a handle.
- Keep all tools clean and replace them in a suitable box or cabinet.
- Do not use a screwdriver as a pry bar.
- Always follow manufacturers' recommendations (you cannot remember everything).
- Look after your tools and they will look after you!

3.1.3 Accuracy of test equipment

Accuracy can mean a number of slightly different things:

- careful and exact
- free from mistakes or errors; precise
- adhering closely to a standard

Consider measuring a length of wire with a steel rule. How accurately could you measure it To the nearest 0.5 mm? This raises a number of issues. Firstly, you could make an error reading the ruler. Secondly, why do we need to know the length of a bit of wire to the nearest 0.5 mm? Thirdly the ruler may have stretched and not give the correct reading!

The first and second of these issues can be dispensed with by knowing how to read the test equipment correctly and also knowing the appropriate level of accuracy required. A micrometer for a plug gap? A ruler for valve clearances? I think you get the idea. The accuracy of the equipment itself is another issue.

Accuracy is a term meaning how close the measured value of something is to its actual value. For example, if a length of about 30 cm is measured with an ordinary wooden ruler, then the error may be up to 1 mm too high or too low. This is quoted as an accuracy of ± 1 mm. This may also be given as a percentage which in this case would be 0.33%.

Resolution, or in other words the 'fineness' with which a measurement can be made, is related to accuracy. If a steel ruler was made to a very high standard but only had markings of one per centimetre it would have a very low resolution even though the graduations were very accurate. In other words the equipment is accurate but your reading will not be!

To ensure instruments are, and remain, accurate there are just two simple guidelines.

- Look after the equipment; a micrometer thrown on the floor will not be accurate.
- Ensure that instruments are calibrated regularly – this means being checked against known good equipment.

Here is a summary of the steps to ensure a measurement is accurate:

Step	Example
Decide on the level of accuracy required	Do we need to know that the battery voltage is 12.6 V or 12.635 V?

Choose the correct instrument for the job	A micrometer to measure the thickness of a shim
Ensure that the instrument has been looked after and calibrated when necessary	Most instruments will go out of adjustment after a time. You should arrange for adjustment at regular intervals. Most tool suppliers will offer the service or in some cases you can compare older equipment to new stock
Study the instructions for the instrument in use and take the reading with care. Ask yourself if the reading is about what you expected	Is the piston diameter 70.75 mm or 170.75 mm?
Make a note if you are taking several readings	Don't take a chance, write it down

3.1.4 Multimeters

An essential tool for working on vehicle electrical and electronic systems is a good digital multimeter. Digital meters are most suitable for accuracy of reading as well as available facilities. The following list of functions, broadly in order from essential to desirable, should be considered.

Function	Range	Accuracy
DC voltage	500 V	0.3%
DC current	10 A	1.0%
Resistance	0 to 10 M Ω	0.5%
AC voltage	500 V	2.5%
AC current	10 A	2.5%
Dwell	3,4,5,6,8 cylinders	2.0%
RPM	10 000 rev/min	0.2%
Duty cycle	% on/off	0.2% (kHz)
Frequency	100 kHz	0.01%
Temperature	>900°C	0.3% +3°C
High current clamp	1000 A (DC)	Depends on conditions
Pressure	3 bar	10.0% of standard scale

A way of determining the quality of a meter, as well as by the facilities provided, is to consider the following:

- accuracy;
- loading effect of the meter;
- protection circuits.

The loading effect is a consideration for any form of measurement. With a multimeter this relates to the internal resistance of the meter. It is recommended that the internal resistance of a meter should be a minimum of 10 MΩ. This not only ensures greater accuracy but also prevents the meter from damaging sensitive circuits.

Figure 3.2 shows two equal resistors connected in series across a 12 V supply. The voltage across each resistor should be 6 V. However, the internal resistance of the meter will affect the

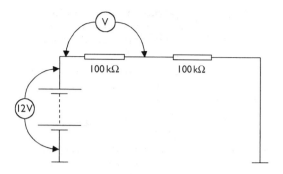

Figure 3.2 Loading effect of a test meter

circuit conditions and change the voltage reading. If the resistor values were 100 kΩ the effect of meter internal resistance would be as follows.

Meter resistance 1 MΩ

With a parallel combined value of 1 MΩ and 100 k Ω = 91 k Ω the voltage drop in the circuit across this would be:

$$91/(100 + 91) \times 12 = 5.71\ V$$

This is an error of about 5%.

Meter resistance 10 MΩ

With parallel combined value of 10 MΩ and 100 KΩ = 99 KΩ the voltage drop in the circuit across this would be:

$$99/(100 + 99) \times 12 = 5.97\ V$$

This is an error of about 0.5%.

Note: This 'invasive measurement' error is in addition to the basic accuracy of the meter.

Figure 3.3 Multimeter and accessories

Figure 3.4 Logic probe

Figure 3.5 Analogue oscilloscope principle

Figure 3.3 shows a digital multimeter. Now that this is recognised, only two further skills are required – where to put the probes and what the reading you get actually means!

3.1.5 Logic probe

This device is a useful way of testing logic circuits but it is also useful for testing some types of sensor. Figure 3.4 shows a typical logic probe. Most types consist of two power supply wires and a metal 'probe'. The display consists of two or three LEDs labelled 'high', 'low' and on some devices 'pulse'. These LEDs light up, together with an audible signal in some cases, when the probe touches either a high, low or pulsing voltage. Above or below 2.5 V is often used to determine high or low on a 5 V circuit.

3.2 Oscilloscopes

3.2.1 Introduction

Two types of oscilloscope are available: analogue or digital. Figure 3.5 shows the basic operation of an analogue oscilloscope. Heating a wire creates a source of electrons, which are then accelerated by suitable voltages and focused into a beam. This beam is directed towards a fluores-

cent screen where it causes light to be given off. This is the basic cathode ray tube.

The plates as shown in the figure are known as X and Y plates as they make the electron beam draw a 'graph' of a voltage signal. The X plates are supplied with a saw tooth signal, which causes the beam to move across the screen from left to right and then to 'fly back' and start again. Being attracted towards whichever plate has a positive potential the beam moves simply. The Y plates can now be used to show voltage variations of the signal under test. The frequency of the saw tooth signal, known as the time base, can be adjusted either automatically as is the case with many analysers or manually on a stand alone oscilloscope. The signal from the item under test can either be amplified or attenuated (reduced), much like changing the scale on a voltmeter. The trigger, in other words when the trace across the screen starts, can be caused internally or externally. In the case of the engine analyser triggering is often external, each time an individual spark fires or each time number one spark plug fires.

A digital oscilloscope has much the same end result as the analogue type but the signal can be thought of as being plotted rather than drawn on the screen. The test signal is A/D converted and the time base is a simple timer or counter circuit. Because the signal is plotted digitally on a screen from data in memory, the 'picture' can be saved, frozen or even printed. The speed of data conversion and the sampling rate as well as the resolution of the screen are very important in ensuring accurate results. This technique is becoming the norm as including scales and notes or superimposing two or more traces for comparison can enhance the display.

A very useful piece of equipment becoming very popular is the 'Scopemeter' or 'MultiScope' as shown in (Figure 3.6). This is a hand-held digital oscilloscope, which allows data to be stored and transferred to a PC for further

Figure 3.6 Multiscope

investigation. The Scopemeter can be used for a large number of vehicle tests. The waveforms used as examples in this book were 'captured' using this device. This type of test equipment is highly recommended.

3.2.2 Waveforms

You will find the words 'waveform', 'pattern' and 'trace' are used in books and workshop manuals but they mean the same thing. When you look at a waveform on a screen you must remember that the height of the scale represents voltage and the width represents time. Both of these axes can have their scales changed. They are called axes because the 'scope' is drawing a graph of the voltage at the test points over a period of time. The time scale can vary from a few μs to several seconds. The voltage scale can vary from a few mV to several kV. For most test measurements only two connections are needed just like a voltmeter. The time scale will operate at intervals preset by the user. It is also possible to connect a 'trigger' wire so that, for example, the time scale starts moving across the screen each time the ignition coil fires. This keeps the display in time with the speed of the engine. When you use a full engine analyser, all the necessary connections are made as listed in the table in section 3.4.1. A hand-held scope has to be connected for each waveform as required. Figure 3.7 shows an example waveform.

All the waveforms shown in various parts of this book are from a correctly operating vehicle. The skill you will learn by practice is to note when your own measurements vary from those shown here.

Figure 3.7 An example waveform transferred from the Multiscope to a PC for annotation and storage – timebase setting (milliseconds per division)

3.3 Scanners/fault code readers

3.3.1 Serial port communications

A special interface of the type that is stipulated by ISO 9141 is required to read data. This standard is designed to work with a single or two wire port allowing many vehicle electronic systems to be connected to a central diagnostic plug. The sequence of events to extract data from the ECU is as listed below:

- test unit transmits a code word;
- ECU responds by transmitting a baud rate recognition word;
- test unit adopts the appropriate setting;
- ECU transmits fault codes.

The test unit converts these to suitable output text. Further functions are possible which include the following.

- Identification of ECU and system to ensure that the test data is appropriate to the system currently under investigation.
- Read out of current live values from sensors. Spurious figures can be easily recognised. Information such as engine speed, temperature, airflow and so on can be displayed and checked against test data.
- System function stimulation to allow actuators to be tested by moving them and watching for suitable response.
- Programming of system changes such as basic idle CO or changes in basic timing can be programmed into the system.

3.3.2 The scanner/fault code reader

Serial communication is an area that is continuing to grow. A special interface is required to read data. This standard is designed to work with a single or two wire port, which connects vehicle electronic systems to a diagnostic plug. Many functions are then possible when a scanner is connected. They include the following.

- Identification of ECU and system to ensure that the test data is appropriate to the system currently under investigation.
- Read out of current live values from sensors so that spurious figures can be easily recognised. Information such as engine speed, temperature air flow and so on can be displayed and checked against test data.
- System function stimulation allows actuators to be tested by moving them and watching for suitable response.
- Programming of system changes. Basic idle CO or changes in basic timing can be programmed into the system.

At present several standards exist which means several different types of serial readers are needed or at best several different adapters and program modules. A standard called On Board Diagnostics II (OBD II) has been developed by the Society of Automotive Engineers

Figure 3.8 Scanner

(SAE). In the USA all new vehicles must conform to this standard. This means that just one scan tool will work with all new vehicles. This standard has also recently been adopted in Europe (EOBD).

Figure 3.8 shows a scanner from a company called GenRad, produced to meet these standards. This scanner allows the technician to perform all the necessary operations, such as fault code reading, via a single common connector. The portable hand-held tool has a large graphics display allowing clear instructions and data. Context-sensitive help is available to eliminate the need to refer back to manuals to look up fault code definitions. It has a memory so that data can be reused even after disconnecting power from the tool. This scanner will even connect to a controller area network (CAN) system with a suitable adapter.

3.4   Engine analysers

3.4.1   Engine analysers

Some form of engine analyser has become an almost essential tool for faultfinding modern vehicle engine systems. The latest machines are now generally based around a PC. This allows more facilities that can be added to by simply changing the software. Whilst engine analysers are designed to work specifically with the motor vehicle, it is worth remembering that the machine consists basically of three parts:

- multimeter;
- gas analyser;
- oscilloscope.

This is not intended to imply that other available tests, such as cylinder balance, are less valid, but to show that the analyser is not magic, it is just able to present results of electrical tests in a convenient way to allow diagnosis of faults. The key component of any engine analyser is the oscilloscope facility, which allows the user to 'see' the signal under test.

The following is a description of the facilities available on a typical engine analyser. The new concept in garage equipment design is based on a PC, specially engineered for workshop use and enabling a flexibility of use far exceeding the ability of machines previously available.

Software is used to give the machine its 'personality' as an engine analyser, system tester, wheel aligner or even any of the other uses made of PCs. Either an infrared handset or a standard 'qwerty' keyboard controls the machine. The information is displayed on a super VGA monitor giving high resolution colour graphics. Output can be sent to a standard printer when a hard copy is required for the customer.

A range of external measurement modules and software application programmes is available. The modules are connected to the host computer by high speed RS422 or RS232 serial communication links. Application software is loaded onto a hard disk. Vehicle specific data can also be stored on disk to allow fast easy access to information but also to allow a guided test procedure.

The modern trend with engine analysers seems to be to allow both guided test procedures with pass/fail recommendations for the less skilled technician, and freedom to test any electrical device using the facilities available in any reasonable way. This is more appropriate for the highly skilled technician. Some of the routines available on modern engine analysers are listed below.

Tune-up

This is a full prompted sequence that assesses each component in turn with results and diagnosis displayed at the end of each component test. Stored data allows pass/fail diagnosis by automatically comparing results of tests with

data on the disk. Printouts can be taken to show work completed.

Symptom analysis

This allows direct access to specific tests relating to reported driveability problems.

Waveforms

A comprehensive range of digitised waveforms can be displayed with colour highlights. The display can be frozen or recalled to look for intermittent faults. A standard lab scope mode is available to allow examination of EFI (electronic fuel injection) or ABS traces for example. Printouts can be made from any display. An interesting feature is 'transient capture' which ensures that even the fastest spikes and intermittent signals are captured and displayed for detailed examination.

Adjustments

Selecting specific components from a menu can make simple quick adjustments. Live readings are displayed appropriate to the selection.

MOT emissions (annual UK test)

Full MOT procedure tests are integrated and displayed on the screen with pass/fail diagnosis to the department of transport specifications for both gas analysis and diesel smoke if appropriate options are fitted. The test results include engine rev/min and oil temperature as well as the gas readings. These can all be printed for garage or customer use.

The connections to the vehicle for standard use are much the same for most equipment manufacturers. These are listed as follows.

Connection	Purpose or one example of use
Battery positive	Battery and charging voltages
Battery negative	A common earth connection
Coil positive	To check supply voltage to coil
Coil negative (adapters for DIS – distributorless ignition systems)	To look at dwell, rev/min and primary waveforms
Coil HT lead clamp (adapters are available for DIS)	Secondary waveforms
Number one cylinder plug lead clamp	Timing light and sequence of waveforms
Battery cable amp clamp	Charging and starting current
Oil temperature probe (dip stick hole)	Oil temperature
Vacuum connection	Engine load

Figure 3.9 shows a 'Sun' digital oscilloscope engine analyser. This test equipment has many features as listed previously and others such as the following.

- **High tech test screens** Vacuum waveform, cylinder time balance bar graph, power balance waveform and dual trace lab scope waveform.
- **Scanner interface** This allows the technician to observe all related information at the same time.
- **Expanded memory** This feature allows many screens to be saved at once, then recalled at a later time for evaluation and reference.

The tests are user controlled whereas some machines have pre-programmed sequences. Some of the screens available are as follows.

Primary	Secondary	Diagnostic	Cylinder test
Primary waveform	Secondary waveform	Voltage waveform	Vacuum waveform
Primary parade waveform	Secondary parade waveform	Lab scope waveform	Power balance waveform
Dwell bar graph	kV histogram	Fuel injector waveform	Cylinder time balance bar graph
Duty cycle/dwell bar graph	kV bar graph	Alternator waveform	Cylinder shorting even/odd bar graph
Duty cycle/voltage bar graph	Burn time bar graph		Cranking amps bar graph

3.4.2 Exhaust gas measurement

It has now become standard to measure four of the main exhaust gases namely:

- carbon monoxide (CO);
- carbon dioxide (CO_2);
- hydrocarbons (HC);
- oxygen (O_2).

The emission test module is often self-contained with its own display but can be linked to the main analyser display. Often lambda value and the air fuel ratio are displayed in addition to the four gasses. The Greek symbol lambda (λ) is used to represent the ideal air fuel ratio (AFR) of 14.7:1 by mass. In other words just the right amount of air to burn up all the fuel. Typical gas, lambda and AFR readings are given in Table 3.1 for a closed loop lambda control system, before (or without) and after the catalytic converter. These are for a modern engine in excellent condition (examples only – always check current data).

The composition of exhaust gas is now a critical measurement and hence a certain degree of accuracy is required. To this end the infrared measurement technique has become the most suitable for CO, CO_2 and HC. Each individual gas absorbs infrared radiation at a specific rate.

Figure 3.9 Engine analyser

Table 3.1

Reading	CO%	$H_{C(ppm)}$	CO_2%	O_2%	Lambda (λ)	AFR
Before catlayst	0.6	120	14.7	0.7	1.0	14.7
After catalyst	0.2	12	15.3	0.1	1.0	14.7

Oxygen is measured by electro-chemical means in much the same way as the on vehicle lambda sensor. CO is measured using a beam of infrared light. A similar technique is used for the measurement of CO_2 and HC. At present it is not possible to measure NOx without more sophisticated laboratory equipment.

Good four-gas emission analysers often have the following features.

● Stand alone unit not dependent on other equipment.
● Graph screen simultaneously displays up to four values as graphs and the graph display order is user selectable. Select from HC, CO, CO_2, O_2 and rev/min for graph display.
● User can create personalised letterhead for screen printouts.
● Uses the non-dispersive infrared (NDIR) method of detection (each individual gas absorbs infrared light at a specific rate).
● Display screens may be frozen or stored in memory for future retrieval.
● Recalibrate at the touch of a button (if calibration gas and a regulator are used).
● Display exhaust gas concentrations in real time numerics or create live exhaust gas data graphs in selectable ranges.
● Calculate and display lambda (λ) (the ideal air fuel ratio of about 14.7:1).

● Display engine rev/min in numeric or graph form and display oil temperature along with current time and date.
● Display engine diagnostic data from a scanner.
● Operate from mains supply or a 12 V battery.

Accurate measurement of exhaust gas is not only required for annual tests but is essential to ensure an engine is correctly tuned. Table 3.1 lists typical values measured from a typical exhaust. Note the toxic emissions are small, but none-the-less dangerous.

3.5 Specialist equipment

3.5.1 Pressure testing

Measuring the fuel pressure on a fuel injection engine is of great value when faultfinding. Many types of pressure testers are available and they often come as part of a kit consisting of various adapters and connections. The principle of the gauges is that they contain a very small tube wound in a spiral. As fuel under pressure is forced into a spiral tube it unwinds causing the needle to move over a graduated scale. Figure 3.10 shows a fuel pressure gauge as part of a kit.

Measuring engine cylinder compression or leakage is a useful test. Figure 3.11 shows an

Figure 3.10 Pressure gauge and kit

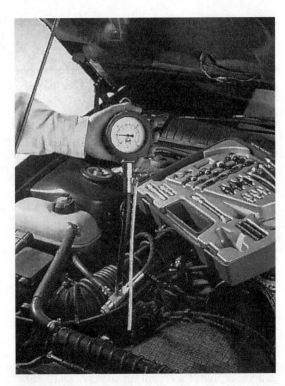

Figure 3.11 Compression tester

engine compression tester. This device is used more to compare cylinder compressions than to measure actual values.

3.5.2 Laser 2000 electronic systems tester

The Lucas Laser 2000 tester (Figure 3.12) is designed to find faults on vehicles with electronic systems. These may include fuelling, antilock braking traction control, etc. Faultfinding on such systems can be difficult and slow due to the complexity of the electronics.

Many ECUs have OBD which means the ECU monitors its inputs and outputs and, if any are incorrect, stores a fault code. A warning lamp will also be illuminated to alert the driver. These codes can be read out and a test procedure followed.

More advanced ECUs have a data link (serial communication) so that fault codes can be displayed using a tester, either as a number or with a text description. Other information such as operating values can also be passed to the tester. Commands can also be sent from the tester to the ECU, for example to operate a solenoid.

Depending upon the diagnostic features of the ECU, Laser 2000 can provide all these options. Further, data may be logged whilst driving the vehicle, fault codes can be erased and

Figure 3.12 Lucas Laser 2000 tester

results of up to four tests may be stored within Laser 2000. Output may be printed if required.

The Laser 2000 is configured for different systems by a hardware module, a software module, a master cable and an adaptor cable. The hardware module is to allow future upgrades; one module covers most current systems. The software contains the test routines for a system or range of systems. Adaptor cables are required to connect to each vehicle diagnostic connector. The Laser 2000 is designed to be user friendly; it is menu driven by function keys relating to the menu on the screen.

One of the most interesting features, besides those mentioned above, is the Laser 2000 snapshot mode. In this mode as well as displaying live data the tester can record values over a period. This is very useful for identifying intermittent faults as the recorded data can be replayed slowly, the results being displayed in numerical as well as graphical format. Figure 3.13 shows a typical snapshot screen on the Laser 2000. Gradual changes are to be expected but sudden changes in say air flow could indicate a fault in the air flow sensor or wiring. Snapshot data may also be printed in tabular form via the RS232 interface.

3.5.3 GenRad diagnostic system (GDS)

This system as shown in Figure 3.14 is a fully featured measurement system, integrated with guided diagnostics for fast and accurate fault diagnosis on complex electrical and electronic

Figure 3.13 Laser 2000 screen

Figure 3.14 GenRad diagnostic system

systems. Hand-held and portable, the unit is much more than a fault code reader. Capable of capturing intermittent faults as well as multiple and inter-related faults, the diagnostic system known as the GDS can save significant amounts of service time.

The system is highly user friendly; communication with the technician takes place via an easy-to-read liquid crystal display (LCD) with rugged touchscreen. The display has also been designed for enhanced visibility in a variety of lighting conditions. GDS is ergonomically designed and features an impact resistant case with integral carrying handle for easy portability. It also features a stand to ease positioning and colour coded connector inserts for probe identification.

The GDS has 1 Mb as standard with optional extra memory giving a total capacity of up to 4 Mb for extended diagnostic routines. The GDS's versatility means that the unit also forms the basis of a comprehensive engine monitoring and analysis system including ignition, cranking, charging and fuel injection diagnostics by the addition of software and transducers.

An optional extra to the GDS is a spread spectrum wireless link, allowing communication between more than one unit and other PC systems. Measurement parameters and data can be communicated allowing remote analysis by an operator where access is limited. Applications can also be loaded to the GDS via a wireless

link, precluding the need for an operator to return to a base station to download software.

General specification

Display	LCD graphics 320 × 240 pixels
Touchscreen	Analogue, 256 × 256 resolution
Memory	1, 2 or 4 Mbyte RAM options. FLASH RAM fitted as standard
Power sources	Internal 1.8 Ah NiCd rechargeable battery or vehicle battery. Base station with automatic three hour fast charge to internal battery
Battery life	Typically 60 minutes with display and stimulus active (4 V into 1000 Ω).
Approx weight	2.5 kg
Approx size	230 mm × 310 mm × 70 mm
Operating temperature range	0°C + 50°C
Storage temperature range	20°C + 60°C
Ingress protection	IP54

Capabilities

- Dual channel AC and DC auto-ranging bi-polar voltage measurement
- Dual channel sampling oscilloscope
- Single channel positive and negative peak voltage detect
- Auto-ranging resistance measurement
- Dual channel timing (period, pulse width, duty cycle and frequency)
- Triggered voltage measurement
- Waveform generator/sensor stimulation/resistance simulation
- Current
- Pressure
- Temperature

Communications

- CAN
- ISO 9141
- J1850 VPW
- J1850 PWM
- KWP2000

Accessories

- Automatic break-out box option
- Base station with CD-ROM drive, unit docking, charge, date download, RS232 or radio modem interface

3.5.4 Multi protocol adapter

GenRad's multi protocol adapter (MPA) shown in Figure 3.15 provides an interface between the serial communications on a vehicle and the host diagnostic unit. The unit provides a communications

Figure 3.15 Multi-protocol adapter

path between the vehicle and the host unit across the selected serial protocol. The host diagnostic unit is also able to download executable code or applications to the MPA, allowing it to be disconnected or freed up to perform other tasks. This increases the diagnostic unit's flexibility and efficiency.

The stand-alone 'flight recorder' capability of the MPA is instrumental in the detection of specific real time events, such as intermittent faults, which are notoriously difficult to trace. This is invaluable for a technician in improving accuracy and efficiency. The MPA also provides a vehicle flash programming output, which may be used to provide vehicle ECU programming 'in-situ' via the vehicle diagnostic connector.

The MPA can be customised to meet specific requirements, for example to allow a vehicle manufacturer to meet environmental protection legislation. Also available as an option to the MPA is a CAN active cable that provides a trouble-free connection directly onto the vehicle's CAN bus. Using an active CAN cable the technician is able to connect off-board test and diagnostic equipment with long cables to the vehicle's CAN bus via the OBDII (J1962) connector.

General specification

Host computer interface	RS485/RS232 (opto-isolated)
Vehicle serial communications interface	ISO 9141–2, J1850, CAN (vers2B)
Vehicle FLASH programming supply	12 V to 19 V @ 100 mA
Auxiliary and ignition relay control	2 × 2 A open drain outputs
RAM (non-volatile to 24 Hours)	128 Kbytes to 4 Mbytes
BOOT ROM	512 Kbytes (in-circuit re-programmable)
Analogue measurements	Ten channels, eight bits
Power switching to hose	Vbatt @ 2 A (non-isolated but switchable under from the host computer)
Vehicle connection	Rugged captive J1962 cable (2 m)
Host connection	6M cable, connector to suit host type

3.5.5 Electronic service bay

The electronic service bay (ESB) is an open system providing electronic information exchange and guided diagnostics for the service technician, serving all aspects of the dealership service operations. With increasingly sophisticated vehicles being brought to market and with the huge variety of vehicle variants throughout the world, the service technician is often faced with a vast amount of information from which specific details need to be retrieved.

In addition, vehicle manufacturers, as information providers, are subject to pressures to disseminate more and more data throughout their networks, including external directives such as new legislation. In short, there has been an exposition of information in the service bay – and at a time when quality of service has itself become a major differentiator. For a correct and timely repair the service technician must be able to access accurate information which is up to date and vehicle specific.

To address this GenRad's ESB brings relevant information from several sources together to either run on a standard PC or to run on a GDS3000. Using a GDS3000 as hardware platform gives the added and powerful advantage of bringing all the sourced information together on one single portable unit for the service technician. It is a rugged unit, making it ideal for workshop or roadside use. Information is presented in a consistent, convenient way and it is designed to be user friendly, so that computing expertise is not essential for the operator.

The information available in the ESB is also valuable to other areas of the dealership – especially the parts counter. Components of GenRad's ESB can also be used on a standard office computer – so the information is available to anyone who may need it. The information stored in the ESB is displayed in data viewers. The following data viewers included.

Service manuals	Information, which is currently delivered in paper manuals, is now presented as an electronic book. Electronic books are much more flexible than their paper equivalents – and can easily be read in random order (rather than sequentially). The ability to navigate freely around a book is very appropriate to a reference manual

Diagnostic sequences	A large proportion of existing service manuals is devoted to faultfinding sequences. In the ESB these sequences are presented as step by step instructions – hence eliminating the need for large sections of existing manuals. These automated sequences are able to take measurements and read values from the vehicle without the need for the technician to use a variety of special tools. In addition, automatic diagnostics are often able to use techniques that would be difficult for a service technician even if he/she had the special tools. As an example, the diagnostic sequence may include oscilloscope functionality with automatic interpretation of the results
Parts catalogues	Apart from ordering parts, assembly and compatibility information can also be made available to the service technician by displaying parts catalogues on the same screen as other information
Service bulletins	Even with electronic publishing and delivery there are always last minute changes caused by unexpected vehicle and component problems. If a technician is to make effective use of service bulletins, it is important that they are presented at the right time. For this reason service bulletins are connected with other elements of the ESB so that they appear alongside the other information

Although the ESB contains all these separate items, it is much more than 'putting them all on one computer.' The real need is to make all this information available at the right time. To make this work, the ESB observes the following principles.

- All the data viewers work in the same way. This means standard buttons and navigation mechanisms, so that once one viewer has been mastered the others are immediately familiar.
- There is never any need to enter the same information twice. Once the system knows about a vehicle, then all the data viewers can use this knowledge.
- The data viewers are simple to operate. They require only a touchscreen for all operations. Keyboards are avoided.

GenRad's ESB runs on a desktop or portable PC, with Windows 95 or Windows NT (minimum specifications 486 DX2 66 MHz, 16 MB RAM, VGA display), or the GDS3000 which allows integration of analogue measurement and vehicle communications.

3.6 On-line diagnostics

3.6.1 Networking

A continuing development in diagnosis and testing is by increased networking of vehicles via adapters to computers locally and then via modems and the telephone lines. It is already quite common practice in the computer industry, with suitable hardware and software, to remotely link one computer to another to carry out diagnostics and in some cases even repairs. This technique can be extended to the

Figure 3.16 Remote diagnostics

computerised systems on modern vehicles. Access to the latest data and test procedures is available at the 'touch of a screen' or the 'click of a mouse'. Figure 3.16 shows a representation of this technique. Some of the latest systems even involve a hand held video camera if it is necessary to communicate with a human and show him/her particular vehicle components!

3.6.2 Compact disks

The incredible storage capacity of compact disks is the reason why they are used more and more as the medium for information storage. When used in conjunction with test equipment as described earlier, the operator will be able to work through the most complex of faults, with interactive help from the computer.

4
Mechanical systems

4.1 Introduction

The main sections in this chapter that relate to an area of the vehicle start with an explanation of the particular system. The sections then conclude with appropriate diagnostic techniques and symptom charts. Extra tests and methods are explained where necessary.

4.2 Engine operation

4.2.1 Four stroke cycle

Figure 4.1 shows a modern vehicle engine. Engines like this can seem very complex at first but keep in mind when carrying out diagnostic work that, with very few exceptions, all engines operate on the four stroke principle. The complexity is in the systems around the engine to make it operate to its maximum efficiency or best performance. With this in mind then, back to basics!

The engine components are combined to use the power of expanding gas to drive the engine. When the term 'stroke' is used it means the movement of a piston from topdead centre (TDC) to bottom dead centre (BDC) or the other way round. The following table explains the spark ignition (SI) and compression ignition (CI) four stroke cycles – for revision purposes! Figure 4.2 shows the SI cycle.

Stroke	Spark ignition	Compression ignition
Induction	The fuel air mixture is forced into the cylinder through the open inlet valve because as the piston moves down it makes a lower pressure. It is acceptable to say the mixture is drawn into the cylinder	Air is forced into the cylinder through the open inlet valve because as the piston moves down it makes a lower pressure. It is acceptable to say the air is drawn into the cylinder
Compression	As the piston moves back up the cylinder the fuel air mixture is compressed to about an eighth of its original volume because the inlet and exhaust valves are closed. This is a compression ratio of	As the piston moves back up the cylinder the fuel air mixture is compressed in some engines to about a sixteenth of its original volume because the inlet and exhaust valves are closed. This is a

Figure 4.1 The BMW 2.8 litre six cylinder engine uses variable camshaft control

| 1 Induction | 2 Compression | 3 Power | 4 Exhaust |

Figure 4.2 Four stroke cycle

	8:1, which is typical for many normal engines	compression ratio of 16:1, which causes a large build up of heat
Power	At a suitable time before top dead centre, a spark at the plug ignites the compressed mixture. The mixture now burns very quickly and the powerful expansion pushes the piston back down the cylinder. Both valves are closed	At a suitable time before top dead centre, very high pressure atomised diesel fuel is injected into the combustion chamber. The mixture burns very quickly and the powerful expansion pushes the piston back down the cylinder. The valves are closed
Exhaust	The final stroke occurs as the piston moves back up the cylinder and pushes the spent gases out of the now open exhaust valve	The final stroke occurs as the piston moves back up the cylinder and pushes the spent gases out of the now open exhaust valve

4.2.2 Cylinder layouts

Great improvements can be made to the performance and balance of an engine by using more than one cylinder. Once this is agreed the actual layout of the cylinders must be considered. The layout can be one of three possibilities as follows.

- **In-line or straight** The cylinders are in a straight line. They can be vertical, inclined or horizontal.
- **Vee** The cylinders are in two rows at a set angle. The actual angle varies but is often 60° or 90°.
- **Opposed** The cylinders are in two rows opposing each other and are usually horizontal.

By far the most common arrangement is the straight four and this is used by all manufactur-

ers in their standard family cars. Larger cars do, however, make use of the 'Vee' configuration. The opposed layout whilst still used is less popular. Engine firing order is important. This means the order in which the power strokes occur. The figures above have the cylinders numbered, and listed by each are some common firing orders. It is important to check in the workshop manual or data book when working on a particular engine.

4.2.3 Camshaft drives

The engine drives the camshaft in one of three ways, gear drive, chain drive or by a drive belt. The last of these is now the most popular as it tends to be simpler and quieter. Note in all cases that the cam is driven at half the engine speed. This is done by the ratio of teeth between the crank and cam cogs which is 1:2, for example 20 crank teeth and 40 cam teeth.

- **Camshaft drive gears** Gears are not used very often on petrol engines but are used on larger diesel engines. They ensure a good positive drive from the crankshaft gear to the camshaft.
- **Camshaft chain drive** Chain drive is still used but was even more popular a few years ago. The problems with it are that a way must be found to tension the chain and also provide lubrication.
- **Camshaft drive belt** Camshaft drive belts have become very popular. The main reasons for this are that they are quieter, do not need lubrication and are less complicated. They do break now and then but this is usually due to lack of servicing. Cam belts should be renewed at set intervals. Figure 4.3 shows an example of the data available relating to camshaft drive belt fitting. This is one of the

many areas where data is essential for diagnostic checks.

4.2.4 Valve mechanisms

A number of methods are used to operate the valves. Three common types are shown as Figure 4.4 and a basic explanation of each follows.

- **Overhead valve with push rods and rockers** The method has been used for many years and although it is not used as much now, many vehicles still on the road are described as overhead valve (OHV). As the cam turns it moves the follower, which in turn pushes the push rod. The push rod moves the rocker, which pivots on the rocker shaft and pushes the valve open. As the cam moves further it allows the spring to close the valve.
- **Overhead cam with followers** Using an overhead cam (OHC) reduces the number of moving parts. In the system shown here the lobe of the cam acts directly on the follower which pivots on its adjuster and pushes the valve open.
- **Overhead cam, direct acting and automatic adjusters** Most new engines now use an OHC with automatic adjustment. This saves on repair and service time and keeps the cost to the customer lower. Systems vary between manufacturers, some use followers and some have the cam acting directly on to the valve. In each case though the adjustment is by oil pressure. A type of plunger, which has a chamber where oil can be pumped under pressure, operates the valve. This expands the plunger and takes up any unwanted clearance.

Valve clearance adjustment is very important. If it is too large the valves will not open fully and will be noisy. If the clearance is too small the valves will not close and no compression will be possible. When an engine is running the valves become very hot and therefore expand. The exhaust valve clearance is usually larger than the inlet, because it gets hotter. Regular servicing is vital for all components but, in particular, the valve operating mechanism needs a good supply of clean oil at all times.

BMW 5 Series 2.5 525i SE	1988–1990
Timing Belt	

A061

BMW–M20

Timing marks

Replacement intervals:
at 36 000 miles

Engine setting position:
TDC at No 1 cylinder

Special tools:
Viscous coupling tool   11.5.040
Pulley retaining tool   11.5.030

Torque settings:
Crank pulley   23 Nm
Tensioner   23 Nm
Fan coupling   43 Nm

Special notes:

The fan coupling has left hand thread. Set timing for camshaft and crankshaft and check TDC mark on the flywheel. Check for rotor arm alignment to distributor casing. After fitting belt rotate engine two full turns and recheck the timing marks.

Figure 4.3 Timing belt data is essential

Pushrod and rocker   Direct OHC   OHC and fingers

Figure 4.4 Valve operating mechanisms

4.2.5 Valve and ignition timing

Valve timing is important. The diagram of Figure 4.5 shows accurately the degrees of rotation of the crankshaft where the inlet and exhaust valves open and close during the four stroke cycle. The actual position in the cycle of operation when valves open and close depends on many factors and will vary slightly with different designs of engine. Some cars now control valve timing by electronics. The diagram is marked to show what is meant by valve lead, lag and overlap. Ignition timing is marked on the diagram. Note how this changes as engine speed changes.

The valve timing diagram shows that the valves of a four stroke engine open just before and close just after the particular stroke. Looking at the timing diagram, if you start at position IVO, the piston is nearly at the top of the exhaust stroke when the inlet valve opens (IVO). The piston reaches the top and then moves down on the intake stroke. Just after starting the compression stroke the inlet valve closes (IVC). The piston continues upwards and, at a point several degrees before top dead centre, the spark occurs and starts the mixture burning.

The maximum expansion is 'timed' to occur after top dead centre, therefore the piston is pushed down on its power stroke. Before the end of this stroke the exhaust valve opens (EVO). Most of the exhaust gases now leave because of their very high pressure. The piston pushes the rest of the spent gases out as it moves back up the cylinder. The exhaust valve closes (EVC) just after the end of this stroke and the inlet has already opened, ready to start the cycle once again.

The reason for the valves opening and closing like this is that it makes the engine more efficient by giving more time for the mixture to enter and the spent gases to leave. The outgoing exhaust gases in fact help to draw in the fuel air mixture from the inlet. Overall this makes the engine have a better 'volumetric efficiency'.

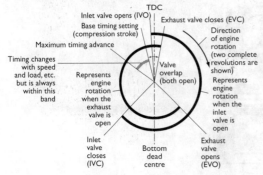

Figure 4.5 Valve and ignition timing

4.3 Diagnostics – engines

4.3.1 Systematic testing example

If the reported fault is excessive use of engine oil proceed as follows.

1. question the customer to find out how much oil is being used.
2. examine the vehicle for oil leaks and blue smoke from the exhaust.
3. for example, oil may be leaking from a gasket or seal – if no leaks are found the engine may be burning the oil.
4. a compression test, if the results were acceptable, would indicate a leak to be the most likely fault. Clean down the engine and run for a while, the leak might show up.
5. For example change the gasket or seals.
6. Run a thorough inspection of vehicle systems particularly those associated with the engine. Double check that the fault has been rectified and that you have not caused any other problems.

4.3.2 Test equipment

> *Note:* You should always refer to the manufacturer's instructions appropriate to the equipment you are using.

Compression tester

With this device the spark plugs are removed and the tester screwed or held in to each spark plug hole in turn. The engine is cranked over by the starter and the gauge will read the compression or pressure of each cylinder.

Cylinder leakage tester

A leakage tester uses compressed air to pressurise each cylinder in turn by a fitting to the spark plug hole. The cylinder under test is set to TDC compression. The percentage of air leaking out and where it is leaking from helps you determine the engine condition. For example if air is leaking through the exhaust pipe then the exhaust valves are not sealing. If air leaks into the cooling system then a leak from the cylinder to the water jacket may be the problem (blown head gasket is possible). Figure 4.6 shows a selection of snap-on diagnostic gauges – vacuum, compression and leakage.

4.3.3 Test results

Some of the information you may have to get from other sources such as data books, or a workshop manual is listed in the following table.

Test carried out	Information required
Compression test	Expected readings for the particular engine under test. For example the pressure reach for each cylinder may be expected to read 800 kPa ±15%
Cylinder leakage test	The percentage leak that is allowed for the tester you are using; some allow about 15% leakage as the limit

4.3.4 Engine fault diagnosis table 1

Symptom	Possible causes or faults	Suggested action
Oil consumption	Worn piston rings and/or cylinders	Engine overhaul
	Worn valve stems, guides or stem oil seals	Replace valves (guides if possible) and oil seals
Oil on engine or floor	Leaking gaskets or seals	Replace appropriate gasket or seal
	Build up of pressure in the crankcase	Check engine breather system
Mechanical knocking noises	Worn engine bearings (big ends or mains for example)	Replace bearings or overhaul engine. Good idea to also check the oil pressure
	Incorrect valve clearances or defective automatic adjuster	Adjust clearances to correct settings or replace defective adjuster
	Piston slap on side of cylinder	Engine overhaul required now or quite soon
Vibration	Engine mountings loose or worn	Secure or renew

Misfiring	Check engine ancillary systems such as fuel and ignition

4.3.5 Engine fault diagnosis table 2

Please note that this section covers related engine systems as well as the engine itself.

Symptom	Possible cause
Engine does not rotate when trying to start	Battery connection loose or corroded
	Battery discharged or faulty
	Broken loose or disconnected wiring in the starter circuit
	Defective starter switch or automatic gearbox inhibitor switch
	Starter pinion or flywheel ring gear loose
	Earth strap broken. Loose or corroded
Engine rotates but does not start	No fuel in the tank!
	Discharged battery (slow rotation)
	Battery terminals loose or corroded
	Air filter dirty or blocked
	Low cylinder compressions
	Broken timing belt
	Damp ignition components
	Fuel system fault
	Spark plugs worn to excess
	Ignition system open circuit
Difficult to start when cold	Discharged battery (slow rotation)
	Battery terminals loose or corroded
	Air filter dirty or blocked
	Low cylinder compressions
	Fuel system fault
	Spark plugs worn to excess
	Enrichment device not working (choke or injection circuit)

Figure 4.6 Diagnostic gauges

Difficult to start when hot	Discharged battery (slow rotation)
	Battery terminals loose or corroded
	Air filter dirty or blocked
	Low cylinder compressions
	Fuel system fault
Starter noisy	Starter pinion or flywheel ring gear loose
	Starter mounting bolts loose
	Starter worn (bearings, etc.)
	Discharged battery (starter may jump in and out)
Starter turns engine slowly	Discharged battery (slow rotation)
	Battery terminals loose or corroded
	Earth strap or starter supply loose or disconnected
	Internal starter fault
Engine starts but then stops immediately	Ignition wiring connection intermittent
	Fuel system contamination
	Fuel pump or circuit fault (relay)
	Intake system air leak
	Ballast resistor open circuit (older cars)
Erratic idle	Air filter blocked
	Incorrect plug gaps
	Inlet system air leak
	Incorrect CO setting
	Uneven or low cylinder compressions (maybe valves)
	Fuel injector fault
	Incorrect ignition timing
	Incorrect valve timing
Misfire at idle speed	Ignition coil or distributor cap tracking
	Poor cylinder compressions
	Engine breather blocked
	Inlet system air leak
	Faulty plugs
Misfire through all speeds	Fuel filter blocked
	Fuel pump delivery low
	Fuel tank ventilation system blocked
	Poor cylinder compressions
	Incorrect plugs or plug gaps
	HT leads breaking down
Engine stalls	Idle speed incorrect
	CO setting incorrect
	Fuel filter blocked
	Air filter blocked
	Intake air leak
	Idle control system not working
Lack of power	Fuel filter blocked
	Air filter blocked
	Ignition timing incorrect
	Low fuel pump delivery
	Uneven or low cylinder compressions (maybe valves)
	Fuel injectors blocked
	Brakes binding or clutch slipping
Backfires	Incorrect ignition timing
	Incorrect valve timing (cam belt not fitted correctly)
	Fuel system fault (air flow sensor on some cars)

Oil pressure gauge low or warning light on	Low engine oil level
	Faulty sensor or switch
	Worn engine oil pump and/or engine bearings
	Engine overheating
	Oil pickup filter blocked
	Pressure relief valve not working
Runs on when switched off	Ignition timing incorrect
	Idle speed too high
	Anti-run on device not working
	Carbon build up in engine
	Engine overheating
Pinking or knocking under load	Ignition timing incorrect
	Ignition system fault
	Carbon build up in engine
	Knock sensor not working
Sucking or whistling noises	Leaking exhaust manifold gasket
	Leaking inlet manifold gasket
	Cylinder head gasket
	Inlet air leak
	Water pump or alternator bearing
Rattling or tapping	Incorrect valve clearances
	Worn valve gear or camshaft
	Loose component
Thumping or knocking noises	Worn main bearings (deep knocking/rumbling noise)
	Worn big end bearings (heavy knocking noise under load)
	Piston slap (worse when cold)
	Loose component
Rumbling noises	Bearings on ancillary component

4.4 Fuel system

4.4.1 Introduction

All vehicle fuel systems consist of the carburettor or fuel injectors, the fuel tank, the fuel pump, and the fuel filter, together with connecting pipes. An engine works by the massive expansion of an ignited fuel air mixture acting on a piston. The job of the fuel system is to produce this mixture at just the right ratio to run the engine under all operating conditions. There are three main ways this is achieved:

- petrol is mixed with air in a carburettor;
- petrol is injected into the manifold, throttle body cylinder or to mix with the air;
- diesel is injected under very high pressure directly into the air already in the engine combustion chamber.

This chapter will only examine the carburettor systems; diesel and injection comes under engine management (Chapter 7).

On idling, high vacuum below the throttle valve draws fuel through a separate circuit

Fuel is drawn from the main outlet as the vacuum around it increases

A flap is used to partially block the barrel for cold starts. It increases vacuum around the fuel outlet and draws more fuel to provide a rich mixture

The accelerator pump squirts an enriching shot of fuel down the barrel to provide rapid response when the throttle is opened quickly, when extra power is needed

Figure 4.7 A simple fixed choke carburettor

4.4.2 Carburation

Figure 4.7 shows a simple fixed choke carburettor operating under various conditions. The float and needle valve assembly ensures a constant level of petrol in the float chamber. The venturi causes an increase in air speed and hence a drop in pressure in the area of the outlet. The main jet regulates how much fuel can be forced into this intake air stream by the higher pressure now apparent in the float chamber. The basic principle is that as more air is forced into the engine then more fuel will be mixed in to the air stream.

The problem with this system is that the amount of fuel forced into the air stream does not linearly follow the increase in air quantity, unless further compensation fuel and air jets are used. A variable venturi carburettor, which keeps the air pressure in the venturi constant but uses a tapered needle to control the amount of fuel, is another method used to control fuel air ratio.

4.4.3 Stages of carburation

The basic principle of a carburettor is to mix fuel and air together in the correct ratios dependent on engine loads and temperature. Fuel flow is caused by the low air pressure around a spray outlet and atmospheric pressure acting on the fuel in the float chamber.

Whilst the engine's requirement for air fuel mixture is infinitely variable, there are six discernible stages to consider. This can help a lot with diagnosing faults because it helps you 'zoom in' on the area where the problem is likely to be found. Although the examples given relate to a standard fixed choke carburettor, the stages are still relevant to all other types. The six stages along with problems and possible solutions are listed below.

Stage	Query or problem	Possible solution or symptoms
Cold starting when a richer mixture is required to reduce the effects of condensation within the inlet manifold and to aid combustion	What would be the result of the choke not closing fully when starting a cold engine? When starting a cold engine with full choke why must the choke valve partially open when the engine is running?	Difficult starting due to a weak mixture To decrease the depression below the choke valve thus preventing the mixture from becoming too rich
Idle when the minimum amount of fuel should be provided to ensure complete combustion and efficiency	A customer complains of erratic idling and hesitation when moving off from rest? What would be the result of exchanging the idle fuel jet for one of a smaller size?	Idling fuel jet restricted Mixture strength too weak at idle Weak idling air to fuel mixture Erratic idle and flat spots when accelerating from stationary
Progression when a smooth sequence of change is necessary from a range of drillings. This is normally from idle until the main jets come into play	What is the purpose of the progression drilling? What would be the result of the progression drillings becoming restricted?	Ensures an even changeover to the main system Lack of response during initial acceleration with warm engine
Acceleration when a measured increase in the supply of fuel is required to sustain an initial burst of speed	What function does the accelerator pump perform? The customer complains of a flat spot during hard acceleration when engine is hot?	Enriches the mixture for hard acceleration Faulty non-return valve in the pump circuit Accelerator pump diaphragm holed
Cruising where the need is for metered fuel to maintain speed at the most efficient setting	What complaint would the customer have if the main air correction jet was restricted? If mixture was too weak on cruise, what would be the effect on operation?	Poor mid throttle range performance combined with high fuel consumption Possible misfiring and poor performance Flat spots on acceleration
High speeds where a slightly richer mixture is required to maintain efficient combustion and to avoid damage to the engine	What operating symptoms could be caused by blocked full load enrichment tube? What symptoms would be observed if the mixture was too rich at high speed?	Reduced top speed Possible poor fuel consumption and reduced engine performance

4.4.4 Electronic control of carburation

Electronic control of a carburettor is made in the following areas.

Idle speed	Controlled by a stepper motor to prevent stalling but still allow a very low idle speed to improve economy and reduce emissions. Idle speed may also be changed in response to a signal from an automatic gearbox to prevent either the engine from stalling or the car from trying to creep
Fast idle	The same stepper motor as above controls fast idle in response to a signal from the engine temperature sensor during the warm up period
Choke	A rotary choke or some other form of valve or flap operates the choke mechanism depending on engine and ambient temperature conditions
Overrun fuel	A small solenoid operated valve or similar
cut off	cuts off the fuel under particular conditions. These conditions are often that the engine temperature must be above a set level, engine speed above a set level and the accelerator pedal is in the off position

The air fuel ratio is set by the mechanical design of the carburettor, so it is very difficult to control by electrical means. Some systems have used electronic control of, say, a needle and jet but this has not proved to be very popular.

Figure 4.8 shows the main components of the system used on some vehicles. As with any control system it can be represented as a series of inputs, a form of control and a number of outputs. The inputs to this system are as follows.

Engine speed	From a signal wire to the negative side of the ignition coil as is common with many systems

Figure 4.8 HIF variable venturi carburettor with electronic control components

Engine coolant temperature	This is taken from a thermistor located in the cylinder head waterways. The same sensor is used for the programmed ignition system if fitted
Ambient temperature	A thermistor sensor is placed such as to register the air temperature. A typical position is at the rear of a headlight
Throttle switch	This switch is placed under the actual pedal and only operates when the pedal is fully off, that is when the butterfly valve in the carburettor is closed

The main controlling actuator of this system is the stepper motor. This motor controls by reduction gears a rotary choke valve for cold starting conditions. The same stepper motor controls idle and fast idle with a rod that works on a snail type cam. The system can operate this way because the first part of the movement of the stepper motor does not affect the choke valve; it only affects the idle speed by opening the throttle butterfly slightly. Further rotation then puts on the choke. The extent, to which the choke is on is determined from engine temperature and ambient temperature.

The ECU 'knows' the position of the stepper motor before setting the choke position by a process known as indexing. This involves the stepper motor being driven to say its least setting on switching off the ignition. When the ignition is next turned on the stepper will drive the idle and choke mechanism by a certain number of steps determined as at the end of the last paragraph.

The other main output is the overrun fuel cut off solenoid. This controls the air pressure in the float chamber and when operated causes pressure in the float chamber and pressure in the venturi at the jet outlet to equalise. This prevents any fuel from being 'drawn' into the air stream.

4.5 Diagnostics – fuel system

4.5.1 Systematic testing example

If the reported fault is excessive fuel consumption proceed as follows.

1. Check that the consumption is excessive for the particular vehicle. Test it yourself if necessary.
2. Are there any other problems with the vehicle, misfiring for example or difficult starting?
3. For example if the vehicle is misfiring as well this may indicate that an ignition fault is the cause of the problem.
4. Remove and examine spark plugs, check HT lead resistance and ignition timing. Check CO emissions.
5. Renew plugs and set fuel mixture.
6. Road test vehicle for correct engine operation.

4.5.2 Test equipment

Note: You should always refer to the manufacturer's instructions appropriate to the equipment you are using.

Exhaust gas analyser (Figure 4.9)

This is a sophisticated piece of test equipment used to measure the make up of the vehicle's exhaust gas. The most common requirement is the measuring of carbon monoxide (CO). A sample probe is placed in the exhaust tail pipe or a special position before the catalytic converter if fitted, and the machine reads out the percentage of certain gases produced. A digital readout is most common. The fuel mixture can then be adjusted until the required readings are obtained.

Fuel pressure gauge

The output pressure of the fuel pump can be tested to ensure adequate delivery. The device is a simple pressure gauge but note the added precautions necessary when dealing with petrol.

Figure 4.9 Exhaust gas analyser

4.5.3 Test results

Some of the information you may have to get from other sources such as data books or a workshop manual is listed in the following table.

Test carried out	Information required
Exhaust gas analysis	CO setting. Most modern vehicles will have settings of about 1% or less. If a 'cat' is fitted then the readings will be even lower when measured at the tail pipe
Fuel pressure	The expected pressure readings will vary depending on the type of fuel system. Fuel injection pressure will be about 2.5 bar whereas fuel pressure for a carburettor will be about 0.3 bar
Fuel delivery	How much fuel the pump should move in a set time. This will again vary with the type of fuel system. 1 litre in 30 seconds is typical for some injection fuel pumps

4.5.4 Fuel fault diagnosis table 1

Symptom	Possible faults	Suggested action
No fuel at carburettor or	Empty tank!
Blocked filter or	Fill it!
Replace filter,

| injection fuel rail | line
Defective fuel pump
No electrical supply to pump | renew/repair line
Renew/check it is being driven
Check fuses/trace fault |
| --- | --- | --- |
| Engine will not or is difficult to start | Choke or enrichment device not working | Check linkages or automatic actuator |
| Engine stalls or will not idle smoothly | Idle speed incorrectly set
Mixture setting wrong
Ignition problem | Look up correct settings and adjust
Look up correct settings and adjust
Check ignition system |
| Poor acceleration | Blockage in carburettor accelerator pump
Partially blocked filter
Injection electrical fault | Strip down and clean out or try a carburettor cleaner first
Renew
Refer to specialist information |
| Excessive fuel consumption | Incorrect mixture settings
Driving technique! | Look up correct settings and adjust
Explain to the customer – but be diplomatic! |
| Black smoke from exhaust | Excessively rich mixture
Flooding | Look up correct settings and adjust
Check and adjust carburettor float settings and operation |

4.5.5 Fuel fault diagnosis table 2

Symptom	Possible cause
Excessive consumption	Blocked air filter
Incorrect CO adjustment
Fuel injectors leaking
Ignition timing incorrect
Temperature sensor fault
Load sensor fault
Low tyre pressures
Driving style!
Fuel leakage	Damaged pipes or unions
Fuel tank damaged
Tank breathers blocked
Fuel smell	Fuel leak
Breather incorrectly fitted
Fuel cap loose
Engine flooding
Incorrect emissions	Incorrect adjustments
Fuel system fault
Air leak into inlet
Blocked fuel filter
Blocked air filter
Ignition system fault

4.6 Air supply and exhaust systems

4.6.1 Exhaust system

A vehicle exhaust system directs combustion products away from the passenger compartment, reduces combustion noise and, on most modern vehicles, reduces harmful pollutants in the exhaust stream. The main parts of the system are the exhaust manifold, the silencer or muffler, the pipes connecting them, and a catalytic converter.

Most exhaust systems are made from mild steel, but some are made from stainless steel which lasts much longer. The system is suspended under the vehicle on rubber mountings. These allow movement because the engine is also rubber mounted, and they also reduce vibration noise.

An exhaust manifold links the engine exhaust ports to the down pipe and main system. It also reduces combustion noise and transfers heat downstream to allow the continued burning of hydrocarbons and carbon monoxide. The manifold is connected to the down pipe, which in turn can be connected to the catalytic converter. Most exhaust manifolds are made from cast iron, as this has the necessary strength and heat transfer properties.

The silencer's main function is to reduce engine noise to an acceptable level. Engine noise is a mixed up collection of its firing frequencies (the number of times per second each cylinder fires). These range from about 100 to 400 Hz (cycles/sec). A silencer reduces noise in two main ways:

- interior chambers using baffles, which are tuned to set up cancelling vibrations;
- absorptive surfaces function like sound-deadening wall and ceiling panels to absorb noise.

When the exhaust gases finally leave the exhaust system, their temperature, pressure and noise have been reduced considerably. The overall length of an exhaust system including the silencers can affect the smooth flow of gases. For this reason do not alter the length or change the layout of an exhaust system. Figure 4.10 shows a silencer/muffler box.

4.6.2 Catalytic converters

Stringent regulations in most parts of the world have made the use of a catalytic converter necessary. The three-way catalyst (TWC) is used to great effect by most manufacturers. It is in effect a very simple device; it looks similar to a standard exhaust silencer box. Note that in order for the 'cat' to operate correctly, the engine must be always be well tuned. This is to ensure that the right 'ingredients' are available for the catalyst to perform its function. A catalytic converter works by converting the dangerous exhaust gases into gases which are non-toxic.

Interference effect
Part of the sound energy is extinguished when it comes together again after different lengths of travel

Twin reactive networks
Long lengths of pipe and corresponding chamber volumes attenuate the low and mid range frequencies

End pipe
The exhaust gases escape into the open air subdued and quietly

Suction resonator
This is where the pipe resonance is 'sucked off'

Classic measures to reduce noise

Intake tube
The hot exhaust gases enter the silencer with unbelievable turbulences and an ear-splitting noise

Reflection chamber
Reflecting obstacles and deflections dissipate part of the sound energy

Choke
Restrictions and perforations in the pipe separate and smooth the pulsating flow

Absorption
Porous material such as basalt fibres absorbs high frequencies and convert these into frictional heat

Figure 4.10 Exhaust noise reduction methods

The core has traditionally been made from ceramic of magnesium aluminium silicate. Due to the several thousand very small channels, this provides a large surface area. It is coated with a wash coat of aluminium oxide, which again increases its effective surface area by about several thousand times. 'Noble' metals are used for the catalysts. Platinum helps to burn off the hydrocarbons (HC) and carbon monoxide (CO), and rhodium helps in the reduction of nitrogen oxides (NO_x). The whole three-way catalytic converter only contains

about three to four grams of these precious metals. Some converters now use metal cores (substrates). Figure 4.11 shows the operation of a catalytic converter and how the lambda window is important.

The engine can damage a catalytic converter in one of two ways:

- firstly by the use of leaded fuel which can cause lead compounds to be deposited on the active surfaces;
- secondly by engine misfire which can cause

During the catalytic conversion of exhaust pollutants into environmentally compatible components carbon monoxide and hydrocarbon become carbon dioxide and water (steam) through oxidation whereas nitrogen is produced from nitrogen oxides through reduction.

Lambda sensor controlled mixture

Since the NO_x emissions behave contrarily to the CO+HC values the exhaust gas purification cannot start from the respective minimum. The smallest common denominator lies at the stoichiometric airfuel ratio of 14.7:1, the lambda window. An oxygen sensor in the exhaust flow, the lambda sensor, controls the optimum mixture via control electronics, thus ensuring this optimum in all engine load cases.

Top: the structure of a ceramic monolith

Below: the active catalytic layer in the exhaust gas flow

Since pollutants behave very differently in the exhaust flow the common optimum has to be determined for conversion: this is lambda = 1.

Figure 4.11 Catalytic converter operation

the catalytic converter to overheat due to burning fuel inside the unit.

Some manufacturers use a system on some vehicles where a sensor checks the output of the ignition HT system and, if the spark is not present, will not allow fuel to be injected. Misfire detection is also part of current on-board diagnostic (OBD) legislation in some countries and future legislation in others.

4.6.3 Air supply system

There are three purposes of the complete air supply system:

- clean the air;
- control air temperature;
- reduce noise.

A filter does the air cleaning and drawing air from around the exhaust manifold helps to control air temperature. When large quantities of air are drawn into the engine it causes the air to vibrate and this makes it noisy. In the same way as with the exhaust system, baffles are used to stop resonance. Resonance means that when vibrations reach a natural level they tend to increase and keep going. A good example of how much noise is reduced by the air intake system is to compare the noise when an engine is run with the air filter removed.

Two types of air filter are in use, the first of these being by far the most popular:

- paper element;
- oil bath and mesh.

The paper element is made of resin-impregnated paper. Air filters using this type of replaceable element are used both for car and commercial vehicles. They provide a very high filtering efficiency and reasonable service life. They can be mounted in any position available under the bonnet. Service intervals vary so check recommendations.

The oil bath and mesh type of air cleaner was widely used on non-turbo charged commercial vehicles. However, it is not very practical for modern low styled bonnets. Because it can be cleaned and fresh oil added, an oil bath air cleaner might still be used for vehicles operating in dusty conditions.

Air temperature control is used to help the vehicle conform to emission control regulations and for good driveability when the engine is cold. Good vaporisation of the fuel is the key. An automatic control is often fitted to make sure

that the air intake temperature is always correct. The air cleaner has two intake pipes, one for cold air and the other for hot air from the exhaust manifold or hot box. The proportion of hot and cold air is controlled by a flap, which is moved by a diaphragm acted on by low pressure from the inlet manifold. The flap rests in the hot air pick up position.

A thermo-valve in the air stream senses the temperature of the air going into the engine. When a temperature of about 25°C is reached, the valve opens. This removes the connection to the manifold, which in turn increases the pressure acting on the diaphragm. The flap is now caused to move and the pick up is now from the cool air position. The flap is constantly moving ensuring that the temperature of air entering the engine remains constant. Picking up hot air when the engine is still cold can also help to prevent icing in a carburettor.

4.7 Diagnostics – exhaust and air supply

4.7.1 Systematic testing

If the reported fault is a noisy exhaust proceed as follows.

1. Check if the noise is due to the exhaust knocking or blowing.
2. Examine the vehicle on the lift.
3. Are further tests required or is it obvious?
4. Cover the end of the exhaust pipe with a rag for a second or two to highlight where the exhaust may be blowing.
5. Renew the exhaust section or complete system as appropriate.
6. Run and test for leaks and knocking.

4.7.2 Test results

Some of the information you may have to get from other sources such as data books or a workshop manual is listed in the following table.

Test carried out	Information required
Air filter condition	Clearly a physical examination but note the required service intervals
Exhaust noise	An idea of the normal noise level – note that 'big bore' exhausts will make more noise than the 'correct' type

4.7.3 Exhaust and air supply fault diagnosis table 1

Symptom	Possible faults	Suggested action
Exhaust noise	Hole in pipe, box or at joints	Renew as appropriate
Knocking noise	Exhaust incorrectly positioned	Reposition
	Broken mountings	Renew
Rich mixture/smoke	Blocked air filter	Replace
Noisy air intake	Intake trunking or filter box leaking or loose	Repair or secure as required
Poor cold driveability	Hot air pick up not operating	Check pipe connections to inlet manifold for leaks. Renew temperature valve or actuator

4.7.4 Exhaust fault diagnosis table 2

Symptom	Possible cause
Excessive noise	Leaking exhaust system or manifold joints Hole in exhaust system
Excessive fumes in car	Leaking exhaust system or manifold joints
Rattling noise	Incorrect fitting of exhaust system Broken exhaust mountings Engine mountings worn

4.8 Cooling

4.8.1 Air-cooled system

Air-cooled engines with multi-cylinders, especially under a bonnet, must have some form of fan cooling and ducting. This is to make sure all cylinders are cooled evenly. The cylinders and cylinder heads are finned. Hotter areas, such as near the exhaust ports on the cylinders, have bigger fins.

Fan-blown air is directed by a metal cowling so it stays close to the finned areas. A thermostatically controlled flap will control airflow. When the engine is warming up, the flap will be closed to restrict the movement of air. When the engine reaches its operating temperature the flap opens and allows the air to flow over the engine. The cooling fan is a large device and is driven from the engine by a belt. This belt must not be allowed to slip or break, because serious damage will occur.

Car heating is not easy to arrange with an air-cooled engine. Some vehicles use a heat exchanger around the exhaust pipe. Air is passed through this device where it is warmed. It can then be used for demisting and heating with the aid of an electric motor and fan.

4.8.2 Water cooled system

The main parts of a water cooled system are as follows:

- water jacket;
- water pump;
- thermostat;
- radiator;
- cooling fan.

Water-cooled engines work on the principle of surrounding the hot areas inside the engine with a water jacket. The water takes on heat from the engine and, as it circulates through the radiator, gives it off to atmosphere. The heat concentration around the top of the engine means a water pump is needed to ensure proper circulation.

The water pump circulates water through the radiator and around the engine when the thermostat is open. Water circulates only round the engine when the thermostat is closed and not through the radiator. Forcing water around the engine prevents vapour pockets forming in very hot areas. This circulation is assisted by the thermo-siphon action. The thermo-siphon action causes the water to circulate because as the water is heated it rises and moves to the top of the radiator. This pushes down on the colder water underneath which moves into the engine. This water is heated rises and so on.

Coolant from the engine water jacket passes through a hose to the radiator at the top. It then passes through thin pipes called the radiator matrix to the lower tank and then back to the lower part of the engine.

Many water passages between the top and bottom tanks of the radiator are used, to increase the surface area. Fins further increase the surface area to make the radiator even more efficient. A cooling fan assists air flow. The heat from the coolant passes to the pipes and fins and then to the air as it is blown by a fan over the fins.

Many modern radiators are made from aluminium pipes and fins with plastic tanks top and bottom (down flow), or at each end (cross flow). The cross flow radiators with tanks at each end are becoming the most popular. The more traditional method was to use copper and brass.

A thermostat is a temperature controlled valve. Its purpose is to allow coolant to heat up more quickly and then be kept at a constant temperature. The total coolant volume in an engine takes time to heat up. Modern engines run more efficiently when at the correct operating temperature. The action of the thermostat is such as to prevent water circulation from the engine to the radiator, until a set temperature is reached. When the valve opens there is a full circuit for the coolant and a good cooling action occurs because of full flow through the radiator. The constant action of the thermostat ensures that the engine temperature remains at a constant level the thermostat used by almost all modern engine is a wax capsule type. If the thermostat is faulty ensure that the correct type for the engine is fitted as some work at different temperatures.

The water pump is driven by a V-belt or multi-V-belt from the crankshaft pulley or by the cam belt. The pump is a simple impeller type and is usually fitted at the front of the engine (where the pulleys are). It assists with the thermo-siphon action of the cooling system, forcing water around the engine block and radiator.

The engine fan, which maintains the flow of air through the radiator, is mounted on the water-pump pulley on older systems. Most cooling fans now are electric. These are more efficient because they only work when needed. The forward motion of the car also helps the air movement through the radiator.

4.8.3 Sealed and semi-sealed systems

Cooling systems on most vehicles today are sealed or semi-sealed. This allows them to operate at pressures as much as 100 N/m^2 (100 Pascal) over atmospheric pressure, raising the boiling point of the coolant to as much as 126.6°C (remember water boils at 100°C at atmospheric pressure). The system can therefore operate at a higher temperature and with greater efficiency.

The pressure buildup is made possible by the radiator pressure cap. The cap contains a pressure valve which opens at a set pressure, and a vacuum valve which opens at a set vacuum. On a semi-sealed system, air is pushed out to atmosphere through the pressure valve as the coolant expands. Air is then drawn back into the radiator through the vacuum valve as the coolant cools and contracts. A sealed system has an expansion tank into which coolant is forced as it expands, and when the engine cools, coolant can flow from the tank back into the cooling system. Figure 4.12 shows a semi-sealed type cooling system.

Correct levels in the expansion tank or in an unsealed radiator are very important. If too much coolant is used it will be expelled on to the floor when the engine gets hot. If not enough is used then the level could become low and overheating could take place.

> **Warning**
> If a pressure cap is removed from a hot system, hot water under pressure will boil the instant pressure is released. This can be very dangerous.

Figure 4.12 Semi-sealed cooling system

Heat from the engine can be used to increase the temperature of the car interior. This is achieved by use of a heat exchanger, often called the heater matrix. Due to the action of the thermostat in the engine cooling system the water temperature remains nearly constant. The air being passed over the heater matrix is therefore heated to a set level.

A source of hot air is now available for heating the vehicle interior. Some form of control is required over how much heat is required. The method used on most modern vehicles is blending. This is a control flap that determines how much of the air being passed into the vehicle is directed over the heater matrix. Some systems use a valve to control the hot coolant flowing to the heater matrix.

By a suitable arrangement of flaps it is possible to direct air of the chosen temperature to selected areas of the vehicle interior. In general, basic systems allow the warm air to be adjusted between the inside of the windscreen and the driver and passenger footwells. Fresh cool air outlets with directional nozzles are also fitted.

One final facility, which is available on many vehicles, is the choice between fresh or recirculated air. The primary reason for this is to decrease the time taken to demist or defrost the vehicle windows and simply to heat the car interior more quickly, and to a higher temperature. The other reason is that for example, in heavy congested traffic, the outside air may not be very clean.

4.9 Diagnostics – cooling

4.9.1 Systematic testing

If the reported fault is loss of coolant proceed as follows.

1. Check coolant level and discuss with customer how much is being lost.
2. Run the engine to see if it is overheating.
3. If the engine is not overheating a leak would seem to be most likely.
4. Pressure test the cooling system and check for leaks from hoses, gaskets and the radiator.
5. Renew a gasket or the radiator, clips or hoses as required. Top up the coolant and check antifreeze content.
6. Road test the vehicle to confirm the fault is cured and that no other problems have occurred.

4.9.2 Test equipment

Note: You should always refer to the manufacturer's instructions appropriate to the equipment you are using.

Cooling system pressure tester (Figure 4.13)

This is a pump with a pressure gauge built in, together with suitable adapters for fitting to the header tank or radiator filler. The system can then be pressurized to check for leaks. The pressure can be looked up or it is often stamped on the filler cap. A good way of doing this test is to pressurise the system when cold and then start the engine and allow it to warm up. You can be looking for leaks but beware of rotating components.

Antifreeze tester

This piece of equipment is a hydrometer used to measure the relative density of the coolant. The relative density of coolant varies with the amount of antifreeze. A table can be used to determine how much more antifreeze should be added to give the required protection.

Temperature meter/thermometer

Sometimes the dashboard temperature gauge reading too high can create the symptoms of an overheating problem. A suitable meter or thermometer can be used to check the temperature. Note though that normal operating temperature

Figure 4.13 Cooling system pressure tester

is often well above 90°C (hot enough to burn badly).

4.9.3 Test results

Some of the information you may have to get from other sources such as data books or a workshop manual is listed in the following table.

Test carried out	Information required
Leakage test	System pressure. Printed on the cap or from data books. About 1 bar is normal
Antifreeze content	Cooling system capacity and required percentage of antifreeze. If the system holds six litres then for a 50% antifreeze content you will need to add three litres of antifreeze. Don't forget you will need to drain out three litres of water to make room for the antifreeze!
Operating temperature	This is about the same as the thermostat opening temperature – 88 to 92°C is a typical range

4.9.4 Cooling fault diagnosis table 1

Symptom	Possible faults	Suggested action
Overheating	Lack of coolant	Top up but then check for leaks
	Thermostat stuck closed	Renew
	Electric cooling fan not operating	Check operation of thermal switch
	Blocked radiator	Renew
	Water pump/fan belt slipping	Check, adjust/renew
Loss of coolant	Leaks	Pressure test when cold and hot, look for leaks and repair as required
Engine does not reach normal temperature or it takes a long time	Thermostat stuck in the open position	Renew

4.9.5 Cooling fault diagnosis table 2

Symptom	Possible cause
Overheating	Low coolant level (maybe due to a leak) Thermostat stuck closed
	Radiator core blocked Cooling fan not operating Temperature gauge inaccurate Airlock in system (some systems have a complex bleeding procedure) Pressure cap faulty
Overcooling	Thermostat stuck open Temperature gauge inaccurate Cooling fan operating when not needed
External coolant leak	Loose or damaged hose Radiator leak Pressure cap seal faulty Water pump leak from seal or bearing Boiling due to overheating or faulty pressure cap Core plug leaking
Internal coolant leak	Cylinder head gasket leaking Cylinder head cracked
Corrosion	Incorrect coolant (antifreeze, etc.) Infrequent flushing
Freezing	Lack of antifreeze Incorrect antifreeze

4.10 Lubrication

4.10.1 Lubrication system

From the sump reservoir under the crankshaft oil is drawn through a strainer into the pump. Oil pumps have an output of tens of litres per minute and operating pressures of over 5 bar at high speeds. A pressure relief valve limits the pressure of the lubrication system to between 2.5 and bar^2. This control is needed because the pump would produce excessive pressure at high speeds. After leaving the pump, oil passes into a filter and then into a main oil gallery in the engine block or crankcase.

Drillings connect the gallery to the crank-shaft bearing housings and, when the engine is running, oil is forced under pressure between the rotating crank journals and the main bearings. The crankshaft is drilled so that the oil supply from the main bearings is also to the big end bearing bases of the connecting rods.

The con-rods are often drilled near the base so that a jet of oil sprays the cylinder walls and the underside of the pistons. In some cases the con-rod may be drilled along its entire length so that oil from the big end bearing is taken directly to the gudgeon pin (small end). The surplus then splashes out to cool the underside of the piston and cylinder.

The camshaft operates at half crankshaft speed, but it still needs good lubrication because as the high pressure loads on the cams. It is usual to supply pressurised oil to the camshaft bearings and splash or spray oil on the cam lobes. On overhead camshaft engines, two systems are used. In the simplest system the rotating cam lobes dip into a trough of oil. Another method is to spray the cam lobes with oil. This is usually done by an oil pipe with small holes in it alongside the camshaft. The small holes in the side of the pipe aim a jet of oil at each rotating cam lobe. The surplus splashes over the valve assembly and then falls back into the sump.

On cars where a chain drives the cam, a small tapping from the main oil gallery sprays oil on the chain as it moves past or the chain may simply dip in the sump oil. Figure 4.14 shows a typical lubrication system.

4.10.2 Oil filters

Even new engines can contain very small particles of metal left over from the manufacturing process or grains of sand which have not been removed from the crankcase after casting. Old engines continually deposit tiny bits of metal worn from highly loaded components such as the piston rings. To prevent any of these lodging in bearings or blocking oil ways, the oil is filtered.

The primary filter is a wire mesh strainer that stops particles of dirt or swarf from entering the oil pump. This is normally on the end of the oil pick-up pipe. An extra filter is also used that stops very fine particles. The most common type has a folded, resin impregnated paper element. Pumping oil through it removes all but smallest solids from the oil.

Most engines use a full-flow system to filter all of the oil after it leaves the pump. The most popular method is to pump the oil into a canister containing a cylindrical filter. From the inner walls of the canister, the oil flows through the filter and out from the centre to the main oil gallery. Full-flow filtration works well provided the filter is renewed at regular intervals. If it is left in service too long it may become blocked. When this happens the buildup of pressure inside the filter forces open a spring-loaded relief valve in the housing and the oil bypasses the filter. This valve prevents engine failure, but the

Figure 4.14 Lubrication system

engine will be lubricated with dirty, oil until the filter is renewed. This is better than no oil!

A bypass filtration system was used on older vehicles. This system only filters a proportion of the oil pump output. The remainder is fed directly to the oil gallery. At first view this seems a strange idea but all of the oil does eventually get filtered. The smaller amount through the filter allows a higher degree of filtration.

4.10.3 Oil pumps

In its simplest form an oil pump consists of two gear wheels meshed together in a tight space so that oil cannot escape past the sides. The engine drives one wheel. As the gears rotate in opposite directions, the gap between each tooth in each wheel traps a small quantity of oil from an inlet port. The trapped oil is carried round by each wheel towards an outlet port on the opposite side where it is forced out by the meshing teeth.

The principle of squeezing oil from an ever-decreasing space is also used in the rotor type pump. An inner and outer rotor are mounted on different axes in the same cylinder. The inner rotor, which commonly has four lobes, is driven by the engine. It meshes with an outer rotor, which has five lobes. As they rotate, the spaces between them change size. The inlet port is at a point where the space between the rotor lobes is increasing. This draws the oil in to the pump. The oil is then carried round the pump. As rotation continues, the space between the lobes gets smaller. This compresses the oil out of the outlet port.

Oil pumps can produce more pressure than is required. A valve is used to limit this pressure to a set value. The pressure relief valve is a simple device, which in most cases works on the ball and spring principle. This means that when the pressure on the ball is greater than the spring, the ball moves. The pressure relief valve is placed in the main gallery so that excess pressure is prevented. When the ball moves oil is simply returned to the sump.

4.10.4 Crankcase ventilation – engine breather systems

Breathing is very important; without being able to breathe, we would die! It is almost as important for an engine breathing system to work correctly. There are two main reasons for engine breathers.

- Prevent pressure buildup inside the engine crankcase due to combustion gases blowing past the pistons. The buildup of pressure will blow gaskets and seals but also there is a high risk of explosion.
- Prevent toxic emissions from the engine. Emission limits are now very strict, for good reason – our health!

Crankcase breathing or ventilation of the engine was first done by what is known as an open system, but this has now been completely replaced by the closed system. The gases escaping from an engine with open crankcase ventilation as described above are very toxic. Legislation now demands a positive closed system of ventilation. This makes the pollution from cylinder blow-by gases negligible. Positive crankcase ventilation is the solution to this problem.

In early types of closed system crankcase ventilation, the lower pressure at the carburettor air cleaner was used to cause an air flow through the inside of the engine. The breather outlet was simply connected by a pipe to the air cleaner. This caused the crankcase gases to be circulated and then burned in the engine cylinders. A flame trap was included in the system, to prevent a crankcase explosion if the engine backfired.

In modern closed systems the much lower pressure within the inlet manifold is used to extract crankcase gases. This has to be controlled in most cases by a variable regulator valve or pressure conscious valve (PCV). The valve is fitted between the breather outlet and the inlet manifold. It consists of a spring-loaded plunger, which opens as the inlet manifold pressure reduces. When the engine is stationary the valve is closed. Under normal running conditions the valve opens to allow crankcase gases to enter the inlet manifold with minimum restriction. At low manifold pressures during idling and overrun (pressure is less than atmospheric), further travel of the valve plunger against its spring closes it in the opposite direction. This reduces gas flow to the inlet manifold. This feature makes sure that the fuel control process is not interfered with under these conditions. The valve also acts as a safety device in case of a backfire. Any high pressure created in the inlet manifold will close the valve completely. This will isolate the crankcase and prevent the risk of explosion.

4.11 Diagnostics – lubrication

4.11.1 Systematic testing

If the reported fault is that the oil pressure light comes on at low speed proceed as follows.

1. Run the engine and see when the light goes off or comes on.
2. Is the problem worse when the engine is hot? Check the oil level! When was it last serviced?
3. If oil level is correct then you must investigate further.
4. Carry out an oil pressure test to measure the actual pressure.
5. If pressure is correct then renew the oil pressure switch. If not engine strip down is likely.
6. Run and test for leaks.

4.11.2 Test equipment

Note: You should always refer to the manufacturer's instructions appropriate to the equipment you are using.

Oil pressure test gauge (Figure 4.15)

This is a simple pressure gauge that can be fitted with suitable adapters into the oil pressure switch hole. The engine is then run and the pressure readings compared to data.

Vacuum gauge

A simple 'U' tube full of water is often used. This is connected to the oil dipstick tube and the engine is run. The gauge should show a pressure less than atmospheric (a partial vacuum). This checks the operation of the crankcase ventilation system.

4.11.3 Test results

Some of the information you may have to get from other sources such as data books, or a workshop manual is listed in the following table.

Test carried out	Information required
Oil pressure	Oil pressure is measured in bars. A typical reading would be about 3 bar
Crankcase pressure	By tradition pressures less than atmosphere are given in strange ways, such as inches of mercury or inches of water! This is why I like to stick to absolute pressure and the bar! Zero bar is no pressure, 1 bar is atmospheric pressure and so on. Two to 3 bar is more than atmospheric pressure like in a tyre. The trouble is standards vary so make sure you compare like with like! Back to crankcase pressure – it should be less than atmospheric, check data
Oil condition	Recommended type of lubricant

4.11.4 Lubrication fault diagnosis table 1

Symptom	Possible faults	Suggested action
Low oil pressure	Lack of oil	Top up
	Blocked filter	Renew oil and filter
	Defective oil pump	Renew after further tests
	Defective oil pressure relief valve	Adjust if possible or renew
High crankcase pressure	Blocked crankcase breather	Clean or replace
	Blocked hose	Clean or renew hose
	Pressure blowing by pistons	Engine overhaul may be required
Loss of oil	Worn piston rings	Engine overhaul may be required
	Leaks	Renew seals or gaskets

Figure 4.15 Oil pressure gauge

4.11.5 Lubrication fault diagnosis table 2

Symptom	Possible cause
Oil leaks	Worn oil seal (check breather system)
	Gasket blown
	Cam or rocker cover loose
	Oil filter seal
Blue smoke	Piston rings
	Valve stem seals
	Head gasket

4.12 Manual transmission

4.12.1 Clutch

A clutch is a device for disconnecting and connecting rotating shafts. In a vehicle with a manual gearbox, the driver pushes down the clutch when changing gear to disconnect the engine from the gearbox. It also allows a temporary neutral position for, say, waiting at traffic lights and a gradual way of taking up drive from rest.

The clutch is made of two main parts, a pressure plate and a driven plate. The driven plate, often termed the clutch disc, is fitted on the shaft, which takes the drive into the gearbox. When the clutch is engaged, the pressure plate presses the driven plate against the engine fly-wheel. This allows drive to be passed to the gearbox. Pushing down the clutch springs the pressure plate away, which frees the driven plate. Figure 4.16 shows some typical clutch components including en electromechanical clutch actuator. The diaphragm type clutch replaced an earlier type with coil springs it has a number of advantages when used on light vehicles:

- not affected by high speeds (coil springs can be thrown outwards);
- low pedal force making for easy operation;
- light and compact;
- clamping force increases or at least remains constant as the friction lining wears.

The method of controlling the clutch is quite simple. The mechanism consists of either a cable or hydraulic system.

4.12.2 Manual gearbox

The driver changes the gears of a manual gearbox by moving a hand-operated lever called a gear stick! All manual gearboxes have a neutral position; three, four, or five forward gears; and a reverse gear. A few even have six forward gears now! The driver puts the gearbox into neutral as the engine is being started, or when a car is parked with the engine left running.

Power travels in to the gearbox via the input shaft. A gear at the end of this shaft drives a gear on another shaft called the countershaft or

Figure 4.16 Clutch components (Valeo)

layshaft. A number of gears of various sizes are mounted on the layshaft. These gears drive other gears on a third motion shaft also known as the output shaft.

The gearbox produces various gear ratios by engaging different combinations of gears. For reverse, an extra gear called an idler operates between the countershaft and the output shaft. It turns the output shaft in the opposite direction to the input shaft. Figure 4.17 shows a front wheel drive gearbox.

Figure 4.18 shows the power flows through this box in each of the different gears. Note how in each case (with the exception of reverse) the gears do not move. This is why this type of gearbox has become known as constant mesh. In other words the gears are running in mesh with each other at all times. Dog clutches are used to select which gears will be locked to the output shaft. These clutches which are moved by selector levers, incorporate synchromesh mechanisms.

A synchromesh mechanism is needed because the teeth of the dog clutches would clash if they met at different speeds. The system works like a friction type cone clutch. The collar is in two parts and contains an outer toothed ring that is spring-loaded to sit centrally on the synchromesh hub. When the outer ring (synchroniser sleeve) is made to move by the action of the selector mechanism the cone clutch is also moved because of the locking keys. The gear speeds up as the cones touch, thus allowing the dog clutches to engage smoothly. A baulking

ring is fitted between the cone on the gear wheel and the synchroniser hub. This is to prevent engagement until the speeds are synchronised.

A detent mechanism is used to hold the selected gear in mesh. In most cases this is just a simple ball and spring acting on the selector shaft(s). Figure 4.19 shows a rear wheel drive gearbox with the detent mechanism marked. Gear selection interlocks are a vital part of a gearbox. These are to prevent more than one gear from being engaged at any one time. On the single rail (one rod to change the gears) gearbox shown in the figure, the interlock mechanism is shown at the rear. As the rod is turned (side to side movement of the gear stick) towards first–second, third–fourth or fifth gear positions, the interlock will only engage with either the first–second, third–fourth or fifth gear selectors as appropriate. Equally when any selector clutch is in mesh the interlock will not allow the remaining selectors to change position.

4.12.3 Driveshafts and wheel bearings

Light vehicle driveshafts now fall into one of two main categories, the first being by far the most popular.

● **Drive shafts with constant velocity joints (FWD)** transmit drive from the output of the final drive to each front wheel. They must also allow for suspension and steering movements.

Final drive gear

Interlock

Layshaft

Figure 4.17 Five-speed gearbox (FWD)

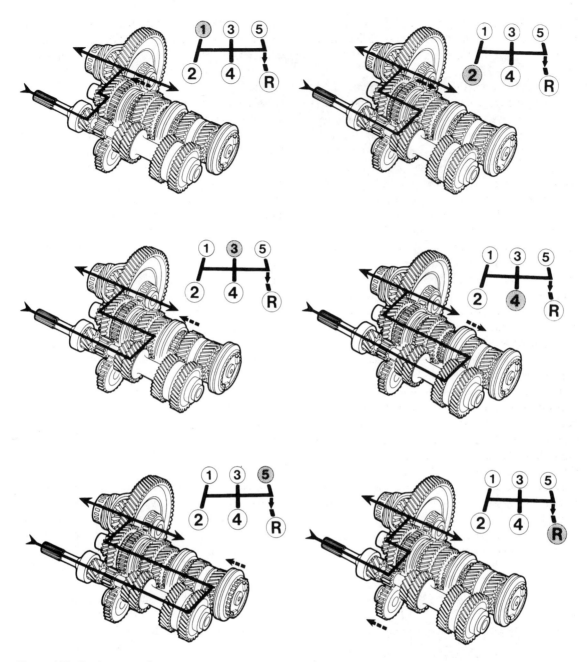

Figure 4.18 Gearbox power flows

- **Propshaft with universal joints (RWD) F** transmits drive from the gearbox output to the final drive in the rear axle. Drive then continues through the final drive and differential, via two half shafts to each rear wheel. The propshaft must also allow for suspension movements.

Wheel bearings are also very important. They allow smooth rotation of the wheel but must also be able to withstand high stresses such as from load in the vehicle and when cornering.

Front bearings

Seal	Keeps out dirt and water, and keeps in the grease lubrication
Spacer	Ensures the correct positioning of the seal
Inner bearing	Supports the weight of the vehicle at the front, when still or moving. Ball bearings are used for most vehicles with specially shaped tracks for the balls. This is so the bearings can stand side loads when cornering
Swivel hub	Attachment for the suspension and steering as well as supporting the bearings

Figure 4.19 Real wheel drive gearbox

Outer bearing	As for inner bearing
Drive flange	Runs inside the centre race of the bearings. The wheel is bolted to this flange

Rear bearings

Stub axle	Solid mounted to the suspension arm, this stub axle fits in the centre of the two bearings
Seal	Keeps out dirt and water, and keeps in the grease lubrication
Inner bearing	Supports the weight of the vehicle at the rear, when still or moving. Ball bearings are used for most vehicles with specially shaped tracks for the balls. This is so the bearings can stand side loads when cornering
Spacer	To ensure the correct spacing and pressure between the two bearings
Drum	For the brakes and attachment of the wheel
Outer bearing	As for inner bearing
Washer	The heavy washer acts as a face for the nut to screw against
Castle nut and split pin	Holds all parts in position securely. With this type of bearing, no adjustment is made because both bearings are clamped on to the spacer. Some older cars use tapered bearings and adjustment is very important
Grease retainer cap	Retains grease, but should not be over packed. Also keeps out the dirt and water

4.12.4 Final drive and differential

Because of the speed at which an engine runs, and in order to produce enough torque at the road wheels, a fixed gear reduction is required. This is known as the final drive, and consists of just two gears. These are fitted after the output of the gearbox, on front wheel drive, or in the rear axle after the propshaft on rear wheel drive vehicles. The gears also turn the drive through ninety degrees on rear wheel drive vehicles. The ratio is normally about 4:1; in other words when the gearbox output is turning at 4000 rev/min the wheels will turn at 1000 rev/min.

Many cars now have a transverse engine, which drives the front wheels. The power of the engine therefore does not have to be carried through a right angle to the drive wheels. The final drive contains ordinary reducing gears rather than bevel gears.

The differential is a set of gears that divide the torque evenly between the two drive wheels. The differential also allows one wheel to rotate faster than the other does when necessary. When a car goes around a corner, the outside drive wheel travels further than the inside one. The outside wheel must therefore rotate faster than the inside one to cover the greater distance in the same time.

Some higher performance vehicles use limited slip differentials. The clutch plates are connected to the two output shafts and hence if controlled will in turn control the amount of slip. This can be used to counteract the effect of one wheel losing traction when high power is applied.

Differential locks are used on many off-road type vehicles. A simple dog clutch or similar device prevents the differential action. This allows far better traction on slippery surfaces.

4.12.5 Four-wheel drive systems

Four-wheel drive (4WD) provides good traction on rough or slippery surfaces. Many cars are now available with 4WD. In some vehicles, the driver can switch between four-wheel drive and two-wheel drive (2WD). A vehicle with four-wheel drive delivers power to all four wheels. A transfer box is used to distribute the power between the front and rear wheels. Figure 4.20 shows the layout of the system used on the Ford Maverick. Note the extra components compared to a normal two-wheel drive system:

- **transfer gearbox** to provide an extra drive output;
- **differential on each axle** to allow cornering speed variations;
- **centre differential** to prevent wind up between the front and rear axles;
- **extra drive shafts** to supply drive to the extra axle.

The transfer gearbox on some vehicles may also contain extra reduction gears for low ratio drive.

One problem to overcome, however, with 4WD is that if three differentials are used then the chance of one wheel slipping actually increases. This is because the drive will always be transferred to the wheel with least traction – like running a 2WD car with one driving wheel jacked up. To overcome this problem and take advantage of the extra traction available a viscous coupling is combined with an epicyclic gear train to form the centre differential.

The drive can now be distributed proportionally. A typical value is about 35% to the front and 65% to the rear wheels. However, the viscous clutch coupling acts so that if, a wheel starts to slip, the greater difference in speed across the coupling will cause more friction and hence more drive will pass through the coupling. This tends to act so that the drive is automatically distributed to the most effective driving axle. A 'Hyvo' or silent chain drive is often used to drive from the transfer box.

4.13 Diagnostics – manual transmission

4.13.1 Systematic testing

If the reported fault is a slipping clutch proceed as follows.

1. Road test to confirm when the fault occurs.
2. Look for oil leaking from the bell housing or general area of the clutch. Check adjustment if possible.
3. If adjustment is correct then the clutch must be examined.
4. In this example the clutch assembly must be removed for visual examination.
5. Replace parts as necessary; this is often done as a kit comprising the clutch plate and cover as well as a bearing in some cases.

Figure 4.20 Ford Maverick 4WD transmission

6. Road test and check operation of all the transmission.

4.13.2 Test equipment

Note: You should always refer to the manufacturer's instructions appropriate to the equipment you are using.

Stethoscope (Figure 4.21 shows a basic type as well as electronic versions)

This is a useful device that can be used in a number of diagnostic situations. In its basic form it is a long screwdriver! The probe (or screwdriver blade) is placed near the suspected component such as a bearing. The ear piece (or screwdriver handle placed next to the ear) amplifies the sound. Take care though; even a good bearing can sound rough using this method. Compare a known good noise with the suspected one.

4.13.3 Test results

Some of the information you may have to get from other sources such as data books or a workshop manual is listed in the following table.

Test carried out	Information required
Backlash or freeplay	Backlash data is often given, as the distance component will move. The backlash between two gears for example should be very small
Overdrive operation	Which gears the overdrive is meant to operate in!

4.13.4 Manual transmission fault diagnosis table 1

Symptom	Possible causes or faults	Suggested action
Clutch slipping	Clutch worn out	Renew
	Adjustment incorrect	Adjust or check auto-adjuster
	Oil contamination	Rectify oil leak – clutch may also need to be renewed
Jumps out of gear	Gearbox detent fault	Gearbox may require overhaul
Noisy when changing gear	Synchromesh worn	Gearbox may require overhaul
Rapid knocking noise when cornering	Driveshaft CV joints worn or without lubrication	Renew or lubricate joint Ensure gaiter is in place and in good condition
Whining noise	Wheel bearing worn Other bearings	Renew Investigate and renew if possible
Difficult to change gear	Clutch out of adjustment	Adjust or check auto-adjuster
	Clutch hydraulic fault	Check system for air and/or leaks
	Gearbox selectors worn	Gearbox may require overhaul

4.13.5 Manual gearbox fault diagnosis table 2

Symptom	Possible cause
Noisy in a particular gear (with engine running)	Damaged gear Worn bearing
Noisy in neutral (with engine running)	Input shaft bearings worn (goes away when clutch is pushed down?) Lack of lubricating oil Clutch release bearing worn (gets worse when clutch is pushed down?)
Difficult to engage gears	Clutch problem Gear linkage worn or not adjusted correctly Work synchromesh units Lack of lubrication
Jumps out of gear	Gear linkage worn or not adjusted correctly Worn selector forks Detent not working Weak synchromesh units
Vibration	Lack of lubrication Worn bearings Mountings loose

Figure 4.21 Stethoscopes

Oil leaks	Gaskets leaking
	Worn seals

4.13.6 Clutch faults diagnosis table

Symptom	Possible cause
No pedal resistance	Broken cable
	Air in hydraulic system
	Hydraulic seals worn
	Release bearing or fork broken
	Diaphragm spring broken
Clutch does not disengage	As above
	Disc sticking in gearbox splines
	Disc sticking to flywheel
	Faulty pressure plate
Clutch slip	Incorrect adjustment
	Worn disc linings
	Contaminated linings (oil or grease)
	Faulty pressure plate
Judder when engaging	Contaminated linings (oil or grease)
	Worn disc linings
	Distorted or worn pressure plate
	Engine mountings worn, loose or broken
	Clutch disc hub splines worn
Noisy operation	Broken components
	Release bearing seized
	Disc cushioning springs broken
Snatching	Disc cushioning springs broken
	Operating mechanism sticking (lubrication?)

4.13.7 Drive shafts fault diagnosis table

Symptom	Possible cause
Vibration	Incorrect alignment of propshaft joints
	Worn universal or CV joints
	Bent shaft
	Mountings worn
Grease leaking	Gaiters split or clips loose
Knocking noises	Dry joints
	Worn CV joints (gets worse on tight corners)

4.13.8 Final drive fault diagnosis table

Symptom	Possible cause
Oil leaks	Gaskets split
	Drive shaft oil seals
	Final drive output bearings worn (drive shafts drop and cause leaks)
Noisy operation	Low oil level
	Incorrect preload adjustment
	Bearings worn
Whining noise	Low oil level
	Worn differential gears

4.14 Automatic transmission

4.14.1 Introduction

An automatic gearbox contains special devices that automatically provide various gear ratios, as they are needed. Most automatic gearboxes have three or four forward gears and reverse. Instead of a gearstick, the driver moves a lever called a selector. Most automatic gearboxes now have selector positions for park, neutral, reverse, drive, 2 and 1 (or 3, 2 and 1 in some cases). The engine will only start if the selector is in either the park or neutral position. In park, the drive shaft is locked so that the drive wheels cannot move. It is now quite common when the engine is running to be able to move the selector out of park only if you are pressing the brake pedal. This is a very good safety feature as it prevents sudden movement of the vehicle.

For ordinary driving, the driver moves the selector to the drive position. The transmission starts out in the lowest gear and automatically shifts into higher gears as the car picks up speed. The driver can use the lower positions of the gearbox for going up or down steep hills or driving through mud or snow. When in position 3, 2, or 1, the gearbox will not change above the lowest gear specified.

4.14.2 Torque converter operation

The torque converter is a device that almost all automatic transmissions now use. It delivers power from the engine to the gearbox like a basic fluid flywheel but also increases the torque when the car begins to move. The torque converter resembles a large doughnut sliced in half. One half, called the pump impeller, is bolted to the drive plate or flywheel. The other half, called the turbine, is connected to the gearbox-input shaft. Each half is lined with vanes or blades. The pump and the turbine face each other in a case filled with oil. A bladed wheel called a stator is fitted between them.

The engine causes the pump to rotate and throw oil against the vanes of the turbine. The force of the oil makes the turbine rotate and send power to the transmission. After striking the turbine vanes, the oil passes through the stator and returns to the pump. When the pump reaches a specific rate of rotation, a reaction between the oil and the stator increases the torque. In a fluid flywheel oil returning to the impeller tends to slow it down. In a torque converter the stator or reactor diverts the oil towards the centre of the impeller for extra thrust. Figure 4.22 shows a gearbox with a cutaway torque converter.

When the engine is running slowly, the oil may not have enough force to rotate the turbine. But when the driver presses the accelerator pedal, the engine runs faster and so does the impeller. The action of the impeller increases the force of the oil. This force gradually becomes strong enough to rotate the turbine and move the vehicle. A torque converter can double the applied torque when moving off from rest. As engine speed increases the torque multiplication tapers off until at cruising speed there is no increase in torque. The reactor or stator then freewheels on its one-way clutch at the same speed as the turbine.

The fluid flywheel action reduces efficiency because the pump tends to rotate faster than the turbine. In other words some slip will occur (about 2%). To improve efficiency, many transmissions now include a lock-up clutch. When the pump reaches a specific rate of rotation, this clutch locks the pump and turbine together, allowing them to rotate as one.

Figure 4.22 This cut-away gearbox shows the components of the torque converter

4.14.3 Epicyclic gearbox operation

Epicyclic gears are a special set of gears that are part of most automatic gearboxes. They consist of three elements:

- a sun gear, located in the centre;
- the carrier that holds two, three, or four planet gears, which mesh with the sun gear and revolve around it;
- an internal gear or annulus is a ring with internal teeth, which surrounds the planet gears and meshes with them.

Any part of a set of planetary gears can be held stationary or locked to one of the others. This will produce different gear ratios. Most of the automatic gearboxes of the type shown earlier have two sets of planetary gears that are arranged in line as shown in Figure 4.23. This provides the necessary number of gear ratios. The appropriate elements in the gear train are held stationary by a system of hydraulically operated brake bands and clutches. These are worked by a series of hydraulically operated valves in the lower part of the gearbox. Oil pressure to operate the clutches and brake bands is supplied by a pump. The supply for this is the oil in the sump of the gearbox.

Unless the driver moves the gear selector to operate the valves, automatic gear changes are made depending on just two factors:

- **throttle opening** a cable is connected from the throttle to the gearbox;
- **road speed** when the vehicle reaches a set speed a governor allows pump pressure to take over from the throttle.

The cable from the throttle also allows a facility known as 'kick down'. This allows the driver to change down a gear, such as for overtaking, by pressing the throttle all the way down.

Many modern automatic gearboxes now use gears the same as in manual boxes. The changing of ratios is similar to the manual operation except that hydraulic clutches and valves are used.

4.14.4 Constantly variable transmission

Figure 4.24 shows the Ford CTX (Constantly variable TransaXle) transmission. This kind of automatic transmission called a continuously variable transmission uses two pairs of cone-

First gear: the line shows power flow through the two epicyclic gears. Driving the front annulus and braking the rear planet carrier gives two gear reductions

Second gear: one gear reduction is achieved by driving the first annulus and braking the common sun wheel

Top gear: all gears are held stationary in relation to each other, and the complete assembly rotates to provide direct drive

Reverse: braking the second planet carrier causes the rear annulus and output shaft to turn in the opposite direction

Figure 4.23 Two epicyclic gear sets can produce three forward gears and reverse

Figure 4.24 Ford CTX transmission

shaped pulleys connected by a metal belt. The key to this system is the high friction drive belt. The belt is made from high performance steel and transmits drive by thrust rather than tension. The ratio of the rotations, often called the gear ratio, is determined by how far the belt rides from the centres of the pulleys. The transmission can produce an unlimited number of ratios. As the car changes speed the ratio is continuously adjusted. Cars with this system are said to use fuel more efficiently than cars with set gear ratios. Within the gearbox hydraulic control is used to move the pulleys and hence change the drive ratio. An epicyclic gear set is used to provide a reverse gear as well as a fixed ratio.

4.14.5 Electronic control of transmission

The main aim of electronically controlled automatic transmission (ECAT) is to improve on conventional automatic transmission in the following ways:

- gear changes should be smoother and quieter;
- improved performance;
- reduced fuel consumption;
- reduction of characteristic changes over system life;
- increased reliability.

The important points to remember are that gear changes and lock-up of the torque converter are controlled by hydraulic pressure. In an ECAT system electrically controlled solenoid valves can influence this hydraulic pressure. Most ECAT systems now have a transmission ECU that is in communication with the engine control ECU.

With an ECAT system the actual point of gearshift is determined from pre-programmed memory within the ECU. Data from other sensors is also taken into consideration. Actual gearshifts are initiated by changes in hydraulic pressure, which is controlled by solenoid valves.

The two main control functions of this system are hydraulic pressure and engine torque. A temporary reduction in engine torque during gear shifting allows smooth operation. This is because the peak of gearbox output torque which causes the characteristic surge during gear changes on conventional automatics is suppressed. Because of these control functions smooth gearshifts are possible and, due to the

learning ability of some ECUs, the characteristics remain throughout the life of the system.

The ability to lock-up the torque converter has been used for some time even on vehicles with more conventional automatic transmission. This gives better fuel economy, quietness and improved driveability. Lock-up is carried out using a hydraulic valve, which can be operated gradually to produce a smooth transition. The timing of lock-up is determined from ECU memory in terms of the vehicle speed and acceleration.

4.14.6 Semi-automatic transmission

A number of different types of semi-automatic transmission are either in use or under development. An interesting system is the electronically controlled clutch. This technology is a spin off formula from and top rally cars. The electronic clutch was developed for these racing vehicles to improve the get away performance and speed of gear changes.

For production vehicles a system has been developed which can interpret the driver's intention. With greater throttle openings the clutch operation changes to prevent abuse and driveline damage. Electrical control of the clutch release bearing position is by a solenoid actuator or electric motor with worm gear reduction. This allows the time to reach the ideal take off position to be reduced and the ability of the clutch to transmit torque to be improved.

This technique has now been developed to the stage where it will operate the clutch automatically as the stick is moved to change gear. Sensors are fitted to monitor engine and road speed as well as gear position. The Ferrari Mondiale uses a system similar to the one described here.

4.15 Diagnostics – automatic transmission

4.15.1 Systematic testing

If the reported fault is that the kick down does not operate proceed as follows.

1. Road test to confirm the problem.
2. Is the problem worse when the engine is hot? Check the transmission fluid level! Has work been done to the engine?
3. If fluid level is correct then you must investigate

further. Work on the engine may have disturbed the kick down cable.
4. Check the adjustment/fitting of the kick down cable.
5. Adjust if incorrect.
6. Run and repeat road test.

4.15.2 Test equipment

Note: You should always refer to the manufacturer's instructions appropriate to the equipment you are using.

Revcounter

A revcounter may be used during a stall test to check the operation of the torque converter and the automatic gearbox.

Pressure gauge

This is a standard type of gauge but with suitable adapters for connection to a gearbox. Figure 4.25 shows where various tests can be carried out on an automatic gearbox.

4.15.3 Test results

Some of the information you may have to get from other sources such as data books or a workshop manual is listed in the following table.

Test carried out	Information required
Stall test	Highest revs expected and the recommended duration of the test
Kick down test	Rev range in which the kick down should operate. For example, above a certain number of engine revs it may not be allowed to work

Line pressure
Throttle pressure 'B'
Governor pressure
Throttle pressure 'A'
2nd clutch pressure
1st clutch pressure
3rd clutch pressure
1st clutch pressure
4th clutch pressure

Figure 4.25 Transmission pressure testing

4.15.4 Automatic gearbox fault diagnosis table 1

Symptom	Possible faults	Suggested action
Slip, rough shifts, noisy operation or no drive	There are numerous faults that can cause these symptoms	Check the obvious such as fluid levels and condition. Carry out a stall test. Refer to a specialist if necessary

4.15.5 Automatic gearbox fault diagnosis table 2

Symptom	Possible cause
Fluid leaks	Gaskets or seals broken or worn Dip stick tube seal Oil cooler or pipes leaking
Discoloured and/or burnt smell to fluid	Low fluid level Slipping clutches and/or brake bands in the gearbox Fluid requires changing
Gear selection fault	Incorrect selector adjustment Low fluid level Incorrect kick down cable adjustment Load sensor fault (maybe vacuum pipe, etc.)
No kick down	Incorrect kick down cable adjustment Kick down cable broken Low fluid level
Engine will not start or starts in gear	Inhibitor switch adjustment incorrect Faulty inhibitor switch Incorrect selector adjustment
Transmission slip, no drive or poor quality shifts	Low fluid level Internal automatic gearbox faults often require the attention of a specialist

4.15.6 ECAT fault diagnosis table

Symptom	Possible fault
ECAT system reduced performance or not working	Communication link between engine and transmission ECUs open circuit Power supply/earth to ECU low or not present Transmission mechanical fault Gear selector switch open/short circuit Speed sensor inoperative Position switch fault Selection switch fault

4.15.7 Automatic transmission – stall test

To assist with the diagnosis of automatic transmission faults a stall test is often used. The duration of a stall test must not be more than about seven seconds. You should also allow at least two minutes before repeating the test. Refer to manufacturer's recommendations if necessary.

> **Warning**
> If the precautions mentioned are not observed, the gearbox will overheat.

The function of this test is to determine the correct operation of the torque converter and that there is no transmission clutch slip. Proceed as follows.

1. Run engine up to normal operating temperature by road test if possible.
2. Check transmission fluid level and adjust if necessary.
3. Connect a revcounter to the engine.
4. Apply handbrake and chock the wheels.
5. Apply foot brake, select 'D' and fully press down the throttle for about seven seconds.
6. Note the highest rev/min obtained (2500 to 2750 is a typically acceptable range).
7. Allow two minutes for cooling and then repeat the test in '2' and 'R'.

4.16 Brakes

4.16.1 Introduction

The main braking system of a car works by hydraulics. This means that when the driver presses the brake pedal, liquid pressure forces pistons to apply brakes on each wheel. A handbrake system, usually operated by a lever and cables, is used for parking. Most hand brakes operate on the rear wheels.

Two types of light vehicle brakes are used. Disc brakes are used on the front wheels of some cars and on all wheels of sports and performance cars. Braking pressure forces brake pads against both sides of a steel disc. Drum brakes are fitted on the rear wheels of some cars and on all wheels of older vehicles. Braking pressure forces brake shoes to expand outwards into contact with a drum. The important part of brake pads and shoes is a friction lining that grips well and withstands wear.

4.16.2 Principle of hydraulic braking

A complete system includes a master cylinder operating several wheel cylinders. The system is designed to give the power amplification needed for braking the particular vehicle. On any vehicle, when braking, a lot of the weight is transferred to the front wheels. Most braking effort is therefore designed to work on the front brakes. Some cars have special hydraulic valves to limit rear wheel braking. This reduces the chance of the rear wheels locking and skidding.

The main merits of hydraulic brakes are as follows:

- almost immediate reaction to pedal pressure (no free play as with mechanical linkages);
- automatic even pressure distribution (fluid pressure effectively remains the same in all parts of the system);
- increase in force (liquid lever).

Caution and regular servicing is required to ensure the following:

- no air must be allowed in the hydraulic circuits (air compresses and would not transfer the force);
- correct adjustment must be maintained between shoe linings to drums and pads to discs (otherwise the pedal movement would be too large);
- lining materials must be free from contamination (such as oil, grease or brake fluid).

A separate mechanical system is a good safety feature. Most vehicles have the mechanical hand brake working on the rear wheels but a few have it working on the front – take care.

Note the importance of flexible connections to allow for suspension and steering movement. These flexible pipes are made of high quality rubber and are covered in layers of strong mesh to prevent expansion when under pressure.

Extra safety is built into braking systems by using a double acting master cylinder (Figure 4.26). This is often described as tandem and can be thought of as two cylinders in one housing. The pressure from the pedal acts on both cylinders but fluid cannot pass from one to the other. Each cylinder is then connected to a complete circuit. This can be by a number of methods:

- diagonal split;
- separate front and rear;
- duplicated front.

Figure 4.26 Double acting master cylinder

4.16.3 Disc and drum brake systems

Figure 4.27 shows a typical disc brake, calliper pads and disc. The type shown is known as single acting sliding calliper. This is because only one cylinder is used but pads are still pressed equally on both sides of the disc by the sliding action. Disc brakes keep cooler because they are in the air stream and only part of the disc is heated as the brakes are applied. They also throw off water better than drum brakes. In most cases servicing is minimal. Disc brakes are self adjusting and replacing pads is usually a simple task. In the type shown just one bolt has to be removed to hinge the calliper upwards.

Disc brakes provide for good braking and are less prone to brake fade than drum brakes. This is because they are more exposed and can get rid of heat more easily. Brake fade occurs when the brakes become so hot they cannot transfer energy any more, and stop working! This type of problem can happen say after keeping the car brakes on for a long time when travelling down a long steep hill. This is why a lower gear should be used to employ the engine as a brake. It is

Figure 4.27 Disc brake calliper and brake pads

clearly important to use good quality pads and linings because inferior materials can fail if over-heated.

Drum brakes operate by shoes being forced on to the inside of drum. A common type with a ratchet for automatic adjustment is shown as Figure 4.28. Shoes can be moved by double or single acting cylinders. The most common layout is to use one double acting cylinder and brake shoes on each rear wheel of the vehicle, and disc brakes on the front wheels. A double acting cylinder simply means that as fluid pressure acts through a centre inlet, pistons are forced out of both ends.

Drum brakes more affected by wet and heat than disc brakes because both water and heat are trapped inside the drum. However, they are easier to fit with a mechanical hand brake linkage.

4.16.4 Brake adjustments

Brakes must be adjusted so that the minimum movement of the pedal starts to apply the brakes. The adjustment in question is the gap between the pads and disc and/or the shoes and drum.

Disc brakes are self-adjusting because as pressure is released it moves the pads just away from the disc. Drum brakes are different because the shoes are moved away from the drum to a set position by a pull off spring. The set position is adjustable and this can be done in a number of ways.

- Self-adjusting drum brakes are almost universal now. On light vehicles a common type uses an offset ratchet which clicks to a wider position if the shoes move beyond a certain amount when operated. Modern cars frequently have a self-adjusting hand brake.
- Screwdriver adjustment through a hole in the wheel and drum is also used. This is often a type of nut on a threaded bar which pushes the shoes out as it is screwed along the thread.

This method can also have an automatic adjuster fitted.

- An adjustment screw on the back plate is now quite an old method in which a screw or square head protruding from the back plate moves the shoes by a snail cam.

The adjustment procedure stated by the manufacturer must be followed. As a guide, though, most recommend tightening the adjuster until the wheels lock and then moving it back until the wheel is just released. You must ensure that the brakes are not rubbing as this would build up heat and wear the friction material very quickly.

As an aid to fault diagnosis, the effects of incorrect adjustment are as follows:

- reduced braking efficiency;
- unbalanced braking;
- excessive pedal travel.

4.16.5 Servo-assisted braking

Servo systems are designed to give little assistance for light braking but increase the assistance as pedal pressure is increased. A common servo system uses low pressure (vacuum) from the manifold on one side, and the higher atmospheric pressure on the other side of a diaphragm. The low pressure is taken via a non-return safety valve from the engine inlet manifold. This pressure difference causes a force, which is made to act on the master cylinder. Figure 4.29 shows a vacuum servo.

Hydraulic power brakes use the pressure from an engine driven pump. This pump will often be the same one used to supply the power assisted steering. Pressure from the pump is made to act on a plunger in line with the normal master cylinder. As the driver applies force to the pedal, a servo valve opens in proportion to the force applied by the driver. The hydraulic assisting force is therefore also proportional. This maintains the important 'driver feel'.

Figure 4.28 Drum brake adjusters – ratchet type

Figure 4.29 Vacuum operated brake servo

A hydraulic accumulator (a reservoir for fluid under pressure) is incorporated into many systems. This is because the pressure supplied by the pump varies with engine speed. The pressure in the accumulator is kept between set pressures in the region of 70 bar.

> **Warning**
> If you have to disconnect any components from the braking system on a vehicle fitted with an accumulator, you must follow the manufacturer's recommendations on releasing the pressure first.

4.16.6 Brake fluid

Always use new and approved brake fluid when topping up or renewing the system. The manufacturer's recommendations must always be followed. Brake fluid is hygroscopic which means that over a period of time it absorbs water. This increases the risk of the fluid boiling due to the heat from the brakes. Pockets of steam in the system would not allow full braking pressure to be applied. Many manufacturers recommend that the fluid should be changed at regular intervals – in some cases once per year or every 30 000 km. Make sure the correct grade of fluid is used.

4.17 Diagnostics – brakes

4.17.1 Systematic testing

If the reported fault is the hand brake not holding proceed as follows.

1. Confirm the fault by trying to pull away with the hand brake on.
2. Check the foot brake operation. If correct this suggests the brake shoes and drums (or pads and discs) are likely to be in good order.
3. Consider this: do you need to remove the wheels and drums or could it be a cable fault?
4. Check cable operation by using an assistant in the car while you observe.
5. Renew the cable if seized.
6. Check hand brake operation and all associated systems.

4.17.2 Test equipment

> *Note:* You should always refer to the manufacturer's instructions appropriate to the equipment you are using.

Brake fluid tester

Because brake fluid can absorb a small amount of water it must be renewed or tested regularly. It becomes dangerous if the water turns into steam inside the cylinders or pipes, causing the brakes to become ineffective. The tester measures the moisture content of the fluid.

Brake roller test (Figure 4.30)

This is the type of test carried out as part of the annual safety test. The front or rear wheels are driven into a pair of rollers. The rollers drive each wheel of the car and as the brakes are applied the braking force affects the rotation. A measure of braking efficiency can then be worked out.

4.17.3 Test results

Some of the information you may have to get from other sources such as data books or a workshop manual is listed in the following table.

Test carried out	Information required
Brake roller test	Required braking efficiency: 50% for first line brakes, 25% for second line brakes and 16% for the parking brake. On modern vehicles half of the main system is the second line (dual line brakes). Old vehicles had to use the parking brake as the second line, therefore it had to work at 25%
Brake fluid condition	Manufacturers specify maximum moisture content

Figure 4.30 Rolling road brake tester

4.17.4 Brakes fault diagnosis table 1

Symptom	Possible faults	Suggested action
Excessive pedal travel	Incorrect adjustment	Adjust it! But check condition as well
Poor performance when stopping	Pad and/or shoe linings worn	Renew
	Seized calliper or wheel cylinders	Renew or free off if possible and safe
	Contaminated linings	Renew (both sides)
Car pulls to one side when braking	Seized calliper or wheel cylinder on one side	Overhaul or renew if piston or cylinder is worn
	Contaminated linings on one side	Renew (both sides)
Spongy pedal	Air in the hydraulic system	Bleed system and then check for leaks
	Master cylinder seals failing	Overhaul or renew
Pedal travels to the floor when pressed	Fluid reservoir empty	Refill, bleed system and check for leaks
	Failed seals in master cylinder	Overhaul or renew
	Leak from a pipe or union	Replace or repair as required
Brakes overheating	Shoe return springs broken	Renew (both sides)
	Callipers or wheel cylinders sticking	Free off or renew if in any doubt
Brake judder	Linings worn	Renew
	Drums out of round	Renew
	Discs have excessive run-out	Renew
Squeaking	Badly worn linings	Renew
	Dirt in brake drums	Clean out with proper cleaner
	Anti-squeal shims missing at rear of pads	Replace and smear with copper grease

4.17.5 Brakes fault diagnosis table 2

Symptom	Possible cause
Brake fade	Incorrect linings
	Badly lined shoes
	Distorted shoes
	Overloaded vehicle
	Excessive braking
Spongy pedal	Air in system
	Badly lined shoes
	Shoes distorted or incorrectly set
	Faulty drums

	Weak master cylinder mounting
Long pedal	Discs running out pushing pads back
	Distorted damping shims
	Misplaced dust covers
	Drum brakes need adjustment
	Fluid leak
	Fluid contamination
	Worn or swollen seals in master cylinder
	Blocked filler cap vent
Brakes binding	Brakes or handbrake maladjusted
	No clearance at master cylinder push rod
	Seals swollen
	Seized pistons
	Shoe springs weak or broken
	Servo faulty
Hard pedal – poor braking	Incorrect linings
	Glazed linings
	Linings wet, greasy or not bedded correctly
	Servo unit inoperative
	Seized calliper pistons
	Worn dampers causing wheel bounce
Brakes pulling	Seized pistons
	Variation in linings
	Unsuitable tyres or pressures
	Loose brakes
	Greasy linings
	Faulty drums, suspension or steering
Fall in fluid level	Worn disc pads
	External leak
	Leak in servo unit.
Disc brake squeal – pad rattle	Worn retaining pins
	Worn discs
	No pad damping shims or springs
Uneven or excessive pad wear	Disc corroded or badly scored
	Incorrect friction material
Brake judder	Excessive disc or drum run-out
	Calliper mounting bolts loose
	Worn suspension or steering components

4.17.6 Brake hydraulic faults

Brake hose clamps will assist in diagnosing hydraulic faults and enable a fault to be located quickly. Proceed as follows.

1 Clamp all hydraulic flexible hoses and check the pedal.
2 Remove the clamps one at a time and check the pedal again (each time).
3 The location of air in the system or the faulty part of the system will now be apparent.

4.18 Steering and tyres

4.18.1 Tyres

The tyre performs two basic functions.

- It acts as the primary suspension, cushioning the vehicle from the effects of a rough surface.
- It provides frictional contact with the road surface. This allows the driving wheels to move the vehicle. The tyres also allow the front wheels to steer and the brakes to slow or stop the vehicle.

The tyre is a flexible casing which contains air. Tyres are manufactured from reinforced synthetic rubber. The tyre is made of an inner layer of fabric plies, which are wrapped around bead wires at the inner edges. The bead wires hold the tyre in position on the wheel rim. The fabric plies are coated with rubber, which is moulded to form the side walls and the tread of the tyre. Behind the tread is a reinforcing band, usually made of steel, rayon, or glass fibre. Modern tyres are mostly tubeless, so they have a thin layer of rubber coating the inside to act as a seal.

4.18.2 Construction of a tubeless radial tyre

The wheel is made with a leak-proof rim and the valve is rubber mounted into a hole formed in the well of the rim. The tyre is made with an accurate bead, which fits tightly on to the rim. A thin rubber layer in the interior of the tyre makes an air tight seal.

The plies of a radial tyre pass from bead to bead at 90° to the circumference, or radially. There is a rigid belt band consisting of several layers of textile or metallic threads running round the tyre under the tread. Steel wire is often used in the construction of radial tyres. The radial tyre is flexible but retains high strength. It has good road holding and cornering power. In addition, radial tyres are economical due to their low 'rolling resistance'.

A major advantage of a radial tyre is its greatly improved grip even on wet roads. This is because the rigid belt band holds the tread flat on the road surface, when cornering. The rigid belt band also helps with the escape of water from under the tyre. Figure 4.31 shows some modern tyres.

Figure 4.31 Tyres!

4.18.3 Steering box and rack

Steering boxes contain a spiral gear known as a worm gear which rotates with the steering column. One form of design has a nut wrapped round the spiral and is therefore known as a worm and nut steering box. The grooves can be filled with re-circulating ball bearings, which reduce backlash or slack in the system and also reduce friction, making steering lighter. On vehicles with independent front suspension, an idler unit is needed together with a number of links and several joints. The basic weakness of the steering box system is in the number of swivelling joints and connections. If there is just slight wear at a number of points, the steering will not feel or be positive.

The steering rack (Figure 4.32) is now used almost without exception on light vehicles. This is because it is simple in design and very long lasting. The wheels turn on two large swivel joints. Another ball joint (often called a track rod end) is fitted on each swivel arm. A further ball joint to the ends of the rack connects the track rods. The rack is inside a lubricated tube and gaiters protect the inner ball joints. The pinion meshes with the teeth of the rack, and as it is turned by the steering wheel, the rack is made to move back and forth, turning the front wheels on their swivel ball joints. On many vehicles now, the steering rack is augmented with hydraulic power assistance.

4.18.4 Power-assisted steering

Rack and pinion steering requires more turning effort than a steering box, although this is not too noticeable with smaller vehicles. However, heavier cars with larger engines or with wider tyres which scrub more, often benefit from power steering.

Many vehicles use a belt driven hydraulic

Steering propshaft

Inner ball joint

Gaiter

Track rod end

Figure 4.32 Steering rack

pump to supply fluid under pressure for use in the system. Inside the rack and pinion housing is a hydraulic valve, which is operated as the pinion is turned for steering. The valve controls the flow of oil into a cylinder, which has a piston connected to the rack. This assists with the steering effort quite considerably.

A well designed system will retain 'feel' of road conditions for the driver to control the car. Steering a slow moving heavier vehicle when there is little room can be tiring, or even impossible for some drivers. This is where power steering has its best advantage. Many modern systems are able to make the power steering progressive. This means that as the speed of the vehicle increases, the assistance provided by the power steering reduces. This maintains better driver feel.

Very modern systems are starting to use electric power steering. This employs a very powerful electric motor as part of the steering linkage. There are two main types of electric power steering:

● Replacing the conventional hydraulic pump with an electric motor whilst the ram remains much the same.
● A drive motor, which directly assists with the steering and which has no hydraulic components.

The second system uses a small electric motor acting directly on the steering via an epicyclic gear train. This completely replaces the hydraulic pump and servo cylinder. It also eliminates the fuel penalty of the conventional pump and greatly simplifies the drive arrangements. Engine stall when the power steering is operated at idle speed is also eliminated. Figure 4.33 shows an electric power steering system.

An optical torque sensor is used to measure driver effort on the steering wheel. The sensor works by measuring light from an LED which is shining through holes which are aligned in discs at either end of a 50 mm torsion bar fitted into the steering column.

4.18.5 Steering characteristics

The steering characteristics of a vehicle, or in other words the way in which it reacts when cornering, can be described by one of three headings:

● oversteer;
● understeer;
● neutral.

Oversteer occurs when the rear of the vehicle tends to swing outward more than the front during cornering. This is because the slip angle on the rear axle is significantly greater than the

Figure 4.33 Electric power steering

front axle. This causes the vehicle to travel in a tighter circle, hence the term oversteer. If the steering angle is not reduced the vehicle will break away and all control will be lost. Turning the steering towards the opposite lock will reduce the front slip angle.

Understeer occurs when the front of the vehicle tends to swing outward more than the rear during cornering. This is because the slip angle on the rear axle is significantly smaller than the front axle. This causes the vehicle to travel in a greater circle, hence the term understeer. If the steering angle is not increased the vehicle will be carried out of the corner and all control will be lost. Turning the steering further into the bend will increase the front the slip angle. Front-engined vehicles tend to understeer because the centre of gravity is situated in front of the vehicle centre. The outward centrifugal force therefore has a greater effect on the front wheels than on the rear.

Neutral steering occurs when the centre of gravity is at the vehicle centre and the front and rear slip angles are equal. The cornering forces are therefore uniformly spread. Note, however, that understeer or oversteer can still occur if the cornering conditions change.

4.18.6 Camber

| *Note:* Typical value is about 0.5° (values will vary so check specs).

On many cars, the front wheels are not mounted vertically to the road surface. Often they are tilted outwards at the top. This is called positive camber (Figure 4.34) and has the following effects:

- easier steering, less turning effort required;
- less wear on the steering linkages;
- less stress on main components;
- smaller scrub radius, which reduces the effect of wheel forces on the steering.

Negative camber has the of giving effect good cornering force. Some cars have rear wheels with negative camber. With independent suspension systems, wheels can change their camber from positive through neutral, to negative as the suspension is compressed. This varies, however, with the design and position of the suspension hinge points.

4.18.7 Castor

| *Note:* Typical value is about 2 to 4° (values will vary so check specs).

The front wheels tend to straighten themselves out after cornering. This is due to a castor action. Supermarket trolley wheels automatically run straight when pushed because the axle on which they rotate is behind the swivel mounting. Vehicle wheels get the same result by leaning

Figure 4.34 Camber angle

the swivel pin mountings back so that the wheel axle is moved slightly behind the line of the swivel axis. The further the axle is behind the swivel, the stronger will be the straightening effect. The main effects of a positive castor angle (Figure 4.35) are:

- self centring action;
- helps determine the steering torque when cornering.

Negative castor is used on some front wheel drive vehicles to reduce the return forces when cornering. Note that a combination of steering geometry angles is used to achieve the desired effect. This means that in some cases the swivel axis produces the desired self-centre action so the castor angle may need to be negative to reduce the return forces on corners.

4.18.8 Swivel axis inclination

Note: Typical value is about 7 to 9° (values will vary so check specs).

The swivel axis is also known as the steering axis. Swivel axis inclination (Figure 4.36) means the angle compared to vertical made by the two swivel joints when viewed from the front or rear. On a strut type suspension system the angle is broadly that made by the strut. This angle always leans in towards the middle of the vehicle. The swivel axis inclination (also called kingpin inclination) is mainly for:

- producing a self-centre action;
- improving steering control on corners;
- giving a lighter steering action.

Scrub radius, wheel camber and swivel axis inclination all have an effect on one another. The swivel axis inclination mainly affects the self-

centring action, also known as the aligning torque. Because of the axis inclination the vehicle is raised slightly at the front as the wheels are turned. The weight of the vehicle therefore tries to force the wheels back into the straight-ahead position.

4.18.9 Tracking

As a front wheel drive car drives forward the tyres pull on the road surface taking up the small amount of free play in the mountings and joints. For this reason the tracking is often set toe-out so that the wheels point straight ahead when the vehicle is moving. Rear wheel drive tends to make the opposite happen because it pushes against the front wheels. The front wheels are therefore set toe-in. When the car moves, the front wheels are pushed out taking up the slack in the joints, so the wheels again end up straight ahead. The amount of toe-in or toe-out is very small, normally not exceeding 5 mm (the difference in the distance between the front and rear of the front wheels). Correctly set tracking ensures true rolling of the wheels and therefore reduced tyre wear. Figure 4.37 shows wheels set toe-in and toe-out.

4.18.10 Scrub radius

The scrub radius is the distance between the contact point of the steering axis with the road and the wheel centre contact point. The purpose of designing in a scrub radius is to reduce the steer-

Figure 4.35 Positive castor

Figure 4.36 Swivel axis

Toe-in

L_1

L_2

Toe-out

L_1

L_2

Figure 4.37 Tracking

ing force and to prevent steering shimmy. It also helps to stabilise the straight-ahead position.

It is possible to design the steering with a negative, positive or zero scrub radius as described below.

Scrub radius	Description	Properties
Negative	The contact point of the steering axis hits the road between the wheel centre and the outer edge of the wheel	Braking forces produce a torque which tends to make the wheel turn inwards. The result of this is that the wheel with the greatest braking force is turned in with greater torque. This steers the vehicle away from the side with the heaviest braking producing a built in counter steer action which has a stabilising effect
Positive	The contact point of the steering axis hits the road between the wheel centre and the inner edge of the wheel	A positive scrub radius makes turning the steering easier. However, braking forces produce a torque which tends to make the wheel turn outwards. The result of this is that the wheel with the greatest braking force is turned out with greater torque. Under different road conditions this can have the effect of
		producing an unwanted steering angle
Zero	The contact point of the steering axis hits the road at the same place as the wheel centre	This makes the steering heavy when the vehicle is at rest because the wheel cannot roll at the steering angle. However, no separate turning torque about the steering axis is created

From the information given you will realise that decisions about steering geometry are not clear-cut. One change may have a particular advantage in one area but a disadvantage in another. To assist with fault diagnosis a good understanding of steering geometry is essential.

4.19 Diagnostics – steering and tyres

4.19.1 Systematic testing

If the reported fault is heavy steering proceed as follows.

1. Ask if the problem has just developed. Road test to confirm.
2. Check the obvious such as tyre pressures. Is the vehicle loaded to excess? Check geometry?
3. Assuming tyre pressure and condition is as it should be we must move on to further tests.
4. For example, jack up and support the front of the car. Operate the steering lock to lock. Disconnect one track rod end and move the wheel on that side, and so on.
5. If the fault is in the steering rack then this should be replaced and the tracking should be set.
6. Test the operation with a road test and inspect all other related components for security and safety.

4.19.2 Test equipment

Note: You should always refer to the manufacturer's instructions appropriate to the equipment you are using.

Tyre pressure gauge and tread depth gauge

Often under-rated pieces of test equipment. Correctly inflated tyres make the vehicle handle better, stop better and use less fuel. The correct depth of tread means the vehicle will be significantly safer to drive, particularly in wet conditions.

Figure 4.38 Tracking gauges

Tracking gauges (Figure 4.38)

The toe-in and toe-out of a vehicle's front wheels is very important. Many types of tracking gauges are available. One of the most common uses a frame placed against each wheel with a mirror on one side and a moveable viewer on the other. The viewer is moved until marks are lined up and the tracking can then be measured.

Wheel balancer (Figure 4.39)

This is a large fixed piece of equipment in most cases. The wheel is removed from the car, fixed on to the machine and spun at high speed. Sensors in the tester measure the balance of the wheel. The tester then indicates the amount of weight which should be added to a certain position. The weight is added by fitting small lead weights.

4.19.3 Test results

Some of the information you may have to get from other sources such as data books or a workshop manual is listed in the following table.

Test carried out	Information required
Tracking	The data for tracking will be given as either an angle or a distance measurement. Ensure that you use the appropriate data for your type of test equipment. Distance will be a figure such as 3 mm toe-in, and angle one such as 50' toe-in (50' means 50 minutes). The angle of 1° is split into 60 minutes, so in this case the angle is 50/60 or 5/6 of a degree
Pressures	A simple measurement which should be in bars. You will find, however that many places still use PSI (pounds per square inch). As in all other cases only compare like with like.
Tread depth	The minimum measurement (e.g. 1.6 mm over 75% of the tread area but please note the current local legal requirements)

4.19.4 Tyres fault diagnosis table

The following table lists some of the faults which can occur if tyres and/or the vehicle are not maintained correctly. Figure 4.40 shows the same.

Figure 4.39 Wheel balancer

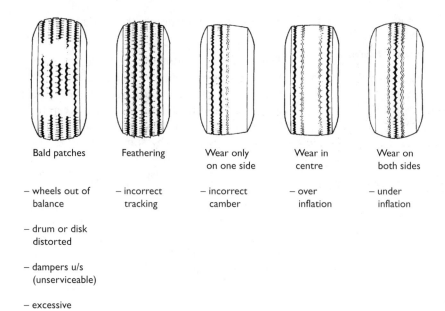

Bald patches   Feathering   Wear only   Wear in   Wear on
                              on one side   centre   both sides

– wheels out of – incorrect   – incorrect   – over   – under
  balance   tracking   camber   inflation   inflation

– drum or disk
  distorted

– dampers u/s
  (unserviceable)

– excessive
  braking

Figure 4.40 Tyre faults

Symptom	Possible cause/fault
Wear on both outer edges of the tread	Under inflation
Wear in the centre of the tread all round the tyre	Over inflation
Wear just on one side of the tread	Incorrect camber
Feathering	Tracking not set correctly
Bald patches	Unbalanced wheels or unusual driving technique!

4.19.5 Tyre inflation pressures

The pressure at which the tyres should be set is determined by a number of factors such as:

● load to be carried;
● number of plies;
● operating conditions;
● section of the tyre.

Tyre pressures must be set at the values recommended by the manufacturers. Pressure will vary according to the temperature of the tyre – this is affected by operating conditions. Tyre pressure should always be adjusted when the tyre is cold and be checked at regular intervals.

4.19.6 Steering fault diagnosis table 1

Symptom	Possible faults	Suggested action
Excessive free play at steering wheel	Play between the rack and pinion or in the steering box	Renew in most cases but adjustment may be possible
	Ball joints or tie rod joints worn	Renew
	Column coupling loose or bushes worn	Secure or renew
Vehicle wanders, hard to keep in a straight line	As above	As above
	Alignment incorrect	Adjust to recommended setting
	Incorrect tyre pressure or mix of tyre types is not suitable	Adjust pressures or replace tyres as required
	Worn wheel bearings	Renew
Stiff steering	Wheel alignment incorrect	Adjust to recommended setting
	Tyre pressures too low	Adjust pressures
	Ball joints or rack seizing	Renew
Wheel wobble	Wheels out of balance	Balance or renew
	Wear in suspension linkages	Renew

	Alignment incorrect	Adjust to recommended setting
Understeer or oversteer	Tyre pressures incorrect	Adjust pressures
	Dangerous mix of tyre types	Replace tyres as required
	Excessive freeplay in suspension or steering system	Renew components as required

4.19.7 Steering, wheels and tyres fault diagnosis

Symptom	Possible cause
Wandering or instability	Incorrect wheel alignment Worn steering joints Wheels out of balance Wheel nuts or bolts loose
Wheel wobble	Front or rear Wheels out of balance Damaged or distorted wheels/tyres Worn steering joints
Pulling to one side	Defective tyre Excessively worn components Incorrect wheel alignment
Excessive tyre wear	Incorrect wheel alignment Worn steering joints Wheels out of balance Incorrect inflation pressures Driving style! Worn dampers
Excessive free play	Worn track rod end or swivel joints Steering column bushes worn Steering column universal joint worn
Stiff steering	Lack of steering gear lubrication Seized track rod end joint or suspension swivel joint Incorrect wheel alignment Damage to steering components

4.20 Suspension

4.20.1 Introduction

The purpose of a suspension system can best be summarised by the following requirements:

- cushion the car, passengers and load from road surface irregularities;
- resist the effects of steering, braking and acceleration, even on hills and when loads are carried;
- keep tyres in contact with the road at all times;
- work in conjunction with the tyres and seat springs to give an acceptable ride at all speeds.

The above list is difficult to achieve completely, so some sort of compromise has to be reached. Because of this many different methods have been tried, and many are still in use. Keep these four main requirements in mind and it will help you to understand why some systems are constructed in different ways.

A vehicle needs a suspension system to cushion and damp out road shocks so providing comfort to the passengers and preventing damage to the load and vehicle components. A spring between the wheel and the vehicle body allows the wheel to follow the road surface. The tyre plays an important role in absorbing small road shocks. It is often described as the primary form of suspension. The vehicle body is supported by springs located between the body and the wheel axles. Together with the damper these components are referred to as the suspension system.

As a wheel hits a bump in the road it is moved upwards with quite some force. An unsprung wheel is affected only by gravity, which will try to return the wheel to the road surface but most of the energy will be transferred to the body. When a spring is used between the wheel and the vehicle body, most of the energy in the bouncing wheel is stored in the spring and not passed to the vehicle body. The vehicle body will now only move upwards through a very small distance compared to the movement of the wheel.

4.20.2 Suspension system layouts

On older types of vehicle, a beam axle was used to support two stub axles. Beam axles are now rarely used in car suspension systems, although many commercial vehicles use them because of their greater strength and constant ground clearance.

The need for a better suspension system came from the demand for improved ride quality and improved handling. Independent front suspension (IFS) was developed to meet this need. The main advantages of independent front suspension are as follows:

- when one wheel is lifted or drops, it does not affect the opposite wheel;
- the unsprung mass is lower, therefore the road wheel stays in better contact with the road;
- problems with changing steering geometry are reduced;

Figure 4.41 Front wheel drive vehicle showing the suspension layout

- there is more space for the engine at the front;
- softer springing with larger wheel movement is possible.

There are a number of basic suspension systems in common use. Figure 4.41 shows a typical suspension layout.

4.20.3 Front axle suspensions

As with most design aspects of the vehicle, compromise often has to be reached between performance, body styling and cost. The following table compares the common front axle suspension systems.

Name	Description	Advantages	Disadvantages
Double transverse arms	Independently suspended wheels located by two arms perpendicular to direction of travel. The arms support stub axles	Low bonnet line Only slight changes of track and camber with suspension movements	A large number of pivot points is required High production costs
Transverse arms with leaf spring	A transverse arm and a leaf spring locate the wheel	The spring can act as an anti-roll bar, hence low cost	Harsh response when lightly loaded Major changes of camber as vehicle is loaded
Transverse arm with McPherson strut	A combination of the spring, damper, wheel hub, steering arm and axle joints in one unit	Only slight changes in track and camber with suspension movement Forces on the joints are reduced because of the long strut	The body must be strengthened around the upper mounting A low bonnet line is difficult to achieve
Double trailing arms	Two trailing arms support the stub axle. These can act on torsion bars often formed as a single assembly	No change in castor, camber or track with suspension movement Can be assembled and adjusted off the vehicle	Lots of space is required at the front of the vehicle Expensive to produce Acceleration and braking cause pitching movements which in turn changes the wheel base

Figure 4.42 shows a suspension system with front struts and rear trailing arms.

4.20.4 Rear axle suspensions

The following table compares the common rear axle suspension systems.

Name	Description	Advantages	Disadvantages
Rigid axle with leaf springs	The final drive, differential and axle shafts are all one unit	Rear track remains constant reducing tyre wear Good directional stability because no camber change causes body roll on corners Low cost Strong design for load carrying	High unsprung mass The interaction of the wheels causes lateral movement reducing tyre adhesion when the suspension is compressed on one side
Rigid axle with A-bracket	Solid axle with coil springs and a central joint supports the axle on the body	Rear of the vehicle pulls down on braking which stabilises the vehicle	High cost Large unsprung mass
Rigid axle with compression/tension struts	Coil springs provide the springing and the axle is located by struts	Suspension extension is reduced when braking or accelerating The springs are isolated from these forces	High loads on the welded joints High weight overall Large unsprung mass
Torsion beam trailing arm axle	Two links are used, connected by a 'U' section that has low torsional stiffness but high resistance to bending	Track and camber does not change Low unsprung mass Simple to produce Space saving	Torsion bar springing on this system can be more expensive than coil springs
Torsion beam axle with Panhard rod	Two links are welded to an axle tube or 'U' section and lateral forces are taken by a Panhard rod	Track and camber does not change Simple flexible joints to the bodywork	Torsion bar springing on this system can be more expensive than coil springs
Trailing arms	The pivot axis of the trailing arms is at 90° to the direction of vehicle travel	When braking the rear of the vehicle pulls down giving stable handling Track and camber does not change Space saving	Slight change of wheel base when the suspension is compressed
Semi-trailing arms – fixed length drive shafts	The trailing arms are pivoted at an angle to the direction of travel. Only one UJ is required because the radius of the suspension arm is the same as the driveshaft when the suspension is compressed	Only very small dive when braking Lower cost than when variable length shafts are used	Sharp changes in track when the suspension is compressed resulting in tyre wear Slight tendency to oversteer
Semi-trailing arms – variable length drive shafts	The final drive assembly is mounted to the body and two UJs are used on each shaft	The two arms are independent of each other Only slight track changes	Large camber changes High cost because of the drive shafts and joints

4.20.5 Anti-roll bar

The main purpose of an anti-roll bar (Figure 4.43) is to reduce body roll on corners. The anti-roll bar can be thought of as a torsion bar. The centre is pivoted on the body and each end bends to make connection with the suspension/wheel assembly. When the suspension is compressed on both sides, the anti-roll bar has no effect because it pivots on its mountings.

As the suspension is compressed on just one side, a twisting force is exerted on the anti-roll bar. The anti-roll bar is now under torsional load. Part of this load is transmitted to the opposite wheel, pulling it upwards. This reduces the amount of body roll on corners. The disadvantages are that some of the 'independence' is lost and the overall ride is harsher. Anti-roll bars can be fitted to both front and rear axles.

4.20.6 Springs

The requirements of the springs can be summarised as follows:

- absorb road shocks from uneven surfaces;
- control ground clearance and ride height;
- ensure good tyre adhesion;
- support the weight of the vehicle;
- transmit gravity forces to the wheels.

Front

Rear

Figure 4.42 Suspension system with front struts and rear trailing arms

Rubber bushes for attachment to transverse arms

Anti-roll (torsion) bar

Rubber mounts for pivoting attachment to body

Figure 4.43 Anti-roll bar and mountings

There are a number of different types of spring in use on modern light vehicles. The following table lists these together with their main features.

Name	Comments	Characteristics
Coil springs	The most common spring currently in use on light vehicles. The coil spring is a torsion bar wound into a spiral	Can be progressive if the diameter of the spring is tapered conically. Cannot transmit lateral or longitudinal forces, hence the need for links or arms. Little internal damping. Little or no maintenance. High travel
Leaf springs	These springs can be single or multiple leaf. They are most often mounted longitudinally. Nowadays they are only ever used on commercial vehicles	Can transmit longitudinal and lateral forces. Short travel. High internal damping. High load capacity. Maintenance may be required. Low height but high weight
Torsion bar springs	A torsion bar is a spring where twisting loads are applied to a steel bar. They can be round or square section, solid or hollow. Their surface must be finished accurately to eliminate pressure points, which may cause cracking and fatigue failure. They can be fitted longitudinally or laterally	Maintenance-free but can be adjusted. Transmit longitudinal and lateral forces. Limited self-damping. Linear rate. Low weight. May have limited fatigue life
Rubber springs	Nowadays rubber springs are only used as a supplement to other forms of springs. They are, however, popular on trailers and caravans	Progressive rate. Transmit longitudinal and lateral forces. Short travel. Low weight and low cost. Their springing and damping properties can change with temperature
Air springs	Air springs can be thought of as being like a balloon or football on which the car is supported. The system involves compressors and air tanks. They are not normally used on light vehicles	Expensive. Good quality ride. Electronic control can be used. Progressive spring rate. High production cost
Hydro-pneumatic springs	A hydro-pneumatic spring is a gas spring with hydraulic force transmission. Nitrogen is usually used as the gas. The damper can be built in as part of the hydraulic system.	Progressive rate. Ride height control. Damping built in. Pressurised oil supply is required. Expensive and complicated

The springs can be hydraulically connected together to reduce pitch or roll. Ride height control can be achieved by pumping oil into or out of the working chamber

4.20.7 Dampers

The functions of a damper can be summarised as follows:

- ensure directional stability;
- ensure good contact between the tyres an the road;
- prevent buildup of vertical movements;
- reduce oscillations;
- reduce wear on tyres and chassis components.

There are a number of different types of damper.

Friction damper	Not used on cars today but you will find this system used as part of caravan or trailer stabilisers
Lever type damper	Used on earlier vehicles, the lever operates a piston which forces oil into a chamber
Twin tube telescopic damper	This is a commonly used type of damper consisting of two tubes. An outer tube forms a reservoir space and contains the oil displaced from an inner tube. Oil is forced through a valve by the action of a piston as the damper moves up or down. The reservoir space is essential to make up for the changes in volume as the piston rod moves in and out
Single tube telescopic damper	This is often referred to as a gas damper. However, the damping action is still achieved by forcing oil through a restriction. The gas space behind a separator piston is to compensate for the changes in cylinder volume caused as the piston rod moves. It is at a pressure of about 25 bar
Twin tube gas damper (Fig. 4.44)	The twin tube gas damper is an improvement on the well-used twin tube system. The gas cushion is used in this case to prevent oil foaming. The gas pressure on the oil prevents foaming which in turn ensures constant operation under all operating conditions. Gas pressure is lower than for a single tube damper at about 5 bar
Variable rate damper	This is a special variation of the twin tube gas damper. The damping characteristics vary depending on the

load on the vehicle. Bypass grooves are machined in the upper half of the working chamber. With light loads the damper works in this area with a soft damping effect. When the load is increased the piston moves lower down the working chamber away from the grooves resulting in full damping effect

Electronically controlled dampers	These are dampers where the damping rate can be controlled by solenoid valves inside the units. With suitable electronic control, the characteristics can be changed within milliseconds to react to driving and/or load conditions

4.21 Diagnostics – suspension

4.21.1 Systematic testing

If the reported fault is poor handling proceed as follows.

1. Road test to confirm the fault.
2. With the vehicle on a lift inspect obvious items like tyres and dampers.
3. Consider if the problem is suspension related or in the steering for example. You may have decided this from road testing.
4. Inspect all the components of the system you suspect, for example dampers for correct operation and suspension bushes for condi-

Figure 4.44 Twin-tube gas damper

tion and security. Let's assume the fault was one front damper not operating to the required standard.

5. Renew both of the dampers at the front to ensure balanced performance.
6. Road test again and check for correct operation of the suspension and other systems.

4.21.2 Test equipment

Note: You should always refer to the manufacturer's instructions appropriate to the equipment you are using.

Damper tester

This is a device that will draw a graph to show the response of the dampers. It may be useful for providing paper evidence of the operating condition but a physical examination is normally adequate.

The operating principle is shown as Figure 4.45 which indicates that the damper is not operating correctly in this case.

4.21.3 Test results

Some of the information you may have to get from other sources such as data books or a workshop manual is listed in the following table.

Test carried out	Information required
Damper operation	The vehicle body should move down as you press on it, bounce back just past the start point and then return to the rest position
Suspension bush condition	Simple levering if appropriate should not show excessive movement, cracks or separation of rubber bushes
Trim height	This is available from data books as a measurement from say the wheel centre to a point on the car wing above

4.21.4 Suspension fault diagnosis table 1

Symptom	Possible faults	Suggested action
Excessive pitch or roll when driving	Dampers worn	Replace in pairs
Car sits lopsided	Broken spring Leak in hydraulic suspension	Replace in pairs Rectify by replacing unit or fitting new pipes
Knocking noises	Excessive free play in a suspension joint	Renew
Excessive tyre wear	Steering/suspension geometry incorrect (may be due to accident damage)	Check and adjust or replace any 'bent' or out of true components

4.21.5 Suspension fault diagnosis table 2

Symptom	Possible cause
Excessive pitching	Defective dampers Broken or weak spring Worn or damaged anti-roll bar mountings
Wandering or instability	Broken or weak spring Worn suspension joints Defective dampers
Wheel wobble	Worn suspension joints
Pulling to one side	Worn suspension joints Accident damage to suspension alignment
Excessive tyre wear	Worn suspension joints Accident damage to suspension alignment Incorrect trim height (particularly hydro-elastic systems)

Push Down

Pen

Paper Movement

Figure 4.45 Damper testing procedure

5

Sensors, actuators and electronics

5.1 Introduction

Sensors, actuators and electronics have a chapter all to themselves because they are so important! And also because the issues and diagnostic techniques are common to many systems. For example, the testing procedure for an inductive engine speed sensor on a fuel injection system, is the same as for an inductive speed sensor on an ABS system. Basic electronic component testing is likewise common to all systems.

Testing sensors to diagnose faults is usually a matter of measuring their output signal. In some cases the sensor will produce this on its own (an inductive sensor for example). In other cases, it will be necessary to supply the correct voltage to the device to make it work (Hall sensor for example).

Note: It is normal to check that the vehicle circuit is supplying the voltage before proceeding to test the sensor.

After the description of most sensors, and actuators a table is included listing the sensor, equipment necessary, test method(s), results of the tests and a scope waveform. A waveform will be reproduced where appropriate, as this is often the recommended method of testing (see Section 3.2 on the 'ScopeMeter' for more details). The waveform shown will either be the output of a sensor or the signal supplied to an actuator.

Note: any figures given are average or typical values. Refer to a good reference source such as a workshop manual, '*Autodata*' book or '*Autologic*' CD-ROM for specific values.

5.2 Sensors

5.2.1 Thermistors

Thermistors are the most common device used for temperature measurement on the motor vehicle. The principle of measurement is that a change in temperature will cause a change in resistance of the thermistor and hence an electrical signal proportional to the temperature being measured. Figure 5.1 shows a typical thermistor used as an engine coolant temperature sensor.

Most thermistors in common use are of the negative temperature coefficient (NTC) type. The actual response of the thermistors can vary but typical values for those used on motor vehicles will vary from several kΩ at 0°C to a few hundred Ω at 100°C. The large change in resistance for a small change in temperature makes the thermistor ideal for most vehicles uses. It can also be easily tested with simple equipment.

Thermistors are constructed of semiconductor materials. The change in resistance with a change in temperature is due to the electrons being able to break free more easily at higher temperatures.

Figure 5.1 Coolant temperature sensor

Sensor	Equipment	Method(s)	Results

Thermistor
Coolant sensor
Air intake temperature
  sensor
Ambient temperature
  sensor
etc.
	Ohmmeter	Connect across the two terminals
		or, if only one, from this to earth
			Most thermistors have a negative
			temperature coefficient (NTC).
			This means the resistance falls as
			temperature rises. A resistance
			check should give readings broadly
			as follows:
			    0°C = 4500 Ω
			   20°C = 1200 Ω
			 100°C = 200 Ω

The scope waveform is shown in Figure 5.2.

5.2.2 Inductive sensors

Inductive type sensors are used mostly for measuring the speed and position of a rotating component. They work on the very basic principle of electrical induction (a changing magnetic flux will induce an electromotive force in a winding). Figure 5.3 shows a typical device used as a crankshaft speed and position sensor.

The output voltage of most inductive type sensors approximates to a sine wave. The amplitude of this signal depends on the rate of change of flux. This is determined mostly by the original design as in number of turns, magnet strength and the gap between the sensor and the rotating component. Once in use though the output voltage increases with the speed of rotation. In the majority of applications, it is the frequency of the signal that is used.

Sensor	Equipment	Method(s)	Results
Inductive Crankshaft speed and position ABS wheel speed Camshaft position	Ohmmeter AC voltmeter	A resistance test with the sensor disconnected AC voltage output with the engine cranking	Values vary from about 200 to 400 Ω on some vehicles to 800 to 1200 Ω on others. The 'sine wave' output should be about 5 V (less depending on engine speed)

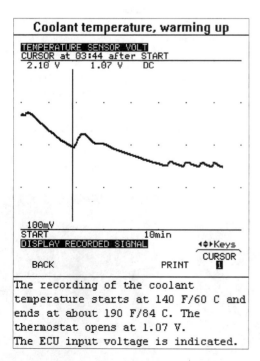

Figure 5.2 Waveform showing output of coolant temperature sensor, warming up

Figure 5.3 Inductive crankshaft sensor and reluctor wheel

The scope waveform is shown in Figure 5.4.

5.2.3 Hall effect sensors

If a conductor is carrying a current in a transverse magnetic field then a voltage will be produced at right angles to the supply current. This voltage is proportional to the supply current and to the magnetic field strength.

Many distributors employ Hall effect sensors. The output of this sensor is almost a square wave with constant amplitude. The Hall effect can also be used to detect current flowing in a cable, the magnetic field produced round the cable being proportional to the current flowing.

Hall effect sensors are becoming increasingly popular. This is partly due to their reliability but also to the fact that they directly produce a constant amplitude square wave in speed measurement applications and a varying DC voltage for either position sensing or current sensing.

Hall effect sensors are being used in place of inductive sensors for applications such as engine speed and wheel speed. The two main advantages are that measurement of lower (or even zero) speed is possible and that the voltage output of the sensors is independent of speed. Figure 5.5 shows a selection of Hall effect sensors.

Figure 5.4 Waveform showing output of crankshaft position sensor

Sensor	Equipment	Method(s)	Results
Hall effect Ignition distributor Engine speed	DC voltmeter	The voltage output is measured as the engine or component is rotated slowly.	This switches between 0 and about 8 V as the Hall chip is magnetised – or not.
Transmission speed Wheel speed Current flow in a wire (ammeter amp clamp)	Logic probe Do *not* use an ohmmeter as this will damage the Hall chip	The sensor is normally supplied with 10 to 12 V	A logic probe will read high and low as the sensor output switches

Figure 5.5 Hall effect sensors (a) transmission, (b) throttle position, (c) tachometer driver

The scope waveform is shown in Figure 5.6.

5.2.4 Optical sensors

An optical sensor for rotational position is a relatively simple device. The optical rotation sensor and circuit shown in Figure 5.7 consists of a phototransistor as a detector and a light emitting diode light source. If the light is focused to a very narrow beam then the output of the circuit shown will be a square wave with frequency proportional to speed.

Figure 5.6 Waveform showing output of Hall effect sensor

Sensor	Equipment	Method(s)	Results
Optical Ignition distributor Rotational speed	DC voltmeter	The device will normally be supplied with a stabilised voltage. Check the output wire signal as the device is rotated slowly.	Clear switching between low and high voltage

Figure 5.7 Optical sensor

The scope waveform is shown in Figure 5.8.

5.2.5 Variable resistance

The two best examples of vehicle applications for variable resistance sensors are the throttle position sensor and the flap type air flow sensor.

Whereas variable capacitance sensors are used to measure small changes, variable resistance sensors generally measure larger changes in position. This is due to lack of sensitivity inherent in the construction of the resistive track.

The throttle position sensor as shown in Figure 5.9 is a potentiometer in which, when supplied

Optical sensor (distributor)

4.40	V	PEAK–PEAK	HOLD
39.0	Hz	FREQUENCY	
52.6	%	DUTY CYCLE 〴	
12.0	ms	PULSE WIDTH 〴	

```
The optical sensor output is a
square wave. The voltage should
remain constant as engine speed
changes.
```

Figure 5.8 Waveform showing output of optical sensor (distributor)

Figure 5.9 Throttle potentiometer

with a stable voltage, often 5 V, the voltage from the wiper contact will be proportional to throttle position. In many cases now the throttle potentiometer is used to indicate rate of change of throttle position. This information is used when implementing acceleration enrichment or inversely over run fuel cut off. The output voltage of a rotary potentiometer is proportional to its position.

The air flow sensor shown as Figure 5.10 works on the principle of measuring the force exerted on the flap by the air passing through it. A calibrated coil spring exerts a counter force on the flap such that the movement of the flap is proportional to the volume of air passing through the sensor. To reduce the fluctuations caused by individual induction strokes a compensation flap is connected to the sensor flap. The fluctuations therefore affect both flaps and are cancelled out. Any damage due to back firing is also minimised due to this design. The resistive material used for the track is a ceramic metal mixture, which is burnt into a ceramic plate at very high temperature. The slider potentiometer is calibrated such that the output voltage is proportional to the quantity of inducted air.

Sensor	Equipment	Method(s)	Results
Variable resistance Throttle potentiometer Flap type air flow sensor	DC voltmeter	This sensor is a variable resistor. If the supply is left conected then check the output on a DC voltmeter.	The voltage should change *smoothly* from about 0 to the supply voltage (often 5 V)
Position sensor	Ohmmeter	With the supply disconnected, check the resistance	Resistance should change smoothly

The scope waveform is shown in Figure 5.11.

5.2.6 Manifold absolute pressure (MAP) sensor (strain gauges)

When a strain gauge is stretched its resistance will increase and when it is compressed its resistance decreases. Most strain gauges consist of a thin layer of film that is fixed to a flexible backing sheet. This in turn is bonded to the part where strain is to be measured. Most resistance strain gauges have a resistance of about 100 Ω.

Strain gauges are often used indirectly to measure engine manifold pressure. Figure 5.12 shows an arrangement of four strain gauges on a diaphragm forming part of an aneroid chamber used to measure pressure. When changes in manifold pressure act on the diaphragm the gauges detect the strain. The output of the circuit is via a differential amplifier as shown, which must have a very high input resistance so as not to affect the bridge balance. The actual size of this sensor may be only a few millimetres in diameter. Changes in temperature are compensated for by using four gauges which when affected in a similar way cancel out any changes.

Figure 5.10 Air flow meter (vane type).

Figure 5.11 Waveform showing output of throttle position sensor

Figure 5.12 Strain gauge pressure sensor

Sensor	Equipment	Method(s)	Results
Strain gauges MAP sensor Torque stress	DC voltmeter	The normal supply to an externally mounted MAP sensor is 5 V. Check the output as manifold pressure changes either by snapping the throttle open, road testing or using a vacuum pump on the sensor pipe	The output should change between about 0 and 5 V as the manifold pressure changes – as a general guide 2.5 V at idle speed

The scope waveform is shown in Figure 5.13.

5.2.7 Variable capacitance

The value of a capacitor is determined by:

- surface area of its plates;
- distance between the plates;
- the dielectric (insulation between the plates).

Sensors can be constructed to take advantage of these properties. Three sensors each using the variable capacitance technique are shown in Figure 5.14. These are:

(a) **Liquid level sensor** the change in liquid level changes the dielectric value.
(b) **Pressure sensor** similar to the strain gauge pressure sensor but this time the distance between capacitor plates changes.

Figure 5.14 Variable capacitance sensors (a) liquid level, (b) presure, (c) position

Figure 5.13 Waveform showing output of mass air flow sensor test

Figure 5.15 Oil quality sensor

(c) **Position sensor** detects changes in the area of the plates.

An interesting sensor used to monitor oil quality is now available. The type shown in Figure 5.15 from the 'Kavlico Corporation' works by monitoring changes in the dielectric constant of the oil. This value increases as antioxidant additives in the oil deplete. The value rapidly increases if coolant contaminates the oil. The sensor output increases as the dielectric constant increases.

Sensor	Equipment	Method(s)	Results
Variable capacitance	DC voltmeter	Measure the voltage at the sensor	Small changes as the input to the sensor is varied – note this is difficult to assess because of very low capacitance values

5.2.8 Knock sensors

A piezoelectric accelerometer is a seismic mass accelerometer using a piezoelectric crystal to convert the force on the mass due to acceleration into an electrical output signal. The crystal not only acts as the transducer but as the suspension spring for the mass. Figure 5.16 shows a typical accelerometer or knock sensor in use on a spark ignition vehicle.

The crystal is sandwiched between the body of the sensor and the seismic mass and is kept under compression by the bolt. Acceleration forces acting on the seismic mass cause variations in the amount of crystal compression and hence generate the piezoelectric voltage. The sensor, when used as an engine knock sensor, will also detect other engine vibrations. These are kept to a minimum by only looking for 'knock' a few degrees before and after top dead centre (TDC). Unwanted signals are also filtered out electrically.

Figure 5.16 Cylinder-specific knock control gets the most out of the fuel consumed, ensuring that the engine runs constantly with maximum efficiency

Sensor	Equipment	Method(s)	Results
Accelerometer Knock sensors	Scope	Tap the engine block lightly (13 mm spanner) near the sensor	Oscillating output that drops back to zero. If the *whole* system is operating the engine will slow down if at idle speed

The scope waveform is shown in Figure 5.17.

5.2.9 Hot wire air flow sensor

The advantage of this sensor is that it measures air mass flow. The basic principle is that as air passes over a hot wire it tries to cool the wire down. If a circuit is created such as to increase the current through the wire then this current will be proportional to the airflow. A resistor is also incorporated to compensate for temperature variations. The 'hot wire' is made of platinum and is only a few millimetres long and about 70 µm thick. Because of its small size the time constant of the sensor is very short, in fact in the order of a few milliseconds. This is a great

```
        Knock sensor test

  3.28  V  PEAK-PEAK        HOLD
  8.33  kHz FREQUENCY

  3V
  .2
  .1
  0
 -1
 -2
 -3V
             500µs/DIV
  KNOCK SENSOR            ◄♦►Keys
             REPEAT
             TEST              RANGE

The engine is not running and the
knock sensor is disconnected. The
signal is displayed after tapping
the engine block near the sensor.
```

Figure 5.17 Waveform showing output of knock sensor under test

Figure 5.18 Hot wire mass air flow meter – insert type

Figure 5.19 Hot film air mass flow meter

advantage as any pulsations of the air flow will be detected and reacted to in a control unit accordingly. The output of the circuit involved with the hot wire sensor is a voltage across a precision resistor. Figure 5.18 shows a hot wire air mass sensor.

The resistance of the hot wire and the precision resistor are such that the current to heat the wire varies between 0.5 A and 1.2 A with different air mass flow rates. High resistance resistors are used in the other arm of the bridge and so current flow is very small. The temperature compensating resistor has a resistance of about 500 Ω which must remain constant other than by way of temperature change. A platinum film resistor is used for these reasons. The compensation resistor can cause the system to react to temperature changes within about three seconds.

The output of this device can change if the hot wire becomes dirty. Heating the wire to a very high temperature for one second every time the engine is switched off prevents this by burning off any contamination. In some air mass sensors a variable resistor is provided to set idle mixture.

The nickel film air flow sensor is similar to the hot wire system. Instead of a hot platinum wire a thin film of nickel is used. The response time of this system is even shorter than the hot wire. Figure 5.19 shows a nickel film air flow sensor.

The advantage which makes a nickel thick-film thermistor ideal for inlet air temperature sensing is its very short time constant. In other words its resistance varies very quickly with a change in air temperature.

Sensor	Equipment	Method(s)	Results
Hot wire *Air flow*	DC voltmeter or duty cycle meter	This sensor includes electronic circuits to condition the signal from the hot wire. The normal supply is either 5 or 12 V. Measure the output voltage as engine speed/load is varied	The output should change between about 0 and 5 V as the air flow changes. 0.4 to 1 V at idle is typical. Or depending on the system in use the output may be digital

The scope waveform is shown in Figure 5.20.

5.2.10 Oxygen sensors

The vehicle application for an oxygen sensor is to provide a closed loop feedback system for engine management control of the air fuel ratio. The amount of oxygen sensed in the exhaust is directly related to the mixture strength or air fuel ratio. The ideal air fuel ratio of 14.7:1 by mass is known as a lambda (λ) value of one. Exhaust gas oxygen (EGO) sensors are placed in the exhaust pipe near to the manifold to ensure adequate heating. The sensors operate reliably at temperatures over 300°C. In some cases, a heating element is incorporated to ensure that this temperature is reached quickly. This type of sensor is known as a heated exhaust gas oxygen sensor or HEGO for short! The heating element (which consumes about 10 W) does not operate all the time to ensure that the sensor does not exceed 850°C at which temperature damage may occur to the sensor. This is why the sensors are not fitted directly in the exhaust manifold. Figure 5.21 shows an EGO sensor in position.

The main active component of most types of oxygen sensors is zirconium dioxide (Z_rO_2). This ceramic is housed in gas permeable electrodes of platinum. A further ceramic coating is applied to the side of the sensor exposed to the exhaust gas as a protection against residue from the combustion process. The principle of operation is that at temperatures in excess of 300°C the zirconium dioxide will conduct the negative oxygen ions. The sensor is designed to be responsive very close to a lambda value of one. As one electrode of the sensor is open to a reference value of atmospheric air a greater quantity of oxygen ions will be present on this side. Due to electrolytic action these ions permeate the electrode and migrate through the electrolyte (Z_rO_2). This builds up a charge rather like a battery. The size of the charge is dependent on the oxygen percentage in the exhaust.

The closely monitored closed loop feedback of a system using lambda sensing allows very accurate control of engine fuelling. Close control of emissions is therefore possible.

Figure 5.20 Waveform showing output of mass air flow sensor at idle speed

Figure 5.21 Lambda sensor in position

Sensor	Equipment	Method(s)	Results
Oxygen Lambda sensor EGO sensor HEGO sensor Lambdasonde	DC voltmeter	The lambda sensor produces its own voltage a bit like a battery. This can be measured with the sensor connected to the system	A voltage of about 450 mV (0.45 V) is the normal figure produced at lambda value of one. The voltage output, however, should vary smoothly between 0.2 and 0.8 V as the mixture is controlled by the ECU

The scope waveform is shown in Figure 5.22.

5.2.11 Dynamic position sensors

A dynamic position or movement or crash sensor can take a number of forms; these can be described as mechanical or electronic. The mechanical system works by a spring holding a roller in a set position until an impact (acceleration/deceleration) above a predetermined limit provides enough force to overcome the spring and the roller moves, triggering a micro switch. The switch is normally open with a resistor in parallel to allow the system to be monitored. Two switches similar to this may be used to ensure that an air bag is deployed only in the case of sufficient frontal impact. Figure 5.23 is a further type of dynamic position sensor. Described as an accelerometer it is based on strain gauges.

There are two types of piezoelectric crystal accelerometer, one much like an engine knock sensor and the other using spring elements. A severe change in speed of the vehicle will cause an output from these sensors as the seismic mass moves or the springs bend. See Section 5.2.8 on knock sensors for further details.

> **Warning**
> For safety reasons, it is *not* recommended to test a sensor associated with an air bag circuit without specialist knowledge and equipment.

Oxygen sensor at idle speed

912 mV   MAXIMUM   HOLD
550 mV   AVERAGE
112 mV   MINIMUM

OXYGEN SENSOR

1s/DIV

◀▲▶Keys

RANGE

Engine running at idle speed and at normal operating temperature.

Figure 5.22 Waveform showing output of oxygen sensor at idle speed

Figure 5.23 Strain gauges accelerometer

Sensor	Equipment	Method(s)	Results
Acceleration switch Dynamic position	DC voltmeter	Measure the supply and output as the sensor is subjected to the required acceleration	A clear switching between say 0 and 12 V

5.2.12 Rain sensor

Rain sensors are used to switch on wipers automatically. Most work on the principle of reflected light. The device is fitted inside the windscreen and light from an LED is reflected back from the outer surface of the glass. The amount of light reflected changes if the screen is wet, even with a few drops of rain. Figure 5.24 shows a typical rain sensor.

Figure 5.24 Rain sensor

Sensor	Equipment	Method(s)	Results
Rain!	DC voltmeter	Locate output wire – by trial and error if necessary and measure dry/wet output (splash water on the screen with the sensor correctly fitted in position)	A clear switching between voltage levels

5.3 Actuators

5.3.1 Introduction

There are many ways of providing control over variables in and around the vehicle. 'Actuators' is a general term used here to describe a control mechanism. When controlled electrically they will either work by the thermal or magnetic effect. In this section the term actuator will be used to mean a device which converts electrical signals into mechanical movement.

5.3.2 Testing actuators

Testing actuators is simple as many are operated by windings. The resistance can be measured with an ohmmeter. Injectors, for example, often have a resistance of about 16 Ω. A good tip is that where an actuator has more than one winding (stepper motor for example), the resistance of each should be about the same. Even if the expected value is not known, it is likely that if the windings all read the same then the device is in order.

With some actuators, it is possible to power them up from the vehicle battery. A fuel injector should click for example and a rotary air bypass device should rotate about half a turn. Be careful with this method as some actuators could be damaged. At the very least use a fused supply (jumper) wire.

5.3.3 Solenoid actuators

The basic operation of solenoid actuators is very simple. The term 'solenoid' means: 'many coils of wire wound onto a hollow tube'. This is often misused but has become so entrenched that terms like 'starter solenoid', when really it is a starter relay, are in common use.

A good example of a solenoid actuator is a fuel injector. Figure 5.25 shows a typical example. When the windings are energised the armature is attracted due to magnetism and compresses the spring. In the case of a fuel injector, the movement is restricted to about 0.1 mm. The period that an injector remains open is very small; under various operating conditions between 1.5 and 10 ms is typical. The time it takes an injector to open and close is also critical for accurate fuel metering. Some systems use ballast resistors in series with the fuel injectors. This allows lower inductance and resistance operating windings to be used, thus speeding up reaction time.

Other types of solenoid actuators, for example door lock actuators, have less critical reaction times. However, the basic principle remains the same.

Figure 5.25 Fuel injector

Actuator	Equipment	Method(s)	Results
Solenoid Fuel injector Lock actuator	Ohmmeter	Disconnect the component and measure its resistance	The resistance of commonly used injectors is about 16 Ω Lock and other actuators may have two windings (e.g. lock and unlock). The resistance values are very likely to be the same

The scope waveform is shown in Figure 5.26. Figure 5.27 shows a variation on the injector signal where current limiting is used to control the open period.

5.3.4 Motorised and solenoid actuators

Permanent magnet electric motors are used in many applications and are very versatile. The output of a motor is of course rotation, and this can be used in many ways. If the motor drives a rotating 'nut' through which a plunger is fitted on which there is a screw thread, the rotary action can easily be converted to linear movement. In most vehicle applications the output of the motor has to be geared down, this is to reduce speed and increase torque. Permanent magnet motors are almost universally used now in place of older and less practical motors with field windings. Some typical examples of the use of these motors are listed as follows:

- windscreen wipers;
- windscreen washers;
- headlight lift;
- electric windows;
- electric sun roof;
- electric aerial operation;
- seat adjustment;
- mirror adjustment;
- headlight washers;
- headlight wipers;
- fuel pumps;
- ventilation fans.

One disadvantage of simple motor actuators is that no direct feedback of position is possible.

Figure 5.26 Waveform showing air supply to fuel injector (normal pulse)

Fuel injector

1.52 ms   INJECTION PULSE   **HOLD**
37.6 v   MAXIMUM

100V
·80
·60
·40
·20
·0
−20V

1ms/DIV

INJECTION   ◄◆►Keys
VEHICLE   RANGE
DATA   MOVE

Fuel injection time, indicated at
idle speed and operating
temperature. This is a 'pulse-width
modulated' fuel injector.

Figure 5.27 Waveform showing supply to fuel injector (pulse-width modulated)

This is not required in many applications; however, in cases such as seat adjustment when a 'memory' of the position may be needed, a variable resistor type sensor can be fitted to provide feedback. Two typical motor actuators are shown in Figure 5.28. They are used as window lift motors. Some of these use Hall effect sensors or an extra brush as a feedback device.

A rotary idle actuator is a type of motor actuator. This device is used to control idle speed by controlling air bypass. There are two basic types in common use. These are single winding types, which have two terminals, and double winding types, which have three terminals. Under ECU control the motor is caused to open and close a shutter controlling air bypass. These actuators only rotate about 90° to open and close the valve. As these are permanent magnet motors the 'single or double windings' refers to the armature.

The single winding type is fed with a square

wave signal causing it to open against a spring and then close again, under spring tension. The on/off ratio or duty cycle of the square wave will determine the average valve open time and hence idle speed.

With the double winding type the same square wave signal is sent to one winding but the inverse signal is sent to the other. As the windings are wound in opposition to each other if the duty cycle is 50% then no movement will take place. Altering the ratio will now cause the shutter to move in one direction or the other.

A further type is an on/off solenoid where a port is opened or closed as the solenoid is operated. This type is shown in Figure 5.29.

(a)   (b)

Figure 5.28 (a) Window lift motor with integrated box for electronic controls, (b) window lift motor for cable lift system

Figure 5.29 Solenoid idle actuator

Actuator	Equipment	Method(s)	Results
Motor See previous list	Battery supply (fused) Ammeter	Most 'motor' type actuators can be run from a battery supply after they are disconnected from the circuit. If necessary the current draw can be measured	Normal operation with current draw appropriate to the 'work' done by the device. For example, a fuel pump motor may draw up to 10 A, but an idle actuator will only draw 1 or 2 A

Actuator	Equipment	Method(s)	Results
Solenoid actuator (idle speed control)	Duty cycle meter	Most types are supplied with a variable ratio square wave	The duty cycle will vary as a change is required

The scope waveform is shown in Figure 5.30.

5.3.5 Stepper motors

Stepper motors are becoming increasingly popular as actuators in the motor vehicle. This is mainly because of the ease with which they can be controlled by electronic systems.

Stepper motors fall into three distinct groups, the basic principles of which are shown in Figure 5.31.

- variable reluctance motors;
- permanent magnet (pm) motors;
- hybrid motors.

The underlying principle is the same for each type. All of them have been and are being used in various vehicle applications.

The basic design for a PM stepper motor comprises two double stators. The rotor is often made of barium-ferrite in the form of a sintered annular magnet. As the windings are energised in one direction then the other the motor will rotate in 90° steps. Half step can be achieved by switching on two windings. This will cause the rotor to line up with the two stator poles and

Figure 5.30 Waveform showing supply to idle air control valve

Figure 5.31 Basic principle of variable reluctance permanent magnet and hybrid stepper motor

implement a half step of 45°. The direction of rotation is determined by the order in which the windings are switched on or off or reversed.

The main advantages of a stepper motor are that feedback of position is not required. This is because the motor can be indexed to a known starting point and then a calculated number of steps will move the motor to any suitable position.

Actuator	Equipment	Method(s)	Results
Stepper motor Idle speed air bypass Carburettor choke control Speedometer drivers	Ohmmeter	Test the resistance of each winding with the motor disconnected from the circuit	Winding resistances should be the same. Values in the region of 10 to 20 Ω are typical

The scope waveform is shown in Figure 5.32.

5.3.6 Thermal actuators

An example of a thermal actuator is the movement of a traditional type fuel or temperature gauge needle. A further example is an auxiliary air device used on many earlier fuel injection systems. The principle of the gauge is shown in Figure 5.33. When current is supplied to the terminals, a heating element operates and causes a bimetallic strip to bend, which moves the pointer.

The main advantage of this type of actuator, when used as an auxiliary device, apart from its simplicity, is that if it is placed in a suitable position its reaction time will vary with the temperature of its surroundings. This is ideal for applications such as fast idle or cold starting control where, once the engine is hot, no action is required from the actuator.

Figure 5.32 Waveform showing supply to idle speed stepper motor

Figure 5.33 Thermal actuator principle

Actuator	Equipment	Method(s)	Results
Thermal Auxiliary air device Instrument display	Ohmmeter Fused battery supply	Check the winding for continuity. If OK power up the device and note its operation (for instruments, power these but use a resistor in place of the sender unit)	Continuity and slow movement (several seconds to a few minutes) to close the valve or move as required

5.3.7 Exhaust gas recirculation (EGR) valve

Various types of EGR valve are in use based on simple solenoid operation. One development in actuator technology is the rotary electric exhaust gas recirculation (EEGR) valve for use in diesel engine applications (LucasVarity). This device is shown in Figure 5.34. It has a self-cleaning action, accurate gas flow control and a fast reaction speed. The waveform shown in the table is not necessarily from this type of valve.

Figure 5.34 Rotary electric exhaust gas recirculation valve

Actuator	Equipment	Method(s)	Results
EGR valve	Ohmmeter Fused battery supply	Check the winding(s) for continuity. If OK power up the device and note its operation	Continuity and rapid movement to close the valve

The scope waveform is shown in Figure 5.35.

5.3.8 Other waveforms

Figures 5.36–5.41 show various waveforms not included in the sections on sensors or actuators. They are included as a useful reference source.

Figure 5.35 Waveform showing supply to EGR valve

5.4 Electronic components and circuits

5.4.1 Introduction

This section describing the principles and applications of various electronic components and circuits is not intended to explain their detailed operation. Overall, an understanding of basic

Figure 5.36 Waveform showing MAP sensor output at idle speed

The mass air flow sensor is an analog type sensor. The signal is displayed at 2500 RPM with the engine at operating temperature. The voltage indicated is a measure for the amount of intake air. The steady voltage is a sign of correct operation.

Figure 5.37 Waveform showing output from mass air flow sensor at 2500 rev/min

The sensor is a magnetic type sensor that uses 4 teeth to indicate the TDC of each cylinder. The engine speed is displayed. The sensor is inside the distributer on this vehicle.

Figure 5.38 Waveform showing TDC signal

Engine is running at idle speed. This camshaft position sensor is a magnetic type sensor that uses one tooth.

Figure 5.39 Camshaft position signal

The frequency of a signal can be displayed

Figure 5.40 Idle air valve showing the frequency measurement

electronic principles will help to show how electronic systems operate. These can range from a simple interior light delay unit to the most complicated engine management system. Testing individual electronic components is a useful diagnostic procedure.

Idle speed valve

30.4	v	PEAK-PEAK	HOLD
30.4	Hz	FREQUENCY	
50.6	%	DUTY CYCLE ↧	
16.8	ms	PULSE WIDTH ↧	

10ms/DIV

GENERAL SENSORS   ◄↕►Keys
VOLT AND   CONTINUITY   RANGE
   TIME   OHM OPEN CLOSE   MOVE

This idle speed valve is duty cycle
controlled. The frequency should
therefore remain stable over the
full load range.

Figure 5.41 Idle speed valve showing how the waveform is not always a perfect square wave

5.4.2 Components

The symbols for the following electronic components are shown in Figure 5.42.

Resistors are probably the most widely used component in electronic circuits. Two factors must be considered when choosing a suitable resistor, the ohms value and the power rating. Resistors are used to limit current flow and provide fixed voltage drops. Most resistors used in electronic circuits are made from small carbon rods; the size of the rod determines the resistance. Carbon resistors have a negative temperature coefficient (NTC) and this must be considered for some applications. Thin-film resistors have more stable temperature properties and are constructed by depositing a layer of carbon on to an insulated former such as glass. The resistance value can be manufactured very accurately by spiral grooves cut into the carbon film. For higher power applications resistors are usually wire wound. Variable forms of most resistors are available. The resistance of a circuit is its opposition to current flow.

A capacitor is a device for storing an electric charge. In its simple form it consists of two plates separated by an insulating material. One plate can have excess electrons compared to the other. On vehicles its main uses are for reducing arcing across contracts and for radio interference suppression circuits as well as in ECUs. Capacitors are described as two plates separated by a dielectric. The area of the plates, the distance between them and the nature of the dielectric determine the value of capacitance. Metal foil sheets insulated by a type of paper are often used to construct capacitors. The sheets are rolled up together inside a tin can. To achieve higher values of capacitance it is necessary to reduce the distance between the plates in order to keep the overall size of the device manageable. This is achieved by immersing one plate in an electrolyte to deposit a layer of oxide typically 10^{-4} mm thick thus ensuring a higher capacitance value. The problem, however, is that this now makes the device polarity conscious and only able to withstand low voltages.

Diodes are often described as one-way valves and for most applications this is an acceptable description. A diode is a PN junction allowing electron flow from the N type material to the P type material. The materials are usually constructed from doped silicon. Diodes are not perfect devices and a voltage of about 0.6 V is required to switch the diode on in its forward biased direction.

Zener diodes are very similar in operation with the exception that they are deigned to breakdown and conduct in the reverse direction at a predetermined voltage. They can be thought of as a type of pressure relief valve.

Transistors are the devices that have allowed the development of today's complex and small electronic systems. The transistor is used as either a solid state switch or as an amplifier. They are constructed from the same P and N type semiconductor materials as the diodes and can be made in either NPN or PNP format. The three terminals are known as the base, collector and emitter. When the base is supplied with the correct bias the circuit between the collector and emitter will conduct. The base current can be in the order of 50 to 200 times less than the emitter current. The ratio of the current flowing through the base compared to the current through the emitter is an indication of the amplification factor of the device.

A Darlington pair is a simple combination of two transistors which will give a high current gain, typically several thousand. The transistors are usually mounted on a heat sink and overall the device will have three terminals marked as a single transistor – base, collector and emitter.

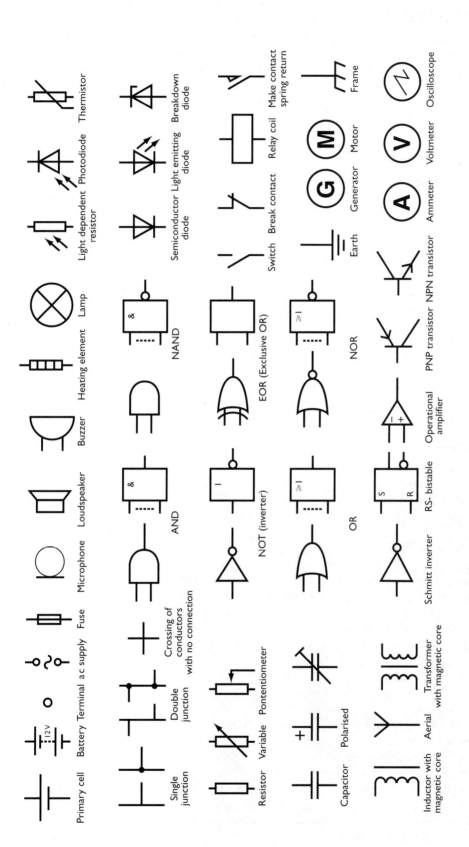

Figure 5.42 Electrical and electronic symbols

The input impedance of this type of circuit is in the order of 1 MΩ; hence it will not load any previous part of a circuit connected to its input. The Darlington pair configuration is used for many switching applications. A common use of a Darlington pair is for the switching of coil primary current in the ignition circuit.

Another type of transistor is the FET or field effect transistor. This device has higher input resistance than the bipolar type described above. They are constructed in their basic form as n-channel or p-channel devices. The three terminals are known as the gate, source and drain. The voltage on the gate terminal controls the conductance of the circuit between the drain and the source.

Inductors are most often used as part of an oscillator or amplifier circuit. The basic construction of an inductor is a coil of wire wound on a former. It is the magnetic effect of the changes in current flow which gives this device the properties of inductance. Inductance is a difficult property to control particularly as the inductance value increases. This is due to magnetic coupling with other devices. Iron cores are used to increase the inductance value. This also allows for adjustable devices by moving the position of the core. Inductors, particularly

of higher values, are often known as chokes and may be used in DC circuits to smooth the voltage.

5.4.3 Integrated circuits

Integrated circuits or ICs are constructed on a single slice of silicon often known as a substrate. Combinations of some of the components mentioned previously can be used to carry out various tasks such as switching, amplifying and logic functions. The components required for these circuits can be made directly on to the slice of silicon. The great advantage of this is not just the size of the ICs but the speed at which they can be made to work due to the short distances between components. Switching speed in excess of 1 MHz is typical.

The range and type of integrated circuits now available is so extensive that a chip is available for almost any application. The integration level of chips is now exceeding VLSI (very large scale integration). This means that there can be more than 100 000 active elements on one chip! Development in this area is moving so fast that often the science of electronics is now concerned mostly with choosing the correct combination of chips and discrete components are only used as final

Figure 5.43 On a surface area of 55 mm^2 this microcontroller contains 230 000 transistors

switching or power output stages. Figure 5.43 shows a highly magnified view of a typical IC.

5.4.4 Digital circuits

With some practical problems, it is possible to express the outcome as a simple yes/no or true/false answer. Let's take a simple example: if the answer to the first or the second question is 'yes', then switch on the brake warning light; if both answers are 'no' then switch it off.

Is the handbrake on?
Is the level in the brake fluid reservoir low?

In this case, we need the output of an electrical circuit to be 'on' when *either one or both* of the inputs to the circuit are 'on'. The inputs will be via simple switches on the handbrake and in the brake reservoir. The digital device required to carry out the above task is an OR gate. An OR gate for use on this system would have two inputs (a and b) and one output (c). Only when 'a' OR 'b' is supplied will 'c' produce a voltage.

Once a problem can be described in logic states then a suitable digital or logic circuit can also determine the answer to the problem. Simple circuits can also be constructed to hold the logic state of their last input, these are in effect simple forms of 'memory'. By combining vast quantities of these basic digital building blocks, circuits can be constructed to carry out the most complex tasks in a fraction of a second. Due to IC technology, it is now possible to create hundreds of thousands if not millions of these basic circuits on one chip. This has given rise to the modern electronic control systems used for vehi-

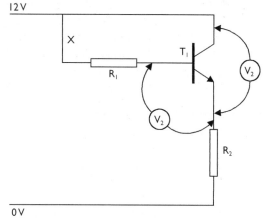

Use resistors R_1 + R_2 of about 1 KΩ when connected as shown V_1 should read 0.6 to 0.7 V and V_2 about 1 V. Disconnect wire X. V_1 should now read 0 V and V_2 12 V.

Figure 5.44 Transistor testing

cle applications as well as all the countless other uses for a computer.

In electronic circuits true/false values are assigned voltage values. In one system known as TTL (transistor-transistor-logic), true or logic '1' is represented by a voltage of 3.5 V and false or logic '0', by 0 V.

5.4.5 Electronic component testing

Individual electronic components can be tested in a number of ways but a digital multimeter is normally the favourite option. The table below suggests some methods of testing components removed from the circuit.

Component	Test method
Resistor	Measure the resistance value with an ohmmeter and compare this to the value written or colour coded on the component
Capacitor	A capacitor can be difficult to test without specialist equipment but try this. Charge the capacitor up to 12 V and connect it to a digital voltmeter. As most digital meters have an internal resistance of about 10 MΩ, calculate the expected discharge time ($T = 5CR$) and see if the device complies! A capacitor from a contact breaker ignition system should take about five seconds to discharge in this way
Inductor	An inductor is a coil of wire so a resistance check is the best method to test for continuity
Diode	Many multimeters have a diode test function. If so the device should read open circuit in one direction and about 0.4 to 0.6 V in the other direction. This is its switch on voltage. If no meter is available with this function then wire the diode to a battery via a small bulb; it should light with the diode one way and not the other
LED	LEDs can be tested by connecting them to a 1.5 V battery. Note the polarity though; the longest leg or the flat side of the case is negative

Transistor (bipolar)

Some multimeters even have transistor testing connections but, if not available, the transistor can be connected into a simple circuit as in Figure 5.44 and voltage tests carried out as shown. This also illustrates a method of testing electronic circuits in general. It is fair to point out that without specific data it is difficult for the non-specialist to test unfamiliar circuit boards. It's always worth checking for obvious breaks and dry joints though!

Digital components

A logic probe can be used. This is a device with a very high internal resistance so it does not affect the circuit under test. Two different coloured lights are used; one glows for a 'logic 1' and the other for 'logic 0'. Specific data is required in most cases but basic tests can be carried out

6

Electrical systems

6.1 Introduction

In this chapter I have covered all the main electrical systems on the vehicle. A main section on the operation of the particular system is followed in each case by appropriate diagnostic techniques. A brief checklist as a reminder of some of the key diagnostic steps is also included. This is also available on my web site as an 'Electrical Help' page. It can also be downloaded as a 'Word' document. Visit the web site at: http://www.automotive-technology.co.uk to check the latest version and lots of other useful information.

6.2 Batteries

6.2.1 Safety

The following points must be observed when working with batteries:

- good ventilation
- protective clothing
- supply of water available (running water preferable)
- first aid equipment available, including eye-wash
- no smoking or naked lights permitted

6.2.2 Lead-acid batteries

Incremental changes over the years have made the sealed and maintenance-free battery, now in common use, very reliable and long lasting. This may not always appear to be the case to some end users, but note that quality is often related to the price the customer pays. Many bottom of the range cheap batteries with a 12 month guarantee will last for 13 months!

The basic construction of a nominal 12 V lead-acid battery consists of six cells connected in series. Each cell producing about 2 V is housed in an individual compartment within a polypropylene or similar case. Figure 6.1 shows a cut-away battery with its main component parts. The active material is held in grids or

Figure 6.1 Lead-acid battery

baskets to form the positive and negative plates. Separators made from a microporous plastic insulate these plates from each other.

The grids, connecting strips and the battery posts are made from a lead alloy. For many years this was lead antimony (PbSb) but this has now been largely replaced by lead calcium (PbCa). The newer materials cause less gassing of the electrolyte when the battery is fully charged. This has been one of the main reasons why sealed batteries became feasible as water loss is considerably reduced.

Modern batteries described as sealed do still have a small vent to stop the pressure buildup due to the very small amount of gassing. A further requirement of sealed batteries is accurate control of charging voltage.

6.2.3 Battery rating

In simple terms the characteristics or rating of a particular battery are determined by how much current it can produce and how long it sustain this current. The rate at which a battery can produce current is determined by the speed of the chemical reaction. This in turn is determined by a number of factors:

● surface area of the plates;
● temperature;
● electrolyte strength;
● current demanded.

The actual current supplied therefore determines the overall capacity of a battery. The rating of a battery has to specify the current output and the time.

Ampere hour capacity	This is now seldom used but describes how much current the battery is able to supply for either 10 or 20 hours. The 20-hour figure is the most common. For example, a battery quoted as being 44 Ah (ampere-hour) will be able, if fully charged, to supply 2.2 a for 20 hours before being completely discharged (cell voltage above 1.75 V)
Reserve capacity	A system used now on all new batteries is reserve capacity. This is quoted as a time in minutes for which the battery will supply 25 A at 25°C to a final voltage of 1.75 V per cell. This is used to give an indication of how long the battery could run the car if the charging system was not working. Typically a 44 Ah battery will have a reserve capacity of about 60 minutes.

Cold cranking amps	Batteries are given a rating to indicate performance at high current output and at low temperature. A typical value of 170 A means that the battery will supply this current for one minute at a temperature of -18°C at which point the cell voltage will fall to 1.4 V (BS).

These cold cranking amps (CCA) capacity rating methods do vary to some extent: British standards, DIN standards and SAE standards are the three main examples!

● BS   60 seconds
● DIN 30 seconds
● SAE 30 seconds

In summary, the capacity of a battery is the amount of electrical energy that can be obtained from it. It is usually given in ampere-hours, reserve capacity (RC) and cold cranking amps.

● A 40 Ah battery means it should give 2 A for 20 hours.
● The reserve capacity indicates the time in minutes for which the battery will supply 25 A at 25°C.
● Cold cranking current indicates the maximum battery current at −18°C (0°F) for a set time (standards vary).

A battery for normal light vehicle use may be rated as follows: 44 Ah, 60 RC and 170 A CCA (BS). A 'heavy duty' battery will have the same Ah rating as its 'standard duty' counterpart, but it will have a higher CCA and RC.

6.3   Diagnosing battery faults

6.3.1 Servicing batteries

In use a battery requires very little attention other than the following when necessary.

● Corrosion should be cleaned from terminals using hot water.
● Terminals should be smeared with petroleum jelly or vaseline *not* ordinary grease.
● Battery tops should be clean and dry.
● If not sealed, cells should be topped up with distilled water 3 mm above the plates.
● Battery should be securely clamped in position.

6.3.2 Maintenance-free

By far the majority of batteries now available are classed as 'maintenance-free'. This implies that little attention is required during the life of the battery. Earlier batteries and some heavier types do, however, still require the electrolyte level to be checked and topped up periodically. Battery posts are still a little prone to corrosion and hence the usual service of cleaning with hot water if appropriate and the application of petroleum jelly or proprietary terminal grease is still recommended. Ensuring that the battery case and in particular the top remains clean will help to reduce the rate of self-discharge.

The state of charge of a battery is still very important and in general it is not advisable to allow the state of charge to fall below 70% for long periods as the sulphate on the plates can harden, making recharging difficult. If a battery is to be stored for a long period (more than a few weeks), then it must be recharged every so often to prevent it from becoming sulphated. Recommendations vary but a recharge every six weeks is a reasonable suggestion.

6.3.3 Charging

The recharging recommendations of battery manufacturers vary slightly. The following methods, however, are reasonably compatible and should not cause any problems. The efficiency of a battery is not 100%. Therefore the recharging process must 'put back' the same Ah capacity as was used on discharge plus a bit more to allow for losses. It is therefore clear that the main question about charging is not how much, but at what rate.

The old recommendation was that the battery should be charged at a tenth of its Ah capacity for about 10 hours or less. This is assuming that the Ah capacity is quoted at the twenty hour rate, as a tenth of this figure will make allowance for the charge factor. This figure is still valid but as Ah capacity is not always used nowadays, a different method of deciding the rate is necessary. One way is to set a rate at a sixteenth of the reserve capacity, again for up to 10 hours. The final suggestion is to set a charge rate at one fortieth of the cold start performance figure, also for up to 10 hours. Clearly if a battery is already half charged, half the time is required to recharge to full capacity.

In summary the ideal charge rate is determined from:

- 1/10 of the Ah capacity;
- 1/16 of the RC
- 1/40 of the CCA

The above suggested charge rates are to be recommended as the best way to prolong battery life. They do all, however, imply a constant current charging source. A constant voltage charging system is often the best way to charge a battery. This implies that the charger, an alternator on a car for example, is held at a constant level and the state of charge in the battery will determine how much current will flow. This is often the fastest way to recharge a flat battery. If a constant voltage of less than 14.4 V is used then it is not possible to cause excessive gassing and this method is particularly appropriate for sealed batteries.

Boost charging is a popular technique often applied in many workshops. It is not recommended as the best method but, if correctly administered and not repeated too often, it is suitable for most batteries. The key to fast or boost charging is that the battery temperature should not exceed 43°C. With sealed batteries it is particularly important not to let the battery gas excessively in order to prevent the buildup of pressure. A rate of about five times the 'normal' charge setting will bring the battery to 70–80% of its full capacity within approximately one hour. The table below summarises the charging techniques for a lead-acid battery. Figure 6.2 shows a typical battery charger.

Charging method	Notes
Constant voltage	Will recharge any battery in seven hours or less without any risk of overcharging (14.4 V maximum)
Constant current	Ideal charge rate can be estimated as: 1/10 of Ah capacity, 1/16 of RC or 1/40 of cold start current (charge time of 10 to 12 hours or pro rata original state)
Boost charging	At no more than five times the ideal rate, a battery can be brought up to about 70% of charge in about one hour

6.3.4 Battery faults

Any electrical device can suffer from two main faults; open circuit or short circuit. A battery is no exception but it can also suffer from other problems such as low charge or low capacity. Often a problem which seems to be with a vehicle battery can be traced to another part of the vehicle such as the charging system. The following Table lists all of the common problems encountered with lead-acid batteries, together with typical causes.

Symptom or fault	Likely causes
Low state of charge	Charging system fault Unwanted drain on battery Electrolyte diluted Incorrect battery for application
Low capacity	Low state of charge Corroded terminals Impurities in the electrolyte Sulphated Old age – active material fallen from the plates
Excessive gassing and temperatures	Overcharging Positioned too near exhaust component
Short circuit cell	Damaged plates and insulators Buildup of active material in sediment trap
Open circuit cell	Broken connecting strap Excessive sulphation Very low electrolyte
Service life shorter than expected	Excessive temperatire Battery has too low a capacity Vibration excessive Contaminated electrolyte Long periods of not being used Overcharging

Repairing modern batteries is not possible. Most of the problems listed will require the battery to be replaced. In the case of sulphation it is sometimes possible to bring the battery back to life with a very long low current charge. A fortieth of the Ah capacity or about a two hundredth of the cold start performance for about 50 hours is an appropriate rate.

6.3.5 Testing batteries

For testing the state of charge of a non-sealed type of battery a hydrometer can be used as shown in Figure 6.3. The hydrometer is a syringe which draws electrolyte from a cell and a float which will float at a particular depth in the electrolyte according to its density. The density or specific gravity is then read from the graduated scale on the float. A fully charged cell should show 1.280, a half charged are 1.200 and a discharged are 1.120.

Most vehicles are now fitted with maintenance free batteries and a hydrometer cannot be used to find the state of charge. This can only be determined from the voltage of the battery, as

Figure 6.2 Battery charger

given in the following table. An accurate voltmeter is required for this test (Figure 6.4).

Battery volts at 20°C	State of charge
12.0 V	Discharged (20% or less)
12.3 V	Half charged (50%)
12.7 V	Charged (100%)

A heavy-duty (HD) discharge tester as shown in Figure 6.5 is an instrument consisting of a low value resistor and a voltmeter connected to a pair of heavy test prods. The test prods are firmly pressed on to the battery terminals. The voltmeter reads the voltage of the battery on heavy discharge of 200–300 A.

Assuming a battery to be in a fully charged condition a serviceable battery should read about 10 V for a period of about ten seconds. A sharply falling battery voltage to below 3 V indicates an unserviceable cell. Note also if any cells are gassing, as this indicates a short circuit. A zero or extremely low reading can indicate an open circuit cell. When using the HD tester the following precautions must be observed.

- Blow gently across the top of the battery to remove flammable gasses.
- The test prods must be positively and firmly pressed into the lead terminals of the battery to minimise sparking.
- It should not be used while a battery is on charge.

1.110–1.130	Discharged
1.230–1.250	70% charged
1.270–1.290	Charged

Reading at 15°C

Figure 6.3 Hydrometer test

Figure 6.4 Battery voltage testing

Figure 6.5 Discharge tester

6.3.6 Scope test

Figure 6.6 shows the result of a battery test using a scope. The minimum voltage and the pulses of voltage help to determine that this battery is 'just' serviceable. However, note that this test could show a faulty battery if the starter was shorted out and drawing excessive current. The

Battery cranking and charging

13.2 V BEGINNING OF SIGNAL **HOLD**
7.28 V MINIMUM
13.9 V END OF SIGNAL

BATTERY TEST

200ms/DIV

VOLT   AMP   REPEAT TEST   RANGE

Note the change in battery voltage
as the starter first engages to
when the engine is running

Figure 6.6 Waveform showing battery cranking and charging output

end voltage of 13.9 V indicates that the charging system is operating correctly.

6.4 Starting

6.4.1 Starter circuit

In comparison with most other circuits on the modern vehicle the starter circuit is very simple. The problem to overcome, however, is that of volt drop in the main supply wires. A spring-loaded key switch usually operates the starter; the same switch also controls the ignition and accessories. The supply from the key switch, via a relay in many cases, causes the starter solenoid to operate and this in turn, by a set of contacts, controls the heavy current. In some cases an extra terminal on the starter solenoid provides an output when cranking, usually used to bypass a dropping resistor on the ignition or fuel pump circuits. The basic circuit for the starting system is shown in Figure 6.7. The problem of volt drop in the main supply circuit is due to the high current required by the starter particularly under adverse starting conditions such as very low temperatures.

A typical cranking current for a light vehicle engine is in the order of 150 A but this may peak in excess of 500 A to provide the initial stalled torque. It is generally accepted that a maximum volt drop of only 0.5 V should be allowed

Figure 6.7 Starter circuit

between the battery and starter when operating. An Ohm's law calculation indicates that the maximum allowed circuit resistance is 2.5 mΩ, when using a 12 V supply. This is a worst case situation and lower resistance values are used in most applications. The choice of suitable conductors is therefore very important.

6.4.2 Inertia starters

In all standard motor vehicle applications it is necessary to connect the starter to the engine ring gear only during the starting phase. If the connection remained permanent, the excessive speed at which the starter would be driven by the engine would destroy the motor almost immediately.

The inertia type of starter motor has been the technique used for over 80 years, but it is now becoming redundant. The starter shown in Figure 6.8 is the Lucas M35J type. It is a four pole, four brush machine and was used on small to medium petrol-engined vehicles. It is capable of producing 9.6 Nm with a current draw of 350 A. The M35J uses a face type commutator and axially aligned brush gear. The fields are wave wound and are earthed to the starter yoke.

The starter engages with the flywheel ring gear by means of a small pinion. The toothed pinion and a sleeve splined on to the armature shaft are threaded such that when the starter is operated via a remote relay, the armature will cause the sleeve to rotate inside the pinion. The pinion remains still due to its inertia and, because of the screwed sleeve rotating inside it, the pinion is moved into mesh with the ring gear.

When the engine fires and runs under its own power the pinion is driven faster than the armature shaft. This causes the pinion to be screwed

Figure 6.8 Inertia type starter

back along the sleeve and out of engagement with the flywheel. The main spring acts as a buffer when the pinion first takes up the driving torque and also acts as a buffer when the engine throws the pinion back out of mesh.

One of the main problems with this type of starter was the aggressive nature of the engagement. This tended to cause the pinion and ring gear to wear prematurely. In some applications the pinion tended to fall out of mesh when cranking due to the engine almost, but not quite, running. The pinion was also prone to seizure often due to contamination by dust from the clutch. This was often compounded by application of oil to the pinion mechanism, which tended to attract even more dust and thus prevent engagement. The pre-engaged starter motor has largely overcome these problems.

6.4.3 Pre-engaged starters

Pre-engaged starters are fitted to the majority of vehicles in use today. They provide a positive engagement with the ring gear, as full power is not applied until the pinion is fully in mesh. They prevent premature ejection as the pinion is held into mesh by the action of a solenoid. A one-way clutch is incorporated into the pinion to prevent the starter motor being driven by the engine. An example of a pre-engaged starter in common use is shown in Figure 6.9.

Figure 6.10 shows the circuit associated with operating this type of pre-engaged starter. The basic operation of the pre-engaged starter is as follows. When the key switch is operated a supply is made to terminal 50 on the solenoid. This causes two windings to be energised, the hold-on winding and the pull-in winding. Note that the pull-in winding is of very low resistance and hence a high current flows. This winding is connected in series with the motor circuit and the current flowing will allow the motor to rotate slowly to facilitate engagement. At the same time the magnetism created in the solenoid attracts the plunger and via an operating lever pushes the pinion into mesh with the flywheel ring gear. When the pinion is fully in mesh the plunger at the end of its travel causes a heavy-duty set of copper contacts to close. These contacts now supply full battery power to the main circuit of the starter motor. When the main contacts are closed the pull-in winding is effectively switched off due to equal voltage supply on both ends. The hold-on winding holds the plunger in position as long as the solenoid is supplied from the key switch.

When the engine starts and the key is released, the main supply is removed and the plunger and pinion return to their rest positions under spring tension. A lost motion spring located on the plunger ensures that the main contacts open before the pinion is retracted from mesh.

Figure 6.9 Pre-engaged starter

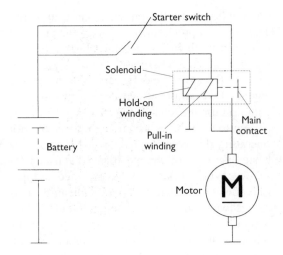

Figure 6.10 Starter circuit (pre-engaged)

During engagement if the teeth of the pinion hit the teeth of the flywheel (tooth to tooth abutment), the main contacts are allowed to close due to the engagement spring being compressed. This allows the motor to rotate under power and the pinion will slip into mesh.

The torque developed by the starter is passed through a one-way clutch to the ring gear. The purpose of this free wheeling device is to prevent the starter being driven at excessively high speed if the pinion is held in mesh after the engine has started. The clutch consists of a driving and driven member with several rollers in between the two. The rollers are spring loaded and either wedge-lock the two members together by being compressed against the springs, or free wheel in the opposite direction.

Many variations of pre-engaged starter are in common use but all work on similar lines to the above description. The wound field type of motor has now largely been replaced by the permanent magnet version.

6.4.4 Permanent magnet (PM) starters

Permanent magnet starters began to appear on production vehicles in the late eighties. The two advantages of these motors, compared to conventional types, are less weight and smaller size. This makes the PM starter a popular choice by vehicle manufacturers as, due to the lower lines of today's cars, less space is now available for engine electrical systems. The reduction in weight provides a contribution towards reducing fuel consumption.

The principle of operation is similar in most respects to the conventional pre-engaged starter motor, the main difference being the replacement of field windings and pole shoes with high quality permanent magnets. The reduction in weight is in the region of 15% and the diameter of the yoke can be reduced by a similar factor.

Permanent magnets provide constant excitation and it would be reasonable to expect the speed and torque characteristic to be constant. However, due to the fall in battery voltage under load and the low resistance of the armature windings, the characteristic is comparable to series wound motors.

Development by some manufacturers has also taken place in the construction of the brushes. A copper and graphite mix is used but the brushes are made in two parts allowing a higher copper content in the power zone and a higher graphite content in the commutation zone. This results in increased service life and a reduction in volt drop giving improved starter power. Figure 6.11 shows three modern PM starters.

For applications with a higher power requirement PM motors with intermediate transmission have been developed. This allows the armature to rotate at a higher and more efficient speed whilst still providing the torque, due to the gear reduction. Permanent magnet starters with intermediate transmission are available with power outputs of about 1.7 kW, suitable for spark ignition engines up to about five litres or compression ignition engines up to about 1.6 litres. This form of PM motor can give a weight saving of up to 40%. The principle of operation is again similar to the conventional pre-engaged starter.

The sun gear is on the armature shaft and the planet carrier drives the pinion. The ring gear or annulus remains stationary and also acts as an intermediate bearing. This arrangement of gears gives a reduction ratio of about 5:1. Figure 6.12 shows a PM starter with intermediate transmission, together with its circuit and operating mechanism.

6.5 Diagnosing starting system faults

6.5.1 Circuit testing procedure

The process of checking a 12 V starting system operation is as follows. (Tests 3 to 8 are all carried out while trying to crank the engine.)

▲ D7 E starter motor ▶

D6 RA starter motor

Figure 6.11 Modern permanent magnet starters

1. Check the battery (at least 70%).
2. Hand and eye checks.
3. Battery volts (minimum 10 V).
4. Solenoid lead (same as battery – if not check starter switch).
5. Starter voltage (no more that 0.5 V less than battery).

If test number 5 is OK then the circuit is working correctly.

6. Insulated line volt drop (maximum 0.25 V).
7. Solenoid contacts volt drop (almost 0 V).
8. Earth line volt drop (maximum 0.25 V).

The idea of these tests is to see if the circuit is supplying all the available voltage at the battery to the starter. If it is, then the starter is at fault, if not, then the circuit is at fault. Figure 6.13 shows a circuit with voltmeters connected. The numbered voltmeters relate to the number of the test in the above list.

Note that connections to the starter should be made to the link between the solenoid contacts and the motor *not* to the main supply terminal. Figure 6.14 shows an example of this link.

6.5.2 Starting fault diagnosis table

Symptom	Possible fault
Engine does not rotate when trying to start	Battery connection loose or corroded
	Battery discharged or faulty
	Broken loose or disconnected wiring in the starter circuit
	Defective starter switch or automatic gearbox inhibitor switch

	Starter pinion or flywheel ring gear loose
	Earth strap broken. Loose or corroded
Starter noisy	Starter pinion or flywheel ring gear loose
	Starter mounting bolts loose
	Starter worn (bearings, etc.)
	Discharged battery (starter may jump in and out)
Starter turns engine slowly	Discharged battery (slow rotation)
	Battery terminals loose or corroded
	Earth strap or starter supply loose or or disconnected
	High resistance in supply or earth circuit
	Internal starter fault

6.6 Charging

6.6.1 Introduction

The 'current' demands made by modern vehicles are considerable. The charging system must be able to meet these demands under all operating conditions and still fast charge the battery.

The main component of the charging system is the alternator and on most modern vehicles, with the exception of its associated wiring, it is the only component in the charging system. Figure 6.15 shows an alternator in common use. The alternator generates AC but must produce DC at its output terminal as only DC can be used to charge the battery and run electronic circuits. The output of the alternator must be a constant voltage regardless of engine speed and current load.

The charging system must meet the following criteria (when the engine is running):

- supply the current demands made by some or all loads;

1 Pinion
2 Ring gear
3 Roller type overrunning clutch
4 Engaging lever
5 Planetary gear
6 Permanent magnet
7 Armature
8 Commutator with carbon brushes
9 Solenoid switch with pull-in and hold-in windings
10 Starter switch
11 Battery

1 Drive end shield, 2 Pinion, 3 Solenoid switch, 4 Terminal, 5 Commutator end shield, 6 Brush plate with carbon brushes, 7 Commutator, 8 Armature, 9 Permanent magnet, 10 Field frame, 11 Planetary gear (intermediate transmission), 12 Engaging lever, 13 Pinion-engaging drive.

Figure 6.12 PM starter with intermediate transmission

- supply whatever charge current the battery demands;
- operate at idle speed;
- constant voltage under all conditions;
- efficient power to weight ratio;
- reliable, quiet, resistance to contamination;
- low maintenance;
- provide indication of correct operation.

6.6.2 Basic principles

Figure 6.16 shows a representation the vehicle charging system as three blocks, the alternator, battery and vehicle loads. When the alternator voltage is less than the battery (engine slow or not running for example), the direction of cur-

rent flow is from the battery to the vehicle loads. The alternator diodes prevent current flowing

Figure 6.13 Starter circuit volt drop testing

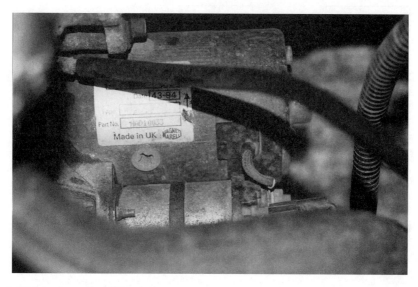

Figure 6.14 Supply link/wire from solenoid terminal to starter motor

into the alternator. When the alternator output is greater than the battery voltage, current will flow from the alternator to the vehicle loads and the battery.

From this simple example it is clear that the alternator output voltage must be above battery voltage at all times when the engine is running. The actual voltage used is critical and depends on a number of factors.

The main consideration for charging voltage is the battery terminal voltage when fully charged. If the charging system voltage is set to this value then there can be no risk of over-

Housing   Stator   Rotor   Transistor   Collector
                             voltage   rings
                             regulator
                             with brush
                             holder

Fan   Fan   Rectifier

Figure 6.15 Bosch compact alternator

charging the battery. This is known as the constant voltage charging technique. The figure of 14.2 ± 0.2 V is the accepted charging voltage for a 12 V system. Commercial vehicles generally employ two batteries in series at a nominal voltage of 24 V; therefore the accepted charge voltage would be doubled. These voltages are used as the standard input for all vehicle loads. For the purpose of clarity the text will just consider a 12 V system.

The other areas for consideration when determining charging voltage are any expected volt drops in the charging circuit wiring and the operating temperature of the system and battery. The voltage drops must be kept to a minimum but it is important to note that the terminal voltage of the alternator may be slightly above that supplied to the battery. Figure 6.17 shows the basic principle of an alternator.

6.6.3 Rectification of AC to DC

In order to full wave rectify the output of a three phase machine six diodes are needed. These are connected in the form of a bridge, which consists of three positive diodes and three negative diodes. The output produced by this configuration is shown compared to the three phase signals.

A further three positive diodes are often included in a rectifier pack. These are usually smaller than the main diodes and are only used to supply a small current back to the field windings in the rotor. The extra diodes are known as the auxiliary, field or excitation diodes.

When a star wound stator is used the addition of the voltages at the neutral point of the star is

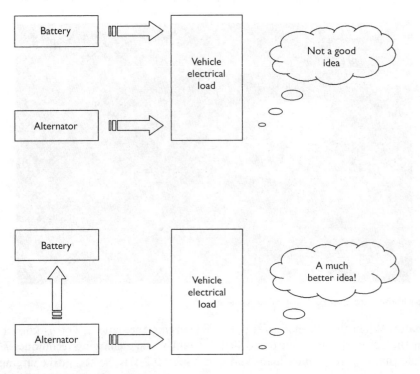

Figure 6.16 Representation of a charging system

in theory 0 V. In practice, however, due to slight inaccuracies in the construction of the stator and rotor a potential develops at this point. By employing two extra diodes, one positive and one negative connected to the star point the energy can be collected. This can increase the power output of an alternator by up to 15%.

Figure 6.18 shows the full circuit of an alternator using an eight diode main rectifier and three field diodes. The voltage regulator, which forms the starting point for the next section, is also shown in this diagram. The warning light in an alternator circuit, in addition to its function in warning of charging faults, also acts to supply the initial excitation to the field windings. An alternator will not always self-excite as the resid-

ual magnetism in the fields is not usually enough to produce a voltage which will overcome the 0.6 or 0.7 V needed to forward bias the rectifier diodes. A typical wattage for the warning light bulb is 2 W. Many manufacturers also connect a resistor in parallel with the bulb to assist in excitation and allow operation if the bulb blows. The charge warning light bulb is extinguished when the alternator produces an output from the field diodes as this causes both sides of the bulb to take on the same voltage (a potential difference across the bulb of 0 V).

6.6.4 Regulation of output voltage

To prevent the vehicle battery from being overcharged the regulated system voltage should be kept below the gassing voltage of the lead-acid battery. A figure of 14.2 ± 0.2 V is used for all 12 V charging systems. Accurate voltage control is vital with the ever-increasing use of electronic systems. It has also enabled the wider use of sealed batteries, as the possibility of overcharging is minimal.

Voltage regulation is a difficult task on a vehicle alternator because of the constantly changing engine speed and loads on the alternator. The output of an alternator without regulation would rise linearly in proportion with engine speed. Alternator output is also proportional to

Figure 6.17 Basic alternator principle

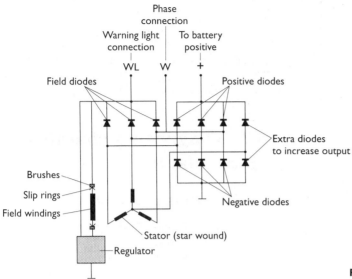

Figure 6.18 Complete internal alternator circuit

magnetic field strength and this in turn is proportional to the field current. It is the task of the regulator to control this field current in response to alternator output voltage. The abrupt switching of the field current does not cause abrupt changes in output voltage due to the very high inductance of the field (rotor), windings. The whole switching process also only takes a few milliseconds.

Regulators can be mechanical or electronic, the latter now almost universal on modern cars. The mechanical type uses a winding connected across the output of the alternator. The magnetism produced in this winding is proportional to output voltage. A set of normally closed contacts is attached to an armature, which is held in position by a spring. The supply to the field windings is via these contacts. When the output voltage rises beyond a pre-set level, say 14 V, the magnetism in the regulator winding will overcome spring tension and open the contacts. This switches off the field correct and causes alternator output to fall. As output falls below a pre-set level the spring will close the regulator contacts again and so the process continues.

The problem with mechanical regulators is the wear on the contacts and other moving parts. This has been overcome with the use of electronic regulators which, due to more accurate tolerances and much faster switching, are far superior, producing a more stable output. Due to the compactness and vibration resistance of electronic regulators they are now fitted almost universally on the alternator reducing the number of connecting cables required.

The key to electronic voltage regulation is the zener diode. This diode can be constructed to breakdown and conduct in the reverse direction at a precise level. This is used as the sensing element in an electronic regulator. Figure 6.19 shows two common electronic voltage regulators.

Electronic regulators can be made to sense either the battery voltage or the machine voltage (alternator) or a combination of the two. Most systems in use at present tend to be machine sensed as this offers some protection against over voltage in the event of the alternator being driven with the battery disconnected.

Over voltage protection is required in some applications to prevent damage to electronic components. When an alternator is connected to a vehicle battery system voltage, even in the event of regulator failure, will not often exceed about 20 V due to the low resistance and swamping effect of the battery. If an alternator is run with the battery disconnected (which is not recommended), a heavy duty Zener diode connected across the output will offer some protection as, if the system voltage exceeds its

Figure 6.19 Voltage regulators

breakdown figure, it will conduct and cause the system voltage to be kept within reasonable limits. This device is often referred to as a surge protection diode.

6.6.5 Charging circuits

On many applications the charging circuit is one of the simplest on the vehicle. The main output is connected to the battery via suitable size cable (or in some cases two cables to increase reliability and flexibility). The warning light is connected to an ignition supply on one side and to the alternator terminal at the other. A wire may also be connected to the phase terminal if it is utilised. Figure 6.20 shows two typical wiring circuits. Note the output of the alternator is often connected to the starter main supply simply for convenience of wiring. If the wires are kept as short as possible this will reduce voltage drop in the circuit. The volt drop across the main supply wire when the alternator is producing full output current should be less than 0.5 V.

Some systems have an extra wire from the alternator to 'sense' battery voltage directly. An ignition feed may also be found and this is often used to ensure instant excitement of the field windings. A number of vehicles link a wire from the engine management ECU to the alternator. This is used to send a signal to increase engine idle speed if the battery is low on charge.

6.7 Diagnosing charging system faults

6.7.1 Testing procedure

After connecting a voltmeter across the battery and an ammeter in series with the alternator output wire(s), as shown in Figure 6.21, the process of checking the charging system operation is as follows.

1. Hand and eye checks (drive belt and other obvious faults) – belt at correct tension, all connections clean and tight.
2. Check battery – must be 70% charged.
3. Measure supply voltages to alternator – battery volts.
4. Maximum output current (discharge battery slightly by leaving lights on for a few minutes, leave lights on and start engine) – ammeter should read within about 10% of rated maximum output.
5. Regulated voltage (run the engine until the ammeter reading is 10 A or less) –14.2 ± 0.2 V (Figure 6.22).
6. Circuit volt drop –0.5 V maximum (voltmeter connected ALT+ to BAT+ and then ALT– to BAT–).

If the alternator is found to be defective then a quality replacement unit is the normal recommendation. Repairs are possible but only if the general state of the alternator is good.

Figure 6.20 Example charging circuits

Figure 6.21 Alternator circuit testing

Figure 6.22 Waveform showing charging voltage

6.7.2 Charging fault diagnosis table

Symptom	Possible fault
Battery loses charge	Defective battery Slipping alternator drive belt Battery terminals loose or corroded Alternator internal fault (diode open circuit, brushes worn or regulator fault, etc.) Open circuit in alternator wiring, either main supply, ignition or sensing wires if fitted Short circuit component causing battery drain even when all switches are off High resistance in the main charging circuit
Charge warning light stays on when engine is running	Slipping or broken alternator drive belt Alternator internal fault (diode open circuit, brushes worn or regulator fault, etc.) Loose or broken wiring/connections
Charge warning light does not come on at any time	Alternator internal fault (brushes worn, open circuit or regulator fault, etc.) Blown warning light bulb Open circuit in warning light circuit

6.7.3 Scope testing

Figure 6.23 shows the result of testing an alternator with a scope (connected across the battery). The ripple is the result of the AC voltage rectified by the diodes. If the ripple is constant

Figure 6.23 Waveform showing alternator ripple voltage

as shown then the diodes must all be in good order. A faulty diode causes a noticeable drop in voltage every third pulse. The larger rise and fall is due to the action of the voltage regulator. From this one test it is possible to be almost certain that the alternator and charging system is in good working order.

6.8 Lighting

6.8.1 External lights

Figure 6.24 shows the rear lights of a Mazda 323. Note how in common with many manufacturers, the lenses are almost smooth. This is because the reflectors now carry out diffusion of the light. Regulations exist relating to external lights. The following is a simplified interpretation of current rules.

Figure 6.24 Rear lights of the Mazda 323

Side lights	A vehicle must have two side lights each with wattage of less than 7 W. Most vehicles have the side light incorporated as part of the headlight assembly
Rear lights	Again two must be fitted each with wattage not less than 5 W. Lights used in Europe must be 'E' marked and show a diffused light. Position must be within 400 mm from the vehicle edge and over 500 mm apart, and between 350 and 1500 mm above the ground
Brake lights	Two lights often combined with the rear lights. They must be between 15 and 36 W each, with diffused light, and must operate when any form of first line brake is applied. Brake lights must be between 350 and 1500 mm above the ground and at least 500 mm apart in a symmetrical position. High level brake lights are now allowed and if fitted must operate with the primary brake lights.
Reverse lights	No more than two lights may be fitted with a maximum wattage each of 24 W. The light must not dazzle and either be switched automatically from the gearbox or with a switch incorporating a warning light. Safety reversing 'beepers' are now often fitted in conjunction with this circuit, particularly on larger vehicles.
Day running lights	Volvo use day running lights as these are in fact required in Sweden and Finland. These lights come on with the ignition and must only work in conjunction with the rear lights. Their function is to indicate that the vehicle is moving or about to move. They switch off when parking or headlights are selected
Rear fog lights	One or two may be fitted but if only one it must be on the off side or centre line of the vehicle. They must be between 250 and 1000 mm above the ground and over 100 mm from any brake light. The wattage is normally 21 W and they must only operate when either the side lights, headlights or front fog lights are in use
Front spot and fog lights	If front spot lights are fitted (auxiliary driving lights), they must between 500 and 1200 mm above the ground and more than 400 mm from the side of the vehicle. If the lights are non-dipping then they must only operate when the headlights are on main beam. Front fog lamps are fitted below 500 mm from the ground and may only be used in fog or falling snow. Spot lamps are designed to produce a long beam of light to illuminate the road in the distance. Fog lights are designed to produce a sharp cut-off line such as to illuminate the road just in front of the vehicle but without reflecting back or causing glare

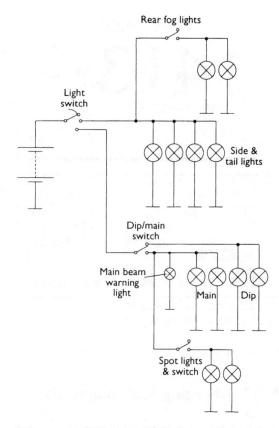

Figure 6.25 Simplified lighting circuits

6.8.2 Lighting circuits

Figure 6.25 shows a simplified lighting circuit. Whilst this representation helps to demonstrate the way in which a lighting circuit operates, it is not now used in this simple form. The circuit does, however, help to show in a simple way how various lights in and around the vehicle operate with respect to each other. For example fog lights can be wired to work only when the side lights are on. Another example is how the head-lights cannot be operated without the side lights first being switched on.

Dim dip headlights are an attempt to stop drivers just using side lights in semi-dark or poor visibility conditions. The circuit is such that when side lights and ignition are on together, then the headlights will come on automatically at about one sixth of normal power.

> *Note:* If there is any doubt as to the visibility or conditions, switch on dipped headlights. If your vehicle is in good order it will not discharge the battery.

Dim dip lights are achieved in one of two ways. The first uses a simple resistor in series with the headlight bulb and the second is to use a 'chop-

Figure 6.26 Complete lighting circuit

per' module which switches the power to the head-lights on and off rapidly. In either case the 'dim-mer' is bypassed when the driver selects normal headlights. The most cost effective method is using a resistor but this has the problem that the resistor (about 1 Ω) gets quite hot and hence has to be positioned appropriately. Figure 6.26 shows a typical modern vehicle lighting circuit.

6.8.3 Gas discharge lighting

Gas discharge headlamps (GDL) are now fitted to some vehicles. They have the potential to provide more effective illumination and new design possi-bilities for the front of a vehicle. The conflict between aerodynamic styling and suitable lighting positions is an economy/safety trade off, which is undesirable. The new headlamps make a signifi-cant contribution towards improving this situa-tion because they can be relatively small. The GDL system consists of three main components.

- **Lamp** this operates in a very different way from conventional incandescent bulbs. A much higher voltage is needed.
- **Ballast system** this contains an ignition and control unit and converts the electrical system voltage into the operating voltage required by the lamp. It controls the ignition stage and run up as well as regulating during continu-ous use and finally monitors operation as a safety aspect.
- **Headlamp** the design of the headlamp is broadly similar to conventional units. How-ever, in order to meet the limits set for dazzle, a more accurate finish is needed and hence more production costs are involved.

Figure 6.27 shows a xenon lamp system.

6.8.4 LED lighting

The advantages of LED lighting are clear, the greatest being reliability. LEDs have a typical rated life of over 50 000 hours compared to just a few thousand for incandescent lamps. The environment in which vehicle lights have to sur-vive is hostile to say the least. Extreme variations in temperature and humidity as well as serious shocks and vibration have to be endured. Figure 6.28 shows some lights employing LEDs.

LEDs are more expensive than bulbs but the potential savings in design costs due to sealed units being used and greater freedom of design could outweigh the extra expense. A further advantage is that they turn on quicker than ordinary bulbs. This time is approxi-mately the difference between 130 mS for the LEDs, and 200 mS for bulbs. If this is related to a vehicle brake light at motorway speeds, then the increased reaction time equates to about a car length. This is potentially a major contribution to road safety. LEDs as high level brake lights are becoming popular because of the shock resistance, which will allow them to be mounted on the boot lid.

Heavy vehicle side marker lights are an area of use where LEDs have proved popu-lar. Many lighting manufacturers are already producing lights for the after market. Being able to use sealed units will greatly increase the life expectancy. Side indicator repeaters are a similar issue due to the harsh environ-mental conditions.

Figure 6.27 Hella xenon lighting

Figure 6.28 Light units with LEDs

6.9 Diagnosing lighting system faults

6.9.1 Testing procedure

The process of checking a lighting system circuit is broadly as follows.

1. Hand and eye checks (loose wires, loose switches and other obvious faults) – all connections clean and tight.
2. Check battery – must be 70% charged.
3. Check bulb(s) – visual check or test with on ohmmeter.
4. Fuse continuity – (do not trust your eyes) voltage at both sides with a meter or a test lamp.
5. If used does the relay click (if yes, jump to stage 8) – this means the relay has operated but it is not necessarily making contact.
6. Supply to switch – battery volts.
7. Supply from switch – battery volts.
8. Supplies to relay – battery volts.
9. Feed out of the relay – battery volts.

10. Voltage supply to the light – within 0.5 V of the battery.
11. Earth circuit (continuity or voltage) – 0Ω or 0 V.

Figure 6.29 shows a simplified dim dip lighting circuit with meters connected for testing. Refer to Chapter 2 for further details about 'volt drop testing'. A simple principle to keep in mind is that the circuit should be able to supply all the available battery voltage to the consumers (bulbs, etc.). A loss of 5 to 10% may be acceptable. With all the switches in the 'on' position appropriate to where the meters are connected the following readings should be obtained:

- V_1 12.6 V (if less check battery condition);
- V_2 0 to 0.2 V (if more the ignition switch contacts have a high resistance);
- V_3 0 to 0.2 V (if more the dim dip relay contacts have a high resistance);
- V_4 0 to 0.2 V (if more there is a high resistance in the circuit between the output of the light switch and the junction for the tail lights);

Figure 6.29 Lighting circuit testing

- V_5 0 to 0.2 V (if more then there is a high resistance in the light switch contacts, the dip switch contacts or the circuit – connect the meter across a smaller section to narrow down the fault);
- V_6 0 to 0.2 V (if more then there is a high resistance in the earth for that bulb);
- V_7 12 to 12.6 V if on normal dip or about 6 V if on dim dip (if less then there is a high resistance in the circuit – check other readings, etc. to narrow down the fault).

6.9.2 Lighting fault diagnosis table

Symptom	Possible fault
Lights dim	High resistance in the circuit
	Low alternator output
	Discoloured lenses or reflectors
Headlights out of adjustment	Suspension fault
	Loose fittings
	Damage to body panels
	Adjustment incorrect
Lights do not work	Bulbs blown
	Fuse blown
	Loose or broken wiring/connections/fuse
	Relay not working
	Corrosion in light units
	Switch not making contact

6.9.3 Headlight beam setting

Many types of beam setting equipment are available and most work on the same principle. This is represented by Figure 6.30. The method is the same as using an aiming board but is more convenient and accurate due to easier working and because less room is required. To set the headlights of a car using an aiming board the following procedure should be adopted.

1. Park the car on level ground square on to a vertical aiming board at a distance of 10 m if possible. The car should be unladen except for the driver.
2. Mark out the aiming board as shown in Figure 6.31.
3. Bounce the suspension to ensure it is level.

Figure 6.30 Principle of a beam setter

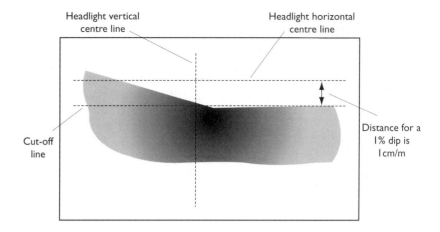

Headlight vertical centre line

Headlight horizontal centre line

Distance for a 1% dip is 1 cm/m

Cut-off line

Ground level

Figure 6.31 Headlight aiming board (Europe RHD)

4. With the lights set on dip beam, adjust the cut-off line to the horizontal mark, which will be 1 cm below the height of the headlight centre for every 1 m the car is away from the board*. The break-off point should be adjusted to the centre line of each light in turn.

Note: If the required dip is 1% then 1 cm per 1 m. If 1.2% is required then 1.2 cm per 1 m, etc.

Figure 6.32 shows the new Jaguar S-type and its interesting headlights!

6.10 Auxiliaries

6.10.1 Wiper motors and linkages

Most wiper linkages consist of series or parallel mechanisms. Some older types use a flexible rack and wheel boxes similar to the operating mechanism of many sunroofs. One of the main considerations for the design of a wiper linkage is the point at which the blades must reverse. This is because of the high forces on the motor and linkage at this time. If the reverse point is set so that the linkage is at its maximum force transmission angle then the reverse action of the blades puts less strain on the system. This also ensures smoother operation. Figure 6.33 shows a typical wiper linkage layout.

Most if not all wiper motors now in use are permanent magnet motors. The drive is taken via a worm gear to increase torque and reduce speed. Three brushes may be used to allow two-speed operation. The normal speed operates through two brushes placed in the usual positions opposite to each other. For a fast speed the third brush is placed closer to the earth brush. This reduces the number of armature windings between them, which reduces resistance hence

Figure 6.32 Interesting headlights on the new Jaguar S-type

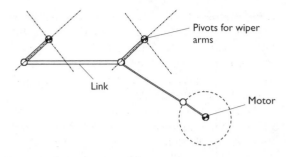

Figure 6.33 Wiper linkage

increasing current and therefore speed. Figure 6.34 shows two typical wiper motors. Typical specifications for wiper motor speed and hence wipe frequency are 45 rev/min at normal speed and 65 rev/min at fast speed. The motor must be able to overcome the starting friction of each blade at a minimum speed of 5 rev/min.

The wiper motor or the associated circuit often has some kind of short circuit protection. This is to protect the motor in the event of stalling, if frozen to the screen for example. A thermal trip of some type is often used or a current sensing circuit in the wiper ECU if fitted.

The maximum time a motor can withstand stalled current is normally specified. This is usually in the region of about 15 minutes.

The windscreen washer system usually consists of a simple DC permanent magnet motor driving a centrifugal water pump. The water, preferably with a cleaning additive, is directed onto an appropriate part of the screen by two or more jets. A non-return valve is often fitted in the line to the jets to prevent water siphoning back to the reservoir. This also allows 'instant' operation when the washer button is pressed. The washer circuit is normally linked in to the wiper circuit such that when the washers are operated the wipers start automatically and will continue for several more sweeps after the washers have stopped.

6.10.2 Wiper circuits

Figure 6.35 shows a circuit for fast, slow and intermittent wiper control. The switches are shown in the off position and the motor is stopped and in its park position. Note that the two main brushes of the motor are connected

Rear motor with electronic components

Front wiper motor

Figure 6.34 Wiper motors

Figure 6.35 Wiper circuit with intermittent/delay operation as well as slow and fast speed together via the limit switch, delay unit contacts and the wiper switch. This causes regenerative braking because of the current generated by the motor due to its momentum after the power is switched off. Being connected to a very low resistance loads up the 'generator' and it stops instantly when the park limit switch closes.

When either the delay contacts or the main switch contacts are operated the motor will run at slow speed. When fast speed is selected the third brush on the motor is used. On switching off, the motor will continue to run until the park limit switch changes over to the position shown. This switch is only in the position shown when the blades are in the parked position.

6.10.3 Headlight wipers and washers

There are two ways in which headlights are cleaned, first by high pressure jets, and second by small wiper blades with low pressure water supply. The second method is in fact much the same as windscreen cleaning but on a smaller scale. The high pressure system tends to be favoured but can suffer in very cold conditions due to the fluid freezing. It is expected that the wash system should be capable of about 50 operations before refilling of the reservoir is necessary. Headlight cleaners are often combined with the windscreen washers. They operate each time the windscreen washers are activated, if the headlights are also switched on.

A retractable nozzle for headlight cleaners is often used. When the water pressure is pumped to the nozzle it is pushed from its retracted position, flush with the bodywork. When the washing is completed the jet is then retracted back into the housing.

6.10.4 Indicators and hazard lights

Direction indicators have a number of statutory requirements. The light produced must be amber, but they may be grouped with other lamps. The flashing rate must be between one and two per second with a relative 'on' time of between 30 and 57%. If a fault develops this must be apparent to the driver by the operation of a warning light on the dashboard. The fault can be indicated by a distinct change in frequency of operation or the warning light remaining on. If one of the main bulbs fails then the remaining lights should continue to flash perceptibly.

Legislation as to the mounting position of the exterior lamps exists such that the rear indicator lights must be within a set distance of the tail lights and within a set height. The wattage of indicator light bulbs is normally 21 W at 6, 12 or 24 V as appropriate. Figure 6.36 shows a typical indicator and hazard circuit.

Flasher units are rated by the number of bulbs they are capable of operating. When towing a trailer or caravan the unit must be able to operate at a higher wattage. Most units use a relay for the actual switching as this is not susceptible to voltage spikes and also provides an audible signal. Figure 6.37 shows the rear lights on a Ford Mondeo!

6.10.5 Brake lights

Figure 6.38 shows a typical brake light circuit. Most incorporate a relay to switch the lights, which is in turn operated by a spring-loaded switch on the brake pedal. Links from this circuit to cruise control may be found. This is to cause the cruise control to switch off as the brakes are operated.

6.10.6 Electric horns

Regulations in most countries state that the horn (or audible warning device) should produce a uniform sound. This makes sirens and melody type fanfare horns illegal! Most horns draw a large current so are switched by a suitable relay.

The standard horn operates by simple electromagnetic switching. Current flow causes an armature to which is attached a tone disc, to be attracted towards a stop. This opens a set of contacts which disconnects the current allowing the armature and disc to return under spring tension. The whole process keeps repeating when the horn switch is on. The frequency of movement and hence the fundamental tone is arranged to lie between 1.8 and 3.5 kHz. This note gives good penetration through traffic noise. Twin horn systems, which have a high and low tone horn, are often used. This produces a more pleasing sound but is still very audible in both town and higher speed conditions. Figure 6.39 shows a typical horn together with its associated circuit.

6.10.7 Engine cooling fan motors

Most engine cooling fan motors (radiator cooling) are simple PM types. The fans used often have the blades placed asymmetrically (balanced but not in a regular pattern) to reduce noise when operating. Figure 6.40 shows a motor in position.

+ Supply

Ignition + Supply

Hazard WL

Hazard switch

Off

On

49a

62   49

31

Flasher
unit

Indicator
switch

Pilot
lights

Left

Right

Figure 6.36 Indicator and
hazard circuit

When twin cooling fans and motors are fitted, they can be run in series or parallel. This is often the case when air conditioning is used as the condenser is usually placed in front of the radiator and extra cooling air speed may be needed. A circuit for series or parallel operation of cooling fans is shown in Figure 6.41.

6.11 Diagnosing auxiliary system faults

6.11.1 Testing procedure

The process of checking an auxiliary system circuit is broadly as follows:

1. Hand and eye checks (loose wires, loose

Figure 6.37 'His Rear Lights' (old Desmond Decker song)!

+

Brake lights

Ignition
switch

Brake light
relay

Brake light
switch

Figure 6.38 Brake light circuit

Figure 6.39 Horn and circuit

switches and other obvious faults) – all connections clean and tight.

2. Check battery – must be 70% charged.
3. Check motor linkage/bulbs – visual check.
4. Fuse continuity – do not trust your eyes (Figure 6.42) but check voltage at both sides with a meter or a test lamp.
5. If used does the relay click (if yes, jump to stage 8) – this means the relay has operated but it is not necessarily making contact.
6. Supply to switch – battery volts.
7. Supply from switch – battery volts.
8. Supplies to relay – battery volts.
9. Feed out of relay – battery volts.
10. Voltage supply to the motor – within 0.5 V of the battery.
11. Earth circuit (continuity or voltage) – 0Ω or 0 V.

Figure 6.40 Cooling fan motor

Slow speed – relay R_2 only (S_2 on)
Full speed – relays R_1, R_2 and R_3 (S_1 and S_2 on)

Figure 6.41 Two-speed twin cooling fan circuit

Figure 6.42 Fuse box

6.11.2 Auxiliaries fault diagnosis table

Symptom	Possible fault
Horn not working or poor sound quality	Loose or broken wiring/connections/fuse Corrosion in horn connections Switch not making contact High resistance contact on switch or wiring Relay not working
Wipers not working or poor operation	Loose or broken wiring/connections/fuse Corrosion in wiper connections Switch not making contact High resistance contact on switch or wiring Relay/timer not working Motor brushes or slip ring connections worn Limit switch contacts open circuit or

high resistance
Blades and/or arm springs in poor condition

Washers not working or poor operation	Loose or broken wiring/connections/fuse Corrosion in washer motor connections Switch not making contact Pump motor poor or not working Blocked pipes or jets Incorrect fluid additive used
Indicators not working or incorrect operating speed	Bulb(s) blown Loose or broken wiring/connections/fuse Corrosion in horn connections Switch not making contact High resistance contact on switch or wiring Relay not working
Heater blower not working or poor operation	Loose or broken wiring/connections/fuse Switch not making contact Motor brushes worn Speed selection resistors open circuit

Figure 6.43 shows the zones of a windscreen as well as a non-circular wiping pattern. The zones are important for assessing if damage to the screen is critical or not.

6.11.3 Wiper motor and circuit testing

Figure 6.44 shows a procedure recommended by Lucas for testing a wiper motor. The expected reading on the ammeter should not be more that about 5 A. Several types of wiper motor are in current use so take care to make the appropriate connections for this test. Remember to use a fused jumper lead as a precaution.

Non-circular wiping

Figure 6.43 Windscreen zones

Figure 6.44 Wiper motor tests

6.12 In car entertainment (ICE) security and communications

6.12.1 ICE

Controls on most sets will include volume, treble, bass, balance and fade. Cassette tape options will include Dolby® filters to reduce hiss and other tape selections such as chrome or metal. A digital display of course, will provide a visual output of operating condition. This is also linked into the vehicle lighting to prevent glare at night. Track selection and programming for one or several compact discs is possible. Figure 6.45 shows a modern 'Pioneer' ICE system

display and control panel together with a top quality speaker (woofer).

Many ICE systems are coded to deter theft. The code is activated if the main supply is disconnected and will not allow the set to work until the correct code has been re-entered. Some systems now include a plug in electronic 'key card', which makes the set worthless when removed.

Good ICE systems include at least six speakers, two larger speakers in the rear parcel shelf to produce good low frequency reproduction, two front door speakers for mid range and two front door tweeters for high frequency notes. Speakers are a very important part of a sound system. No matter how good the receiver or CD player is, the sound quality will be reduced if inferior speakers are used. Equally if the speakers are of

Pi dome mid range with magnetic fluid

IMPP foam composite cone

Black stained design frame

Single conex damper

Butyl rubber edge

High performance strontium magnet

Figure 6.45 'Pioneer' ICE display and speaker

a lower power output rating than the set, distortion will result at best and damage to the speakers at worst. Speakers fall generally into the following categories:

- **tweeters** high frequency reproduction;
- **mid range** middle range frequency reproduction (treble);
- **woofers** low frequency reproduction (bass);
- **sub-woofers** very low frequency reproduction.

The radio data system RDS has become a standard on many radio sets. It is an extra inaudible digital signal which is sent with FM broadcasts in a similar way to how teletext is sent with TV signals. RDS provides information so a receiver can appear to act intelligently. The possibilities available when RDS is used are as follows.

- The station name can be displayed in place of the frequency.
- There can be automatic tuning to the best available signal for the chosen radio station. For example, in the UK a journey from the south of England to Scotland would mean the radio would have to be retuned up to ten times. RDS will do this without the driver even knowing.
- Traffic information broadcasts can be identified and a setting made so that whatever you are listening to at the time can be interrupted.

The radio broadcast data system (RBDS) is an extension of RDS which has been in use in Europe since 1984. The system allows the broadcaster to transmit text information at the rate of about 1200 bits per second. The information is transmitted on a 57 kHz suppressed sub-carrier as part of the FM MPX signal.

RBDS was developed for the North American market by the National Radio Systems Committee (NRSC), a joint committee composed of the Electronic Industries Association (EIA) and the National Association of Broadcasters (NAB). The applications for the transmission of text to the vehicle are interesting and include:

- song title and artist;
- traffic, accident and road hazard information;
- stock information;
- weather.

In emergency situations, the audio system can be enabled to interrupt the cassette, CD, or normal radio broadcast to alert the user.

Figure 6.46 shows a circuit typical of many ICE systems.

6.12.2 Security systems

Car and alarm manufacturers are constantly fighting to improve security. Building the alarm system as an integral part of the vehicle electronics has made significant improvements. Even so, retro fit systems can still be very effective. Three main types of intruder alarm are used:

- switch operated on all entry points;
- battery voltage sensed;
- volumetric sensing.

There are three main ways to disable the vehicle:

- ignition circuit cut off;

Figure 6.46 ICE circuit

- starter circuit cut off;
- engine ECU code lock.

Most alarm systems are made for 12 V, negative earth vehicles. They have electronic sirens and give an audible signal when arming and disarming. They are all triggered when the car door opens and will automatically reset after a period of time, often one or two minutes. The alarms are triggered instantly when entry point is breached. Most systems are two pieces, with separate control unit and siren; most will have the control unit in the passenger compartment and the siren under the bonnet.

Most systems now come with two infrared (IR) remote 'keys' that use small button type batteries and have an LED that shows when the signal is being sent. They operate with one vehicle only. Intrusion sensors such as car movement and volumetric sensing can be adjusted for sensitivity.

When operating with flashing lights most systems draw about 5 A. Without flashing lights (siren only) the current draw is less than 1 A. The sirens produce a sound level of about 95 dB, when measured 2 m in front of the vehicle.

Figure 6.47 shows a block diagram of a complex alarm system. The system, as is usual, can be considered as a series of inputs and outputs. This is particularly useful for diagnosing faults. Most factory fitted alarms are combined with the central door locking system. This allows the facility mentioned in a previous section known as lazy lock. Pressing the button on the remote

unit, as well as setting the alarm, closes the windows and sunroof and locks the doors.

A security code in the engine ECU is a powerful deterrent. This can only be 'unlocked' to allow the engine to start when it receives a coded signal. Ford and other manufacturers use a special ignition key which is programmed with the required information. Even the correct 'cut' key will not start the engine. Citroen, for example, have used a similar idea but the code has to be entered via a numerical keypad.

Of course nothing will stop the car being lifted on to a lorry and driven away, but this technique will mean a new engine control ECU will be needed. The cost will be high and also

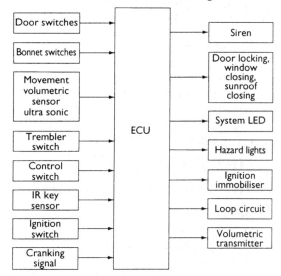

Figure 6.47 Block diagram of a complex alarm system

questions may be asked as to why a new ECU is required.

6.12.3 Mobile communications

If the success of the cellular industry is any indication of how much use we can make of the telephone, the future promises an even greater expansion. Cellular technology started to become useful in the 1980s and has continued to develop from then – very quickly.

The need and desire we perceive to keep in touch with each other is so great that an increasing number of business people now have up to five phone numbers: home, office, pager, fax and cellular. But within the foreseeable future, high-tech digital radio technology and sophisticated telecommunications systems will enable all communications to be processed through a single number.

With personal numbering, a person carrying a pocket-sized phone will need only one phone number. Instead of people calling places, people will call people; we will not be tied to any particular place. Personal numbering will make business people more productive because they will be able to reach and be reached by colleagues and clients, anywhere and anytime, indoors or outdoors. When travelling from home to office or from one meeting to the next, it will be possible to communicate with anyone, whenever the need arises.

But where does this leave communication systems relating to the vehicle? It is my opinion that 'in vehicle' communication equipment for normal business and personal use will be by the simple pocket sized mobile phone and that there is no further market for the car telephone. Hands free conversions will still be important.

CB radios and short range two-way systems such as used by taxi firms and service industries will still have a place for the time being. Even these may decline as the cellular network becomes cheaper and more convenient to use.

6.13 Diagnosing ICE, security and communication system faults

6.13.1 Testing procedure

The process of checking an ICE system circuit is broadly as follow.

1. Hand and eye checks (loose wires, loose switches and other obvious faults) – all connections clean and tight.
2. Check battery – must be 70% charged.
3. Check code is correct for the set (if appropriate).
4. Fuse continuity – do not trust your eyes but check voltage at both sides with a meter or a test lamp.
5. Supply to unit(s) – battery volts.
6. Earth circuit (continuity or voltage) – 0 Ω or 0 V.
7. Aerial earth connection at the set – 0 Ω.
8. Aerial earth connection to the vehicle body – 0 Ω.
9. Speaker resistance checks (refer to specifications but 4 or 8 Ω are the most common).

6.13.2 ICE, security and communication system fault diagnosis table

Symptom	Possible fault
Alarm does not operate	Fuse blown Not set correctly Remote key battery discharged Open circuit connection to alarm unit ECU fault Receiver/transmitter fault Volumetric transmitter/receiver fault
Alarm goes off for no apparent reason	Drain on battery Loose connection Vibration/trembler/movement detection circuit set too sensitive Self-discharge in the battery Window left open allowing wind or even a bird or insect to cause interior movement Somebody really is trying to steal the car ...
Radio interference	Tracking HT components Static buildup on isolated body panels High resistance or open circuit aerial earth Suppression device open circuit
ICE system does not produce sound	Set not switched on! Loose or open circuit connections Trapped wires Connections to separate unit (amplifier, equaliser, etc.) incorrect Fuse blown
Unbalanced sound	Fade or balance controls not set correctly Speakers not wired correctly (front right, front left, rear right, rear left, etc.) Speaker open circuit or reduced output

Phasing	Speaker polarity incorrect. This should be marked but if not use a small battery to check all speakers are connected the same way. A small DC voltage will move the speaker cone in one direction
Speaker rattle	Insecure speaker(s) Trim not secure Inadequate baffles
Crackling noises	If one speaker – then try substitution If one channel – swap connections at the set to isolate the fault If all channels but only the radio then check interference Radio set circuit fault
Vibration	Incorrect or loose mounting
Hum	Speaker cables routed next to power supply wires Set fault
Distortion	Incorrect power rating speakers
Poor radio reception	Incorrect tuning 'Dark' spot/area. FM signals can be affected by tall buildings, etc. Aerial not fully extended Aerial earth loose or high resistance Tuner not trimmed to the aerial (older sets generally) Aerial sections not clean
Telephone reception poor	Low battery power Poor reception area Interference from the vehicle Loose connections on hands free circuit

6.13.3 Interference suppression

The process of interference suppression on a vehicle is to reduce the amount of unwanted noise produced from the speakers of an ICE system. This can, however, be quite difficult. To aid the discussion it is necessary to first understand the different types of interference. Figure 6.48 shows two signals, one clean and the other suffering from interference. The amount of interference can be stated as a signal to noise ratio. This is the useful field strength compared to the interference field strength at the receiver.

There are two overall issues to be considered relating to suppression of interference on a vehicle. These are as follows.

- **Short range** the effect of interference on the vehicle's radio system.
- **Long range** the effect of the vehicle on external receivers such as domestic televisions. This is covered by legislation making it illegal to cause disturbance to radios or televisions when using a vehicle.

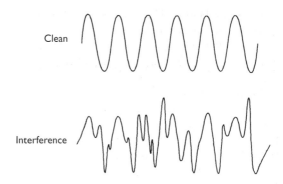

Figure 6.48 Radio signals

Interference can propagate in one of four ways:

- line borne conducted through the wires;
- air borne radiated through the air to the aerial;
- capacitive coupling by an electric field;
- inductive coupling magnetic linking.

The sources of interference in the motor vehicle can be summarised quite simply as any circuit which is switched or interrupted suddenly. This includes the action of a switch and the commutation process in a motor, both of which produce rapidly increasing signals. The secret of suppression is to slow down this increase. Interference is produced from four main areas of the vehicle:

- ignition system;
- charging system;
- motors and switches;
- static discharges.

The ignition system of a vehicle is the largest source of interference, in particular the high tension side. Voltages up to 30 kV are now common and the current for a fraction of a second when the plug fires can peak in excess of 100 A. The interference caused by the ignition system is mostly above 30 Mhz and the energy can peak for fractions of a second in the order of 500 kW.

The charging system produces noise because of the sparking at the brushes. Electronic regulators produce few problems but regulators with vibrating contacts can cause trouble.

Any motor or switch including relays is likely to produce some interference. The most popular sources are the wiper motor and heater motor. The starter is not considered due to its short usage time.

Buildup of static electricity is due to friction between the vehicle and the air, and the tyres and the road. If the static on say the bonnet builds up more than on the wing then a spark can be discharged. Using bonding straps to ensure all panels stay at the same potential easily prevents this. Due to the action of the tyres a potential can build up between the wheel rims and the chassis unless suitable bonding straps are fitted. The arc to ground can be as much as 10 kV.

There are five main techniques for suppressing radio interference:

- resistors;
- bonding;
- screening;
- capacitors;
- inductors.

Resistance is used exclusively in the ignition HT circuit, up to a maximum of about 20 kΩ per lead. This has the effect of limiting the peak current, which in turn limits the peak electromagnetic radiation. Providing excessive resistance is not used, the spark quality is not affected. These resistors effectively damp down the interference waves.

Bonding has been mentioned earlier. It is simply to ensure that all parts of the vehicle are at the same electrical potential to prevent sparking due to the build up of static.

Screening is generally only used for specialist applications such as emergency services and the military. It involves completely enclosing the ignition system and other major sources of noise in a conductive screen, which is connected to the vehicle's chassis earth. This prevents interference waves escaping, it is a very effective technique but expensive. Often a limited amount of screening, metal covers on the plugs for example, can be used to good effect.

Capacitors and inductors are used to act as filters. This is achieved by using the changing value of 'resistance' to alternating signals as the frequency increases. The correct term for this resistance is either capacitive or inductive reactance. By choosing suitable values of capacitor in parallel and/or inductor in series it is possible to filter out unwanted signals of certain frequencies.

The aerial is worth a mention at this stage. Several types are in use; the most popular still being the rod aerial which is often telescopic. The advantage of a rod aerial is that it extends beyond the interference field of the vehicle. For reception in the AM bands the aerial represents a capacitance of 80 pF with a shunt resistance of about 1 MΩ. The set will often incorporate a trimmer to ensure that the aerial is matched to the set. Contact resistance between all parts of the aerial should be less than 20 mΩ. This is particularly important for the earth connection.

When receiving in the FM range the length of the aerial is very important. The ideal length of a rod aerial for FM reception is one quarter of the wavelength. In the middle of the FM band (94 MHz) this is about 80 cm. Due to the magnetic and electrical field of the vehicle and the effect of the coaxial cable, the most practical length is about 1 m. Some smaller aerials are available but whilst these may be more practical the signal strength is reduced. Aerials embedded into the vehicle windows or using the heated rear window element are good from the damage prevention aspect and for insensitivity to moisture, but produce a weaker signal often requiring an aerial amplifier to be included. Note that this will also amplify interference. Some top range vehicles use a rod aerial and a screen aerial, the set being able to detect and use the strongest signal. This reduces the effect of reflected signals and causes less flutter.

Consideration must be given to the position of an external aerial. This has to be a compromise taking into account the following factors:

- **rod length** 1 m if possible;
- **coaxial cable length** longer cable reduces the signal strength;
- **position** as far away as reasonably possible from the ignition system;
- **potential for vandalism** out of easy reach;
- **aesthetic appearance** does it fit with the style of the vehicle;
- **angle of fitting** vertical is best for AM horizontal for FM!

Most quality sets also include a system known as interference absorption. This is a circuit built in to the set consisting of high quality filters and is not adjustable.

6.14 Body electrical systems

6.14.1 Electric seat adjustment

Adjustment of the seat is achieved by using a number of motors to allow positioning of different parts of the seat. A typical motor reverse circuit is shown in Figure 6.49. When the switch is moved *one* of the relays will operate and this changes the polarity of the supply to *one* side of the motor. Movement is possible in the following ways:

- front to rear;
- cushion height rear;

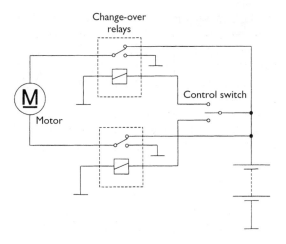

Figure 6.49 Motor reverse circuit

- cushion height front;
- backrest tilt;
- headrest height;
- lumbar support.

When seat position is set some vehicles have position memories to allow automatic repositioning, if the seat has been moved. This is often combined with electric mirror adjustment. Figure 6.50 shows how the circuit is constructed to allow position memory. As the seat is moved a variable resistor, mechanically linked to the motor, is also moved. The resistance value provides feedback to an ECU. This can be 'remembered' in a number of ways; the best technique is to supply the resistor with a fixed voltage such that the output relative to the seat position is proportional to position. This voltage can then be 'analogue to digital' converted, which produces a simple

'number' to store in a digital memory. When the driver presses a memory recall switch the motor relays are activated by the ECU until the number in memory and the number fed back from the seat are equal. This facility is often isolated when the engine is running to prevent the seat moving into a dangerous position as the car is being driven. Position of the seats can still be adjusted by operating the switches as normal.

6.14.2 Electric mirrors

Many vehicles have electrical adjustment of mirrors, particularly on the passenger side. The system used is much the same as has been discussed above in relation to seat movement. Two small motors are used to move the mirror vertically or horizontally. Many mirrors also contain a small heating element on the rear of the glass. This is operated for a few minutes when the ignition is first switched on and can also be linked to the heated rear window circuit. Figure 6.51 shows an electrically operated mirror circuit, which includes feedback resistors for positional memory.

6.14.3 Electric sunroof operation

The operation of an electric sunroof is similar to the motor reverse circuit discussed earlier in this chapter. However, further components and circuitry are needed to allow the roof to slide, tilt and stop in the closed position. The extra components used are a micro switch and a latching relay. A latching relay works in much the same way as a normal relay except that it locks into position each time it is energised. The mechanism

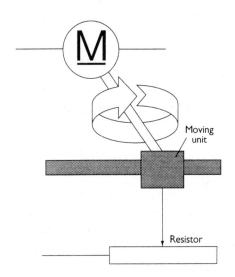

Figure 6.50 Position memory for electric seats

Figure 6.51 Feedback resistors for positional memory and circuit.

Figure 6.52 Sunroof circuit

Figure 6.53 Door lock circuit

used to achieve this is much like that used in ball point pens that use a button on top.

The micro switch is mechanically positioned such as to operate when the roof is in its closed position. A rocker switch allows the driver to adjust the roof. The circuit for an electrically operated sun roof is shown in Figure 6.52. The switch provides the supply to the motor to run it in the chosen direction. The roof will be caused to open or tilt. When the switch is operated to close the roof the motor is run in the appropriate direction until the micro switch closes when the roof is in its closed position. This causes the latching relay to change over which stops the motor. The control switch has now to be released. If the switch is pressed again the latching relay will once more change over and the motor will be allowed to run.

6.14.4 Door locking circuit

When the key is turned in the driver's door lock all the other doors on the vehicle should also lock. Motors or solenoids in each door achieve this. If the system can only be operated from the driver's door key then an actuator is not required in this door. If the system can be operated from either front door or by remote control then all the doors need an actuator. Vehicles with sophisticated alarm systems often lock all the doors as the alarm is set.

Figure 6.53 shows a door locking circuit. The main control unit contains two change over relays, which are actuated by either the door lock switch or, if fitted, the remote infrared key. The motors for each door lock are simply wired in parallel and all operate at the same time.

Most door actuators are now small motors

which, via suitable gear reduction, operate a linear rod in either direction to lock or unlock the doors. A simple motor reverse circuit is used to achieve the required action.

Infrared central door locking is controlled by a small hand-held transmitter and an infrared sensor receiver unit as well as a decoder in the main control unit. This layout will vary slightly between different manufacturers. When the infrared key is operated by pressing a small switch a complex code is transmitted. The number of codes used is well in excess of 50 000 The infrared sensor picks up this code and sends it in an electrical form to the main control unit. If the received code is correct the relays are triggered and the door locks are either locked or unlocked. If an incorrect code is received on three consecutive occasions when attempting to unlock the doors, then the infrared system will switch itself off until the door is opened by the key. This will also reset the system and allow the correct code to again operate the locks. This technique prevents a scanning type transmitter unit from being used to open the doors.

6.14.5 Electric window operation

The basic form of electric window operation is similar to many of the systems discussed so far in this chapter, that is a motor reversing system either by relays or directly by a switch. More sophisticated systems are now becoming more popular for reasons of safety as well as improved comfort. The following features are now available from many manufacturers:

● one-shot up or down;
● inch up or down;
● lazy lock;
● back-off.

When a window is operated in one-shot or one-touch mode the window is driven in the chosen direction until either the switch position is reversed, the motor stalls or the ECU receives a signal from the door lock circuit. The problem with one-shot operation is that if a child, for example, should become trapped in the window there is a serious risk of injury. To prevent this, the back-off feature is used. An extra commutator is fitted to the motor armature and produces a signal via two brushes, proportional to the motor speed. If the rate of change of speed of the motor is detected as being below a certain threshold when closing, then the ECU will reverse the motor until the window is fully open.

By counting the number of pulses received the ECU can also determine the window position. This is important, as the window must not reverse when it stalls in the closed position. In order for the ECU to know the window position it must be initialised. This is often done simply by operating the motor to drive the window first fully open, and then fully closed. If this is not done then the one-shot close will not operate. On some systems Hall effect sensors are used to detect motor speed. Other systems sense the current being drawn by the motor and use this as an indication of speed.

Lazy lock feature allows the car to be fully secured by one operation of a remote infrared key. This is done by the link between the door lock ECU and the window and sunroof ECUs.

A signal is supplied which causes all the windows to close in turn, then the sunroof and finally locks the doors. The alarm will also be set if required. The windows close in turn to prevent the excessive current demand which would occur if they all tried to operate at the same time.

A circuit for electric windows is shown in Figure 6.54. Note the connections to other systems such as door locking and the rear window isolation switch. This is commonly fitted to allow the driver to prevent rear window operation for child safety for example.

6.15 Diagnosing body electrical system faults

6.15.1 Testing procedure

The following procedure is very generic but with a little adaptation can be applied to any electrical system. Refer to manufacturer's recommendations if in any doubt. The process of checking any system circuit is broadly as follows.

1. Hand and eye checks (loose wires, loose switches and other obvious faults) – all connections clean and tight.

Figure 6.54 Electric window circuit

2. Check battery – must be 70% charged.
3. Check motor/solenoid/linkage/bulbs/unit – visual check.
4. Fuse continuity – (do not trust your eyes but check voltage at both sides with a meter or a test lamp.
5. If used does the relay click (if yes, jump to stage 8) – this means the relay has operated but it is not necessarily making contact.
6. Supply to switch – battery volts.
7. Supply from switch – battery volts.
8. Supplies to relay – battery volts.
9. Feed out of relay – battery volts.
10. Voltage supply to the motor – within 0.5 V of the battery.
11. Earth circuit (continuity or voltage) – 0 Ω or 0 V.

6.15.2 Body electrical systems fault diagnosis

Symptom	Possible fault
Electric units not operating	If *all* units not operating: open circuit in main supply main fuse blown
(unit = window, door lock, mirror etc.)	relay coil or contacts open circuit or high resistance
	If *one* unit is not operating: fuse blown control switch open circuit motor seized or open circuit back-off safety circuit signal incorrect (windows)

6.15.3 Circuit systematic testing

The circuit shown in Figure 6.55 is for a power hood on a Rover vehicle. The following faultfinding guide is an example of how to approach a problem with a system such as this in a logical manner.

If the power hood will not operate with the ignition switch at the correct position and the handbrake applied proceed as follows.

1. Check fuses 6 and 13.
2. Check 12 V supply on N wire from fuse 6.
3. Check for 12 V on GS wire at power hood relay.
4. Check continuity from power hood relay to earth on BW wire.
5. Check power hood relay.
6. Check for 12 V on NW wire at hood switch. Check for 12 V on N wire at hood up and down relays.

7. Check continuity from hood up and down relays to earth on B wire.
8. Check switch operation.
9. Check pump motor operation.

If the power hood will operate in one direction only proceed as follows.

1. Check for 12 V on N wire at hood up or down relay as appropriate.
2. Check continuity from hood up or down relay to earth on B wire.
3. Check relay.

6.16 Instrumentation

6.16.1 Gauges

Thermal gauges, which are ideal for fuel and engine temperature indication, have been in use for many years. This will continue because of their simple design and inherent 'thermal' damping. The gauge works by utilizing the heating effect of electricity and the widely adopted benefit of the bimetal strip. As a current flows through a simple heating coil wound on a bimetal strip, heat causes the strip to bend. The bimetal strip is connected to a pointer on a suitable scale. The amount of bend is proportional to the heat, which in turn is proportional to the current flowing. Providing the sensor can vary its resistance in proportion to the measurand (e.g. fuel level), the gauge will indicate a suitable representation as long as it has been calibrated far the particular task. Figure 6.56 shows a representation of a typical thermal gauge circuit.

Thermal type gauges are used with a variable resistor and float in a fuel tank or with a thermistor in the engine water jacket. The resistance of the fuel tank sender can be made non-linear to counteract any non-linear response of the gauge. The sender resistance is at a maximum when the tank is empty.

A constant voltage supply is required to prevent changes in the vehicle system voltage affecting the reading. This is because if system voltage increased the current flowing would increase and hence the gauges would read higher. Most voltage stabilisers are simple zener diode circuits.

Air cored gauges work on the same principle as a compass needle lining up with a magnetic field. The needle of the display is attached to a very small permanent magnet. Three coils of

Figure 6.55 Power hood circuit

wire are used and each produces a magnetic field. The magnet will line up with the resultant of the three fields. The current flowing and the number of turns (ampere-turns) determine the strength of the magnetic flux produced by each coil. As the number of turns remains constant the current is the key factor. Figure 6.57 shows the principle of the air cored gauge together with the circuit for use as a temperature indicator. The ballast resistor on the left is used to limit maximum current and the calibration resistor is used for calibration! The thermistor is the temperature sender. As the thermistor resistance is increased the current in all three coils will change. Current through C will be increased but the current in coils A and B will decrease.

The air cored gauge has a number of advantages. It has almost instant response and as the needle is held in a magnetic field it will not move as the vehicle changes position. The gauge can be arranged to continue to register the last position even when switched off or, if a small 'pull off' magnet is used, it will return to its zero position. As a system voltage change would affect the current flowing in all three coils variations are cancelled out negating the need for voltage stabilisation. Note that the operation is similar to the moving iron gauge.

Figure 6.56 Thermal gauge circuit

Figure 6.57 Priciple of the air cored gauge together with the circuit when used as a fuel lever or temperature indicator and the resultant magnetic fields

6.16.2 Digital instrumentation

The block diagram shown in Figure 6.58 is typical of a digital instrumentation system. All signal conditioning and logic functions are carried out in the ECU. This will often form part of the dashboard assembly. Standard sensors provide information to the ECU, which in turn will drive suitable displays. The ECU contains a ROM (read only memory) section, which allows it to be programmed to a specific vehicle. The gauges used are as described in the above sections. Some of the extra functions available with this system are described briefly as follows.

● **Low fuel warning light**   Can be made to illuminate at a particular resistance reading from the fuel tank sender unit.
● **High engine temperature warning light**   Can be made to operate at a set resistance of the thermistor.
● **Steady reading of the temperature gauge**   To prevent the gauge fluctuating as the cooling system thermostat operates, the gauge can be made to read only at say five set figures. For example, if the input resistance varies from 240 to 200 Ω as the thermostat operates, the

Figure 6.58 Digital instrumentation

ECU will output just one reading corresponding to 'normal' on the gauge. If the resistance is much higher or lower the gauge will read to one of the five higher or lower positions. This gives a low resolution but high readability for the driver.

● **Oil pressure or other warning lights can be made to flash**   This is more likely to catch the driver's attention.
● **Service or inspection interval warning lights can be used**   The warning lights are operated broadly as a function of time but, for example, the service interval is reduced if the engine experiences high speeds and/or high temperatures. Oil condition sensors are also used to help determine service intervals.
● **Alternator warning light**   Works as normal but the same or an extra light can be made to operate if the output is reduced or if the drive belt slips. This is achieved by a wire from one phase of the alternator providing a pulsed signal, which is compared to a pulsed signal from the ignition. If the ratio of the pulses changed this would indicate a slipping belt.

6.16.3 Vehicle condition monitoring

VCM or vehicle condition monitoring is a form of instrumentation. It has now become difficult to separate it from the more normal instrumentation system discussed in the first part of this chapter. Figure 6.59 shows a typical display unit, which also incorporates the vehicle map (see next section). The complete VCM system can include driver information relating to the following list:

- high engine temperature;
- low fuel;
- low brake fluid;
- worn brake pads;
- low coolant level;
- low oil level;
- low screen washer fluid;
- low outside temperature;
- bulb failure;
- doors, bonnet or boot open warning.

A circuit is shown in Figure 6.60, which can be used to operate bulb failure warning lights for whatever particular circuit it is monitoring. The simple principle is that the reed relay is only operated when the bulb being monitored is drawing current. The fluid and temperature level monitoring systems work in a similar way to the systems described earlier but in some cases the level of a fluid is by a float and switch.

Figure 6.59 Trip computer display and a vehicle 'map'

Figure 6.60 Bulb failure warning circuit

Oil level can be monitored by measuring the resistance of a heated wire on the end of the dip stick. A small current is passed through the wire to heat it. How much of the wire is covered by oil will determine its temperature and therefore its resistance.

Many of the circuits monitored use a dual resistance system so that the circuit itself is also checked. Figure 6.61 shows the equivalent circuit for this technique. In effect it will produce one of three possible outputs: high resistance, low resistance or an out of range reading. The high or low resistance readings are used to indicate say correct fluid level and low fluid level. A figure outside these limits would indicate a circuit fault of either a short or open circuit connection.

The display is often just a collection of LEDs or a back lit liquid crystal display (LCD). These are arranged into suitable patterns and shapes such as to represent the circuit or system being monitored. A door open will illuminate a symbol which looks as if the door of the vehicle map (plan view of the car) is open. Low outside temperature or ice warning is often a large snowflake!

6.16.4 Trip computer

The trip computer used on many top range vehicles is arguably an expensive novelty, but is popular none-the-less. The display and key pad of a typical trip computer is shown above. The functions available on most systems are:

- time and date;
- elapsed time or a stop watch;
- estimated time of arrival;
- average fuel consumption;
- range on remaining fuel;
- trip distance.

The above details can usually be displayed in

Figure 6.61 Equivalent circuit of a dual resistance self-testing system

Figure 6.62 Trip computer block diagram

imperial, US or metric units as required. Figure 6.62 shows a block diagram of a trip computer system. Note that several systems use the same inputs and that several systems 'communicate' with each other. This makes the overall wiring very bulky – if not complicated.

6.16.5 Displays

If the junction of a diode is manufactured in a certain way, light will be emitted from the junction when a current is made to pass in the forward biased direction. This is an LED and will produce red, yellow or green light with slight changes in the manufacturing process. LEDs are used extensively as indicators on electronic equipment and in digital displays. They last for a very long time (50 000 hours) and draw only a small current.

LED displays are tending to be replaced for automobile use by the liquid crystal type, which can be back lit to make it easier to read in the daylight. However, LEDs are still popular for many applications.

The actual display will normally consist of a number of LEDs arranged into a suitable pattern for the required output. This can range from the standard seven segment display to show numbers, to a custom designed speedometer display.

Liquid crystals are substances that do not melt directly from a solid to the liquid phase, but first pass through a paracrystalline stage in which the molecules are partially ordered. In this stage a liquid crystal is a cloudy or translucent fluid but still has some of the optical properties of a solid crystal.

Mechanical stress, electric and magnetic fields, pressure and temperature can alter the molecular structure of liquid crystals. A liquid crystal also scatters light that shines on it. Because of these properties, liquid crystals are used to display letters and numbers on calculators, digital watches and automobile instrument displays. LCDs are also used for portable computer screens and even television screens. The LCD has many more areas of potential use and developments are on going. In particular this type of display is now good enough to reproduce pictures and text on computer screens.

When a voltage of about 10 V at 50 Hz is applied to the crystal it becomes disorganised and the light passing through it is no longer twisted by 90°. This means that the light polarised by the first polariser will not pass through the second, and will therefore not be reflected. This will show as a dark area on the display. These areas are constructed into suitable segments in much the same way as with LEDs to provide whatever type of display is required. The size of each individual area can be very small such as to form one pixel of a TV or computer screen if appropriate.

A vacuum fluorescent display works in much the same way as a television tube and screen. It is becoming increasingly popular for vehicle use because it produces a bright light (which is adjustable), and a wider choice of colours than LED or LCD displays. The glass front of the display can be coloured to improve the readability and aesthetic value. This type of display has many advantages but the main problem for automobile use is its susceptibility to shock and vibration. This can be overcome, however, with suitable mountings. Figure 6.63 shows some instrument and other displays using a number of the previously discussed techniques.

6.17 Diagnosing instrumentation system faults

6.17.1 Testing procedure

The process of checking a thermal gauge fuel or temperature instrument system is broadly as follows.

1. Hand and eye checks (loose wires, loose switches and other obvious faults) – all connections clean and tight.
2. *Either* fit a known good 200 Ω resistor in

Figure 6.63 Display techniques

place of the temperature sender – gauge should read full

3. *Or* short fuel tank sender wire to earth – gauge should read full.

4. Check continuity of wire from gauge to sender – 0 to 0.5 Ω.

5. Check supply voltage to gauge – pulsed 0 to 12 V on old systems – a stabilised 10 V on others.

6. If all above tests are OK the gauge head is at fault.

Figure 6.64 shows an interesting and useful test carried out on a temperature sensor using an oscilloscope set to a very slow time base (or sample rate).

6.17.2 Instrumentation fault diagnosis table

Symptom	Possible fault
Fuel and temperature gauges both read high or low	Voltage stabiliser
Gauges read full/hot or empty/cold all the time	Short/open circuit sensors Short or open circuit wiring
Instruments do not work	Loose or broken wiring/connections/fuse Inoperative instrument voltage stabiliser Sender units (sensor) faulty Gauge unit fault (not very common)

Figure 6.64 Waveform showing the output of a coolant temperature sensor warming up

6.17.3 Black box technique for instrumentation

Instrumentation systems, like most others, now revolve around an ECU. The ECU is considered to be a 'black box'; in other words we know what it should do but how it does it is irrelevant! Figure 6.65 shows an instrumenta-

Figure 6.65 Instrument pack warning circuit

tion system where the instrument pack could be considered as a black box. Normal faultfinding or testing techniques can now be applied to the sensors and supply circuits.

Remember also the 'sensor to ECU method' of testing described in Section 2.5.8. A resistance test carried out on a component such as the tank unit (lower right) would give a direct measure of its resistance. A second reading at the instrument pack between the GB and BP wires, if the same as the first, would confirm that the circuit is in good order.

Warning
The circuit supply must always be off when carrying out ohmmeter tests.

6.18 Heating, ventilation and air conditioning (HVAC)

6.18.1 Ventilation and heating

To allow fresh air from outside the vehicle to be circulated inside the cabin, a pressure difference must be created. This is achieved by using a plenum chamber. A plenum chamber by definition holds a gas (in this case air) at a pressure higher than the ambient pressure. The plenum chamber on a vehicle is usually situated just below the windscreen, behind the bonnet. When the vehicle is moving the air flow over the vehicle will cause a higher pressure in this area. Suitable flaps and drains are utilised to prevent water entering the car through this opening.

By means of distribution trunking, control flaps and suitable 'nozzles', the air can be directed as required. This system is enhanced with the addition of a variable speed blower motor. Figure 6.66 shows a typical ventilation and heating system layout.

When extra air is forced into a vehicle cabin the interior pressure would increase if no outlet was available. Most passenger cars have the outlet grilles on each side of the vehicle above or near the rear quarter panels or doors.

6.18.2 Heating system – water-cooled engine

Heat from the engine is utilised to increase the temperature of the car interior. This is achieved by use of a heat exchanger, called the heater

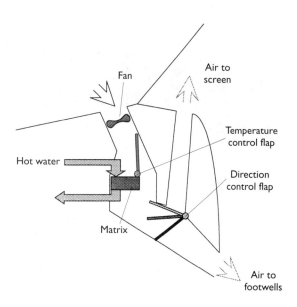

Figure 6.66 Heating and ventilation system

matrix. Due to the action of the thermostat in the engine cooling system the water temperature remains broadly constant. This allows for the air being passed over the heater matrix to be heated by a set amount depending on the outside air temperature and the rate of air flow. A source of hot air is therefore available for heating the vehicle interior. However, some form of control is required over how much heat (if any) is required. The method used on most modern vehicles is the blending technique. This is simply a control flap, which determines how much of the air being passed into the vehicle is directed over the heater matrix. The main drawback of this system is the change in air flow with vehicle speed. Some systems use a valve to control the hot coolant flowing to the heater matrix.

By a suitable arrangement of flaps it is possible to direct air of the chosen temperature to selected areas of the vehicle interior. In general, basic systems allow the warm air to be adjusted between the inside of the windscreen and the driver and passenger footwells. Most vehicles also have small vents directing warm air at the driver's and front passenger's side windows. Fresh cool air outlets with directional nozzles are also fitted.

One final facility, which is available on many vehicles, is the choice between fresh or recirculated air. The main reason for this is to decrease the time it takes to demist or defrost the vehicle windows, and simply to heat the car interior more quickly to a higher temperature. The other reason is that, for example in heavy congested traffic, the outside air may not be very clean.

Figure 6.67 Heating and ventilation motor and fans

6.18.3 Heater blower motors

The motors used to increase air flow are simple permanent magnet two brush motors. The blower fan is often the centrifugal type and in many cases the blades are positioned asymmetrically to reduce resonant noise. Figure 6.67 shows a typical motor and fan arrangement. Varying the voltage supplied controls motor speed. This is achieved by using dropping resistors. The speed in some cases is made 'infinitely' variable, by the use of a variable resistor. In most cases the motor is controlled to three or four set speeds.

Figure 6.68 shows a circuit diagram typical of a three-speed control system. The resistors are usually wire wound and are placed in the air

Figure 6.68 Circuit diagram of a three-speed control system

Figure 6.69 An electronically controlled vehicle heating system

stream to prevent overheating. These resistors will have low values in the region of 1 Ω or less.

6.18.4 Electronic heating control

Most vehicles that have electronic control of the heating system also include air conditioning, which is covered in the next section. However, a short description at this stage will help to lead into the more complex systems. Figure 6.69 shows a block diagram representing an electronically controlled vehicle heating system.

This system requires control of the blower motor, blend flap, direction flaps and the fresh or recirculated air flap. The technique involves one or a number of temperature sensors suitably positioned in the vehicle interior, to provide information for the ECU. The ECU responds to information received from these sensors and sets the controls to their optimum positions. The whole arrangement is in fact a simple closed loop feedback system with the air temperature closing the loop. The ECU has to compare the position of the temperature control switch with the information that is supplied by the sensors and either cool or heat the car interior as required.

6.18.5 Air conditioning introduction

A vehicle fitted with air conditioning allows the temperature of the cabin to be controlled to the ideal or most comfortable value determined by the ambient conditions. The system as a whole still utilises the standard heating and ventilation components, but with the important addition of an evaporator, which both cools and dehumidifies the air.

Air conditioning can be manually controlled or, as is now often the case, combined with some form of electronic control. The system as a whole can be thought of as a type of refrigerator or heat exchanger. Heat is removed from the car interior and dispersed to the outside air.

To understand the principle of refrigeration the following terms and definitions will be useful.

- Heat is a form of energy.
- Temperature means the degree of heat of an object.
- Heat will only flow from a higher to a lower temperature.
- Heat quantity is measured in 'calories' (more often kcal).

- 1 kcal heat quantity changes the temperature of 1 kg of liquid water by 1°C.
- Change of state is a term used to describe the changing of a solid to a liquid, a liquid to a gas, a gas to a liquid or a liquid to a solid.
- Evaporation is used to describe the change of state from a liquid to a gas.
- Condensation is used to describe the change of state from gas to liquid.
- Latent heat describes the energy required to evaporate a liquid without changing its temperature (breaking of molecular bonds), or the amount of heat given off when a gas condenses back into a liquid without changing temperature (making of molecular bonds).

Latent heat in the change of state of a refrigerant is the key to air conditioning. A simple example of this is that if you put a liquid such as methylated spirits on your hand it feels cold. This is because it evaporates and the change of state (liquid to gas) uses heat from your body. This is why the process is often thought of as 'unheating' rather than cooling.

The refrigerant used in many air conditioning systems is known as R134A. This substance changes state from liquid to gas at −26.3°C. R134A is HFC based rather than CFC, due to the problems with atmospheric ozone depletion associated with CFC based refrigerants. A key to understanding refrigeration is to remember that low pressure refrigerant will have low temperature, and high pressure refrigerant will have a high temperature.

Figure 6.70 shows the basic principle of an air conditioning – or refrigeration – system. The basic components are the evaporator, condenser and pump or compressor. The evaporator is situated in the car; the condenser is outside the car, usually in the air stream; and the compressor is driven by the engine.

As the pump operates it will cause the pressure on its intake side to fall, which will allow the refrigerant in the evaporator to evaporate and draw heat from the vehicle interior. The high pressure or output of the pump is connected to the condenser. The pressure causes the refrigerant to condense (in the condenser), thus giving off heat outside the vehicle as it changes state. Figure 6.71 shows some typical components of an air conditioning system.

6.18.6 Air conditioning overview

The operation of the system is a continuous cycle. The compressor pumps low pressure but heat laden vapour from the evaporator, compresses it and pumps it as a super heated vapour under high pressure to the condenser. The temperature of the refrigerant at this stage is much higher than the outside air temperature hence it gives up its heat via the fins on the condenser as it changes state back to a liquid.

This high pressure liquid is then passed to the receiver drier where any vapour which has not yet turned back to a liquid is stored, and a desiccant bag removes any moisture (water) that is contaminating the refrigerant. The high pressure liquid is now passed through the thermostatic expansion valve and is converted back to a low pressure liquid as it passes through a restriction in the valve into the evaporator. This valve is the element of the system that controls the refrigerant flow and hence the amount of cooling provided. As the liquid changes state to a gas in the evaporator, it takes up heat from its surroundings, thus cooling or 'unheating' the air that is forced over the fins. The low pressure vapour leaves the evaporator returning to the pump thus completing the cycle.

If the temperature of the refrigerant increases beyond certain limits, condenser cooling fans can be switched in to supplement the ram air effect. A safety switch is fitted in the high pressure side of most systems. It is often known as a high-low pressure switch, as it will switch off the compressor if the pressure is too high due to a component fault, or if the pressure is too low due to a leakage, thus protecting the compressor.

Figure 6.70 Basic principles of air conditioning

Compressor.

Plate fin evaporator.

Heating and ventilation unit.

Air conditioning unit.

Complete air conditioning system.

Figure 6.71 Heating ventilation and air condition\ing (HVAC) components

6.18.7 Automatic temperature control

Full temperature control systems provide a comfortable interior temperature in line with the passenger controlled input. The ECU has full control of fan speed, air distribution, air temperature, fresh or recirculated air and the air conditioning pump. These systems will soon be able to control automatic demist or defrost when reliable sensors are available. A single button currently will set the system to full defrost or demist.

A number of sensors are used to provide input to the ECU.

● Ambient temperature sensor mounted outside the vehicle to allow compensation for extreme temperature variations. This device is usually a thermistor.
● Solar light sensor mounted on the fascia panel. This device is a photodiode and allows a measurement of direct sunlight from which the ECU can determine whether to increase the air to the face vents.

● The in car temperature sensors are simple thermistors but to allow for an accurate reading a small motor and fan can be used to take a sample of interior air and direct it over the sensing elements.
● A coolant temperature sensor is used to monitor the temperature of the coolant supplied to the heater matrix. This sensor is used to prevent operation of the system until coolant temperature is high enough to heat the vehicle interior.
● Driver input control switches.

The ECU takes information from all of the above sources and will set the system in the most appropriate manner as determined by the software. Control of the flaps can be either by solenoid controlled vacuum actuators or by small motors. The main blower motor is controlled by a heavy-duty power transistor and is constantly variable. These systems are able to provide a comfortable interior temperature in exterior conditions ranging from -10 to +35°C even in extreme sunlight.

6.18.8 Seat heating

The concept of seat heating is very simple. A heating element is placed in the seat, together with an on-off switch and a control to regulate the heat. However the design of these heaters is more complex than first appears. The heater must meet the following criteria.

- The heater must only supply the heat loss experienced by the person's body.
- Heat is to be supplied only at the major contact points.
- Leather and fabric seats require different systems due to their different thermal properties.
- Heating elements must fit the design of the seat.
- The elements must pass the same rigorous tests as the seat, such as squirm, jounce and bump tests.

Figure 6.72 shows a seat containing heating elements.

In order for the passengers (including the driver) to be comfortable rigorous tests have been carried out to find the optimum heat settings and the best position for the heating elements. Many tests are carried out on new designs, using a manikin with sensors attached, to measure the temperature and heat flow.

The cable used for most heating elements consists of multi-strand alloyed copper. This cable may be coated with tin or insulated as the application demands. The heating element is laminated and bonded between layers of polyurethane foam.

6.18.9 Screen heating

Heating of the rear screen involves a very simple circuit as shown in Figure 6.73. The heating elements consist of a thin metallic strip bonded to the glass. When a current is passed through the elements, heat is generated and the window will defrost or demist. This circuit can draw high current, 10 to 15 A being typical. Because of this, the circuit will often contain a timer relay to prevent the heater being left on too long. The timer will switch off after 10 to 15 minutes. The elements are usually positioned to defrost the main area of the screen and the rest position of the rear wiper blade if fitted.

Front windscreen heating is being introduced on many vehicles. This of course presents more problems than the rear screen, as vision must not be obscured. The technology, drawn from the aircraft industry, involves very thin wires cast in to the glass. As with the heated rear window this device can consume a large current and is operated by a timer relay.

6.19 Diagnostics – HVAC

6.19.1 Testing procedure

> **Warning**
> Do not work on the refrigerant side of air conditioning systems unless you have been trained and have access to suitable equipment.

The process of checking an air conditioning system is broadly as follows.

Figure 6.72 Heated seat – great on a cold morning!

Figure 6.73 Screen heating circuit

Figure 6.74 Circuit voltage testing

1. Hand and eye checks (loose wires, loose switches and other obvious faults) – all connections clean and tight.
2. Check voltages on supply and earth cables (battery voltage and 0 V as in Figure 6.74).
3. Check system pressures.
4. Check discharge temperature.
5. Inspect receiver drier sight glass.
6. Inspect for signs of refrigerant leaks (oily deposits).
7. Refer to the next table.
8. Check sensors if fitted.
9. Check operation of compressor clutch.

6.19.2 Air conditioning fault diagnosis table

Symptom	Possible fault
After stopping the compressor, pressure falls quickly to about 195 kPa and then falls gradually	Air in the system or if no bubbles are seen in the sight glass as the condenser is cooled with water then excessive refrigerant may be the fault
Discharge pressure low	Fault with the compressor or, if bubbles are seen, low refrigerant
Discharge temperature is lower than normal	Frozen evaporator
Suction pressure too high	High pressure valve fault, excessive refrigerant or expansion valve open too long
Suction and discharge pressure too high	Excessive refrigerant in the system or condenser not workng due to fan fault or clogged fins
Suction and discharge pressure too low	Clogged or kinked pipes
Refrigerant loss	Oily marks (from the lubricant in the refrigerant) near joints or seals indicate leaks

6.19.3 Heating and ventilation fault diagnosis table

Symptom	Possible fault
Booster fan not operating at any speed	Open circuit fuse/supply/earth Motor inoperative/seized Dropping resistor(s) open circuit Switch open circuit Electronic speed controller not working
Booster fan only works on full speed	Dropping resistor(s) open circuit Switch open circuit Electronic speed controller not working
Control flap(s) will not move	Check vacuum connections (many work by vacuum operated actuators) Inspect cables
No hot air	Matrix blocked Blend flap stuck
No cold air	Blend flap stuck Blocked intake
Reduced temperature when set to 'hot'	Cooling system thermostat stuck open Heater matrix partially blocked Control flap not moving correctly

6.19.4 Air conditioning receiver drier sight glass

A very useful guide to diagnostics is the receiver drier sight glass. Figure 6.75 shows four possible symptoms and suggestions as to the possible fault.

Clear – system OK *or* completely empty

Foamy / bubbles – low on refrigerant and air in system

Streaky – Low on refrigerant and compressor oil circulation

Cloudy – Descicant in receiver dryer contaminating the system

Figure 6.75 Air conditioning receiver dryer sight glass

7
Engine management

7.1 Introduction

Engine management is a general term that describes the control of engine operation. This can range from a simple carburettor to control or manage the fuel, with an ignition distributor with contact breakers to control the ignition, to a very sophisticated electronic control system. The fundamental tasks of an engine management system are to manage the ignition and fuelling, as well as other aspects, and to refine the basic control of an engine.

Many of the procedures and explanations in this chapter are generic. In other words the ignition system explained in the next sections may be the same as the system used by a combined ignition and fuel control system.

7.2 Ignition

7.2.1 Basics

The purpose of the ignition system is to supply a spark inside the cylinder, near the end of the compression stroke, to ignite the compressed charge of air fuel vapour. For a spark to jump across an air gap of 0.6 mm under normal atmospheric conditions (1 bar) a voltage of 2 to 3 kV is required. For a spark to jump across a similar gap in an engine cylinder having a compression ratio of 8:1 approximately 8 kV is required. For higher compression ratios and weaker mixtures, a voltage up to 20 kV may be necessary. The ignition system has to transform the normal battery voltage of 12 V to approximately 8 to 20 kV and, in addition, has to deliver this high voltage to the right cylinder, at the right time. Some ignition systems will supply up to 40 kV to the spark plugs.

Conventional ignition is the forerunner of the more advanced systems controlled by electronics. However, the fundamental operation of most ignition systems is very similar; one wind-

ing of a coil is switched on and off causing a high voltage to be induced in a second winding. A coil ignition system is composed of various components and sub-assemblies; the actual design and construction of these depend mainly on the engine with which the system is to be used. The circuit of a contact breaker ignition system is shown in Figure 7.1.

7.2.2 Advance angle (timing)

For optimum efficiency the ignition advance angle should be such as to cause the maximum combustion pressure to occur about 10° after TDC. The ideal ignition timing is dependent on two main factors, engine speed and engine load. An increase in engine speed requires the ignition timing to be advanced. The cylinder charge, of air fuel mixture, requires a certain time to burn (normally about 2 ms). At higher engine speeds the time taken for the piston to travel the same distance reduces. Advancing the time of the spark ensures that full burning is achieved.

A change in timing due to engine load is also required as the weaker mixture used on low load conditions burns at a slower rate. In this situation further ignition advance is necessary. Greater load on the engine requires a richer mixture, which burns more rapidly. In this case some

Figure 7.1 Contact breaker ignition system

retardation of timing is necessary. Overall, under any condition of engine speed and load an ideal advance angle is required to ensure maximum pressure is achieved in the cylinder just after TDC. The ideal advance angle may also be determined by engine temperature and any risk of detonation.

Spark advance is achieved in a number of ways. The simplest of these is the mechanical system comprising a centrifugal advance mechanism and a vacuum (load sensitive) control unit. Manifold depression is almost inversely proportional to the engine load. I prefer to consider manifold pressure, albeit less than atmospheric pressure; the absolute manifold pressure (MAP) is proportional to engine load. Digital ignition systems may adjust the timing in relation to the temperature as well as speed and load. The values of all ignition timing functions are combined either mechanically or electronically in order to determine the ideal ignition point.

The energy storage takes place in the ignition coil. The energy is stored in the form of a magnetic field. To ensure that the coil is charged before the ignition point a dwell period is required. Ignition timing is at the end of the dwell period.

7.2.3 Electronic ignition

Electronic ignition is now fitted to almost all spark ignition vehicles. This is because the conventional mechanical system has some major disadvantages.

- Mechanical problems with the contact breakers not least of which is the limited lifetime.
- Current flow in the primary circuit is limited to about 4 A or damage will occur to the contacts – or at least the lifetime will be seriously reduced.
- Legislation requires stringent emission limits which means the ignition timing must stay in tune for a long period of time.
- Weaker mixtures require more energy from the spark to ensure successful ignition, even at very high engine speed.

These problems can be overcome by using a power transistor to carry out the switching function and a pulse generator to provide the timing signal. Very early forms of electronic ignition used the existing contact breakers as the signal provider. This was a step in the right direction but did not overcome all the mechanical limitations such as contact bounce and timing slip.

Most (all?) systems nowadays are constant energy ensuring high performance ignition even at high engine speed. Figure 7.2 shows the circuit of a standard electronic ignition system.

The term 'dwell' when applied to ignition is a measure of the time during which the ignition coil is charging, in other words when primary current is flowing. The dwell in conventional systems was simply the time during which the contact breakers were closed. This is now often expressed as a percentage of one charge-discharge cycle. Constant dwell electronic ignition systems have now been replaced almost without exception by constant energy systems discussed in the next section.

Whilst this was a very good system in its time, constant dwell still meant that at very high engine speeds, the time available to charge the coil could only produce a lower power spark. Note that as engine speed increases dwell angle or dwell percentage remains the same but the actual time is reduced.

In order for a constant energy electronic ignition system to operate the dwell must increase with engine speed. This will only be of benefit, however, if the ignition coil can be charged up to its full capacity, in a very short time (the time available for maximum dwell at the highest expected engine speed). To this end constant energy coils are very low resistance and low inductance. Typical resistance values are less than 1 Ω (often 0.5 Ω). Constant energy means that, within limits, the energy available to the spark plug remains constant under all operating conditions.

Due to the high energy nature of constant energy ignition coils, the coil cannot be allowed to remain switched on for more than a certain time. This is not a problem when the engine is running, as the variable dwell or current limiting circuit prevents the coil from overheating. Some

Figure 7.2 Electronic ignition system

form of protection must be provided, however, for when the ignition is switched on but the engine is not running. This is known as stationary engine primary current cut off.

7.2.4 Hall effect distributor

The Hall effect distributor has become very popular with many manufacturers. Figure 7.3 shows a typical example. As the central shaft of the distributor rotates, the chopper plate attached under the rotor arm alternately covers and uncovers the Hall chip. The number of vanes corresponds with the number of cylinders. In constant dwell systems the dwell is determined by the width of the vanes. The vanes cause the Hall chip to be alternately in and out of a magnetic field. The result of this is that the device will produce almost a square wave output, which can then easily be used to switch further electronic circuits.

The three terminals on the distributor are marked '+ 0 -'; the terminals + and - are for a voltage supply and terminal '0' is the output signal. Typically the output from a Hall effect sensor will switch between 0 V and about 8 V. The supply voltage is taken from the ignition ECU and on some systems is stabilised at about 10 V to prevent changes to the output of the sensor when the engine is being cranked.

Hall effect distributors are very common due to the accurate signal produced and long term reliability. They are suitable for use on both constant dwell and constant energy systems. Operation of a Hall effect pulse generator can easily be tested with a DC voltmeter or a logic probe. Note that tests must not be carried out using an ohmmeter as the voltage from the meter can damage the Hall chip.

7.2.5 Inductive distributor

Many forms of inductive type distributors exist and all are based around a coil of wire and a permanent magnet. The example distributor shown in Figure 7.4 has the coil of wire wound on the pick up and as the reluctor rotates the magnetic flux varies due to the peaks on the reluctor. The number of peaks or teeth on the reluctor corresponds to the number of engine cylinders. The gap between the reluctor and pick up can be important and manufacturers have recommended settings.

7.2.6 Current limiting and closed loop dwell

Primary current limiting ensures that no damage can be caused to the system by excessive primary current, but also forms a part of a constant energy system. The primary current is allowed to build up to its pre-set maximum as soon as possible and is then held at this value. The value of this current is calculated and then pre-set during construction of the amplifier module. This technique, when combined with dwell angle control, is known as closed loop control as the actual value of the primary current is fed back to the control stages.

A very low resistance, high power precision resistor is used in this circuit. The resistor is connected in series with the power transistor and the ignition coil. A voltage sensing circuit connected across this resistor will be activated at a pre-set

Figure 7.3 Ignition system with Hall generator

Distributor rotor

Magnet

Vanes

Air gap

Hall IC

Vane switch

3-core Hall generator lead

Ignition-distributor shaft

Carrying plate

Distributor housing

voltage (which is proportional to the current), and causes the output stage to hold the current at a constant value. Figure 7.5 shows a block diagram of a closed loop dwell control system.

Stationary current cut off is for when the ignition is on but the engine not running. This is achieved in many cases by a simple timer circuit, which will cut the output stage after about one second.

7.2.7 Programmed ignition

Programmed ignition is the term used by some manufacturers; others call it electronic spark advance (ESA). Constant energy electronic ignition was a major step forwards and is still used on countless applications. However, its limitations lay in still having to rely upon mechanical components for speed and load advance characteristics. In many cases these did not match ideally the requirements of the engine.

Programmed ignition systems have a major difference compared to earlier systems in that they operate digitally. Information about the operating requirements of a particular engine is programmed in to memory inside the ECU. The data for storage in ROM is obtained from rigorous testing on an engine dynamometer and further development work in the vehicle under various operating conditions. Programmed ignition has several advantages.

- The ignition timing can be accurately matched to the individual application under a range of operating conditions.
- Other control input can be utilised such as coolant temperature and ambient air temperature.

Figure 7.4 Inductive distributor

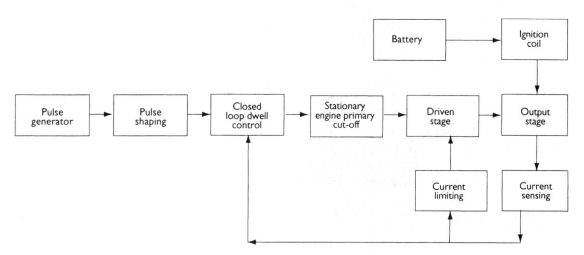

Figure 7.5 Closed loop dwell control system

- Starting is improved, fuel consumption is reduced as are emissions and idle control is better.
- Other inputs can be taken into account such as engine knock.
- The number of wearing components in the ignition system is considerably reduced.

Programmed ignition or ESA can be a separate system or included as part of the fuel control system. In order for the ECU to calculate suitable timing and dwell outputs, certain input information is required.

The crankshaft sensor consists of a permanent magnet, a winding and a soft iron core. It is mounted in proximity to a reluctor disc. The disc has 34 teeth spaced at 10° intervals around to periphery. It has two teeth missing 180° apart, at a known position BTDC. Many manufacturers use this technique with minor differences. As a tooth from the reluctor disc passes the core of the sensor the reluctance of the magnetic circuit is changed. This induces a voltage in the winding, the frequency of the waveform being proportional to the engine speed. The missing tooth causes a 'missed' output wave and hence engine position can be determined.

Engine load is proportional to manifold pressure in that high load conditions produce high pressure and lower load conditions, such as cruise, produce lower pressure. Load sensors are therefore pressure transducers. They are either mounted in the ECU or as a separate unit and are connected to the inlet manifold with a pipe. The pipe often incorporates a restriction to damp out fluctuations and a vapour trap to prevent petrol fumes reaching the sensor.

Coolant temperature measurement is carried out by a simple thermistor. In many cases the same sensor is used for the operation of the temperature gauge and to provide information to the fuel control system. A separate memory map is used to correct the basic timing settings. Timing may be retarded when the engine is cold to assist in more rapid warm up.

Combustion knock can cause serious damage to an engine if sustained for long periods. This knock or detonation is caused by over advanced ignition timing. At variance with this is that an engine in general will run at its most efficient when the timing is advanced as far as possible. To achieve this the data stored in the basic timing map will be as close to the knock limit of the engine as possible. The knock sensor provides a margin for error. The sensor itself is an accelerometer often of the piezoelectric type. It is fitted in the engine block between cylinders two and three on in-line four cylinder engines. Vee engine's require two sensors, one on each side. The ECU responds to signals from the knock sensor in the engine's knock window for each cylinder; this is often just a few degrees each side of TDC. This prevents clatter from the valve mechanism being interpreted as knock. The signal from the sensor is also filtered in the ECU to remove unwanted noise. If detonation is detected the ignition timing is retarded on the fourth ignition pulse after detection (four cylinder engine), in steps until knock is no longer detected. The steps vary between manufacturers but about 2° is typical. The timing is then advanced slowly in steps of say 1° over a number of engine revolutions, until the advance required by memory is restored. This fine control allows the engine to be run very close to the knock limit without risk of engine damage.

Correction to dwell settings is required if the battery voltage falls, as a lower voltage supply to the coil will require a slightly larger dwell figure. This information is often stored in the form of a dwell correction map.

As the sophistication of systems has increased the information held in the memory chips of the ECU has also increased. The earlier versions of programmed ignition system produced by Rover achieved accuracy in ignition timing of ± 1.8° whereas a conventional distributor is ± 8°. The information, which is derived from dynamometer tests as well as running tests in the vehicle, is stored in ROM. The basic timing map consists of the correct ignition advance for 16 engine speeds and 16 engine load conditions.

A separate three-dimensional map is used which has eight speed and eight temperature sites. This is used to add corrections for engine coolant temperature to the basic timing settings. This improves driveability and can be used to decrease the warm up time of the engine. The data is also subjected to an additional load correction below 70°C. Figure 7.6 shows a flow chart representing the logical selection of the optimum ignition setting. Note that the ECU will also make corrections to the dwell angle, both as a function of engine speed to provide constant energy output and due to changes in battery voltage. A lower battery voltage will require a slightly longer dwell and a higher voltage a slightly shorter dwell. A Windows® 95/98/2000 shareware program that simulates

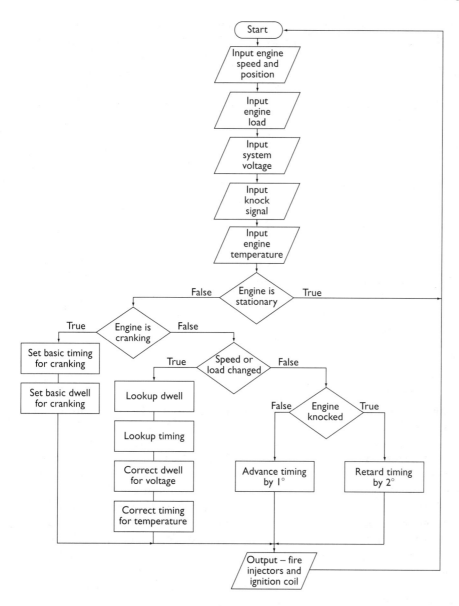

Figure 7.6 Ignition calculation flow diagram

the ignition system (as well as many other systems) is available for download from my web site.

The output of a system such as this programmed ignition is very simple. The output stage, in common with most electronic ignition, consists of a heavy-duty transistor which forms part of, or is driven by, a Darlington pair. This is simply to allow the high ignition primary current to be controlled. The switch off point of the coil will control ignition timing and the switch on point will control the dwell period.

The high tension distribution is similar to a more conventional system. The rotor arm, however, is mounted on the end of the camshaft with the distributor cap positioned over the top. Figure 7.7 shows a programmed ignition system.

7.2.8 Distributorless ignition

Distributorless ignition has all the features of programmed ignition systems but, by using a special type of ignition coil, outputs to the spark plugs without the need for an HT distributor. The system is generally only used on four cylinder engines as the control system becomes too complex for higher numbers. The basic principle is that of the 'lost spark'. The distribution of the spark is achieved by using double ended coils, which are fired alternately by the ECU. The timing is determined from a crankshaft speed and position sensor as well as load and other corrections. When one of the coils is fired a spark is delivered to two engine cylinders, either 1 and 4, or 2 and 3. The spark delivered to

Figure 7.7 Programmed ignition system component layout

the cylinder on the compression stroke will ignite the mixture as normal. The spark produced in the other cylinder will have no effect, as this cylinder will be just completing its exhaust stroke.

Because of the low compression and the exhaust gases in the 'lost spark' cylinder the voltage used for the spark to jump the gap is only about 3 kV. This is similar to the more conventional rotor arm to cap voltage. The spark produced in the compression cylinder is therefore not affected.

An interesting point here is that the spark on one of the cylinders will jump from the earth electrode to the spark plug centre. Many years ago this would not have been acceptable as the spark quality when jumping this way would not have been as good as when it jumps from the centre electrode. However, the energy available from modern constant energy systems will produce a spark of suitable quality in either direction.

The direct ignition system (DIS) consists of three main components, the electronic module, a crankshaft position sensor and the DIS coil. In many systems a MAP sensor is integrated in the module. The module functions in much the same way as has been described for the electronic spark advance system.

The crankshaft position sensor is similar in operation to the one described in the previous

section. It is again a reluctance sensor and is positioned against the front of the flywheel or against a reluctor wheel just behind the front crankshaft pulley. The tooth pattern consists of 35 teeth. These are spaced at 10° intervals with a gap where the 36th tooth would be. The missing tooth is positioned at 90° BTDC for numbers 1 and 4 cylinders. This reference position is placed a fixed number of degrees before TDC, in order to allow the timing or ignition point to be calculated as a fixed angle after the reference mark.

The low tension winding is supplied with battery voltage to a centre terminal. The appropriate half of the winding is then switched to earth in the module. The high tension windings are separate and are specific to cylinders 1 and 4, or 2 and 3. Figure 7.8 shows a typical DIS coil for a six cylinder engine.

7.2.9 Direct ignition

Direct ignition is in a way the follow on from distributorless ignition. This system utilises an inductive coil for each cylinder. These coils are mounted directly on the spark plugs. Figure 7.9 shows a cross section of the direct ignition coil. The use of an individual coil for each plug ensures that the rise time for the low inductance primary winding is very fast. This ensures that a very high voltage, high energy spark is produced. This voltage, which can be in excess of 40 kV,

Figure 7.8 DIS coil

Figure 7.9 Direct ignition system

provides efficient initiation of the combustion process under cold starting conditions and with weak mixtures. Some direct ignition systems use capacitor discharge ignition.

In order to switch the ignition coils igniter units are used. These can control up to three coils and are simply the power stages of the control unit but in a separate container. This allows less interference to be caused in the main ECU due to heavy current switching and shorter runs of wires carrying higher currents.

Ignition timing and dwell are controlled in a manner similar to the previously described programmed system. The one important addition to this on some systems is a camshaft sensor to provide information as to which cylinder is on the compression stroke. A system which does not

require a sensor to determine which cylinder is on compression (engine position is known from a crank sensor) determines the information by initially firing all of the coils. The voltage across the plugs allows measurement of the current for each spark and will indicate which cylinder is on its combustion stroke. This works because a burning mixture has a lower resistance. The cylinder with the highest current at this point will be the cylinder on the combustion stroke.

A further feature of some systems is the case when the engine is cranked over for an excessive time making flooding likely. The plugs are all fired with multisparks for a period of time after the ignition is left in the on position for five seconds. This will burn away any excess fuel.

During difficult starting conditions, multi-sparking is also used by some systems during 70° of crank rotation before TDC. This assists with starting and then once the engine is running, the timing will return to its normal calculated position.

7.2.10 Spark plugs

Figure 7.10 shows a standard spark plug. The centre electrode is connected to the top terminal by a stud. The electrode is constructed of a nickel based alloy. Silver and platinum are also used for some applications. If a copper core is used in the electrode this improves the thermal conduction properties.

The insulating material is ceramic based and of a very high grade. The electrically conductive glass seal between the electrode and terminal stud is also used as a resistor. This resistor has two functions: firstly to prevent burn off of the centre electrode; and secondly to reduce radio interference. In both cases the desired effect is achieved because the resistor damps the current at the instant of ignition.

Flashover or tracking down the outside of the plug insulation is prevented by ribs. These effectively increase the surface distance from the terminal to the metal fixing bolt, which is of course earthed to the engine.

Due to the many and varied constructional features involved in the design of an engine, the range of temperatures a spark plug is exposed to can vary significantly. The operating temperature of the centre electrode of a spark plug is critical. If the temperature becomes too high then pre-ignition may occur as the fuel air mixture may become ignited due to the incandescence of the plug electrode. On the other hand if

Terminal

Thread

Anti flashover

Insulator
aluminium oxide

Conductive
glass seal

Terminal
stud

Body

Washer
seal

Insulator tip
Centre electrode
Earth electrone

Figure 7.10 Construction of a typical spark plug

the electrode temperature is too low then carbon and oil fouling can occur, as deposits are not burnt off. Fouling of the plug nose can cause shunts (a circuit in parallel with the spark gap). It has been shown through experimentation and experience that the ideal operating temperature of the plug electrode is between 400 and 900°C.

The heat range of a spark plug then is a measure of its ability to transfer heat away from the centre electrode. A hot running engine will require plugs with a higher thermal loading ability than a colder running engine. Note that hot and cold running of an engine in this sense refers to the combustion temperature and not to the efficiency of the cooling system.

The following factors determine the thermal capacity of a spark plug.

● insulator nose length
● electrode material
● thread contact length
● projection of the electrode

It has been found that a longer projection of the electrode helps to reduce fouling problems due to low power operation, stop go driving and high altitude conditions. In order to use greater projection of the electrode better quality thermal conduction is required to allow suitable heat transfer at higher power outputs. Figure 7.11 shows the heat conducting paths of a spark plug together with changes in design for heat ranges. Also shown is the range of part numbers for NGK plugs.

For normal applications alloys of nickel are used for the electrode material. Chromium, manganese, silicon and magnesium are examples of the alloying constituents. These alloys exhibit excellent properties with respect to corrosion and burn off resistance. To improve on the thermal conductivity compound electrodes are used. This allows a greater nose projection for the same temperature range as discussed in the last section. A common example of this type of plug is the copper core spark plug.

Silver electrodes are used for specialist applications as silver has very good thermal and electrical properties. Again with these plugs nose length can be increased within the same temperature range. Platinum tips are used for some spark plug applications due to the very high burn off resistance of this material. It is also possible because of this to use much smaller diameter electrodes thus increasing mixture accessibility. Platinum also has a catalytic effect further accelerating the combustion process.

Spark plug electrode gaps in general have

BP 5 ES ← BP 6 ES → BP 7 ES

Low number hot type	**High number cold type**
A large area of the insulator nose is exposed to the combustion gases. The firing end heats up quickly.	A small area of the insulator nose is exposed to the combustion gases. The firing end heats up slowly.

Figure 7.11 'Hot' and 'Cold' spark plugs

increased as the power of the ignition systems driving the spark has increased. The simple relationship between plug gap and voltage required is that as the gap increases so must the voltage (leaving aside engine operating conditions). Further, the energy available to form a spark at a fixed engine speed is constant, which means that a larger gap using higher voltage will result in a shorter duration spark. A smaller gap will allow a longer duration spark. For cold starting an engine and for igniting weak mixtures the duration of the spark is critical. Likewise the plug gap must be as large as possible to allow easy access for the mixture to prevent quenching of the flame.

The final choice is therefore a compromise reached through testing and development of a particular application. Plug gaps in the region of 0.6 to 1.2 mm seem to be the norm at present.

7.3 Diagnostics – ignition systems

7.3.1 Testing procedure

Warning
Caution/Achtung/Attention – high voltages can seriously damage your health!

The following procedure is generic and with a little adaptation can be applied to any ignition system. Refer to manufacturer's recommendations if in any doubt.

1. Check battery state of charge (at least 70%).
2. Hand and eye checks (all connections secure and clean).
3. Check supply to ignition coil (within 0.5 V of battery).
4. Spark from coil via known good HT lead (jumps about 10 mm, but do not try a greater distance).
5. If good spark then check HT system for tracking and open circuits. Check plug condition (leads should be a maximum resistance of about 30 kΩ/m and per lead). Stop here in this procedure.
6. If there is no spark or it will only jump a short distance continue with this procedure (colour of spark is not relevant).
7. Check continuity of coil windings (primary 0.5 to 3 Ω, secondary several kΩ).

8. Supply and earth to 'module' (12 V minimum supply, earth drop 0.5 V maximum).
9. Supply to pulse generator if appropriate (10 to 12 V).
10. Output of pulse generator (inductive about 1 V AC when cranking, Hall type switches 0 V to 8 V DC).
11. Continuity of LT wires (0 to 0.1 Ω).
12. Replace 'module' but only if all tests above are satisfactory.

7.3.2 Ignition fault diagnosis table

Symptom	Possible fault
Engine rotates but does not start	Damp ignition components Spark plugs worn to excess Ignition system open circuit
Difficult to start when cold	Spark plugs worn to excess High resistance in ignition circuit
Engine starts but then stops immediately	Ignition wiring connection intermittent Ballast resistor open circuit (older cars)
Erratic idle	Incorrect plug gaps Incorrect ignition timing
Misfire at idle speed	Ignition coil or distributor cap tracking Spark plugs worn to excess Dwell incorrect (old systems)
Misfire through all speeds	Incorrect plugs or plug gaps HT leads breaking down Timing incorrect
Lack of power	Ignition timing incorrect HT components tracking
Backfires	Incorrect ignition timing Tracking
Runs on when switched off	Ignition timing incorrect Carbon buildup in engine Idle speed too high Anti-run on device inoperative
Pinking or knocking under load	Ignition timing incorrect Ignition system electronic fault Knock sensor not working

Figure 7.12 shows a typical ignition timing light, essential to ensure correct settings where these are adjustable, or to check programmed advance systems for correct operation.

Figure 7.12 Ignition timing light

7.3.3 Conventional ignition components and testing

Component	Description	Test method
Spark plug	Seals electrodes for the spark to jump across in the cylinder. Must withstand very high voltages, pressures and temperatures	Compare nose condition to a manufacturer's chart Inspect ignition secondary waveform when the engine is under load
Ignition coil	Stores energy in the form of magnetism and delivers it to the distributor via the HT lead Consists of primary and secondary windings	Resistance checks of the primary and secondary windings Primary: 1.5 Ω (ballasted) to 3 Ω Secondary: 5 to 10 kΩ
Ignition switch	Provides driver control of the ignition system and is usually also used to cause the starter to crank	Voltage drop across the contacts
Ballast resistor	Shorted out during the starting phase to cause a more powerful spark. Also contributes towards improving the spartk at higher speeds	Resistance (often about 1.5 Ω) or check voltage at coil supply (about 6 or 7 V when the contact breakers are closed)
Contact breakers (breaker points)	Switch the primary ignition circuit on and off to charge and discharge the coil	Volt drop across them should not exceed about 0.2 V General condition
Capacitor (condenser)	Suppresses most of the arcing as the contact breakers open. This allows for a more rapid break of primary current and hence a more rapid collapse of the coil magnetism, which produces a higher voltage output	Charge the capacitor up across a 12 V battery. Connect a digital meter and watch the voltage discharge from 12 V to almost 0 V over about five seconds
HT distributor	Directs the spark from the coil to each cylinder in a pre-set sequence	Visual inspection tracking (conducting lines) and contamination
Centrifugal advance	Changes the ignition timing with engine speed. As speed increases the timing is advanced	Measure the timing at certain speeds using an 'advance' timing light. Refer to data
Vacuum advance	Changes timing depending on engine load. On conventional systems the vacuum advance is most important during cruise conditions	Apply a known vacuum and note timing changes or often just sucking on the pipe and noting movement is adequate

7.3.4 DIS diagnostics

The DIS system is very reliable due to the lack of any moving parts. Some problems can be experienced when trying to examine HT oscilloscope patterns due to the lack of a king lead. This can often be overcome with a special adapter but it is still necessary to move the sensing clip to each lead in turn.

The DIS coil can be tested with an ohmmeter. The resistance of each primary winding should be 0.5 Ω and the secondary windings between 11 and 16 kΩ. The coil will produce in excess of 37 kV in an open circuit condition. The plug leads have integral retaining clips to prevent water ingress and vibration problems. The maximum resistance for the HT leads is 30 kΩ per lead.

No service adjustments are possible with this system with the exception of octane adjustment on some models. This involves connecting two pins together on the module for normal operation, or earthing one pin or the other to change to a different fuel. The actual procedure must be checked with the manufacturer for each particular model.

INTRODUCTION

The appearance of the firing-end of a spark plug graphically reflects the condition of an engine, the suitability of the spark plug heat range, and whether or not the carburettor and ignition timing are properly adjusted. This guide is intended to assist you in correctly choosing your spark plugs and determing the performance condition of your engine.

OPTIMUM PERFORMANCE TEMPERATURE RANGE

The firing and appearances 1-5 are considered to be good.

Good condition   Good condition

Good condition   Good condition

Good condition

Figure 7.13(a)

FOULING RANGE

Lower than the self-cleaning temperature of 400°C– 450°C (750°F – 850°F) Air-fuel mixture richer than 8.1 to 10.1

Wet Black Deposit

The firing-end of the spark plug becomes saturated with fuel and oil and its insulation ability deteriorates and misfiring occurs.

Recommendation
Check for non air/fuel mixture. Check the entire ignition system. If condition recurs, engine overhaul may be necessary.

Black Carbon Fouling

Carbon accumulates in large quantity and, while the firing-end of the plug is dry, its insulation is abnormally decreased. This, too, is regarded as a prime cause of misfiring.

Recommendation
Check for rich air/fuel mixture. Check the entire ignition system and cooling system (excessive cooling).

Carbon Fouled   Wet Fuel Fouled   Oil Fouled

When the firing end of a spark plug is fouled by carbon, wet fuel, as shown in photos 6, 7, and 8 respectively an electrical leakage path is formed and the insulation deteriorates, consequently the available voltage from the ignition system is lowered and a spark can not jump at the spark gap.

Causes of carbon fouling

1. Too rich fuel mixture.

2. Excessive use of choke.

3. Clogged air filter.

4. Deterioration of ignition system, such as breaker points, ignition coil or plug leads.

5. Incorrect spark gap.

6. Over-retarded ignition timing.

7. Compression loss due to imperfect cylinder-piston seal or valve seating.

8. Prolonged low speed driving or idling.

9. Too cold a spark plug fitted.

Causes of oil fouling

1. Lubricating oil entering into combustion chamber.

Figure 7.13(b)

PRE-IGNITION RANGE

Pre-ignition caused by a temperature exceeding 850°C – 1000°C (1600°F – 1800°F)

When a spark plug is overheated the insulator tip is glazed or glossy, accumulated deposits are melted or blistered and electrodes wear out quickly as shown in photos 9 and 10. When excessively overheated, pre-ignition occurs and the electrodes and insulator tip melt and piston damage may occur. Sometimes the insulator nose acn crack and fracture.

Causes of overheating

1. Over-advanced ignition timing
2. Too lean fuel mixture
3. Excessive deposits accumulated in combustion chamber
4. Insufficient cooling
5. Insufficient spark plug tightening or failure to fit gasket.
6. Too low cotane gasoline
7. Toohot a spark plug fitted.

Overheated   Melted

Overheated
The plug has been subjected to a realitively heavy load and evidence of overheating can be seen in the oxidized electrodes and melted deposits which have formed on the insulator surface.

Recommendation
Check for over-advanced ignition timing and too lean fuel mixture. Check spark plug tightening and gasket. If conditions recurs use plug one step colder in heat range.

Melted
Overheated plug with melted electrodes and blistered porcelain insulator surface.

Recommendation
Check for over-advanced ignition timing and too lean fuel mixture. Check spark plug tightening and gasket. If conditions recurs use plug one step colder in heat range.

Figure 7.13(c)

Normal life

A worn spark plug not only wastes fuel but also loads the whole ignition system because the expanded gap requires higher voltage.
As a result, a worn spark plug may also cause engine damage and increased exhaust emissions.

Recommendation
Spark plugs should be replaced.

Deposits

The accumulation of deposits on the firing end is influenced by oil leakage, fuel quality and engine operating period.

Recommendation
Check for excessive amounts of lubricating oil entering into the combustion chamber. High quality oil should be used.

Lead Fouling

Lead fouling usually appears as a yellowish brown deposit on the insulator nose and this cannot be detected on a resistance tester at room temperature. Lead compounds are combined at different temperatures formed at 370°C – 420°C (700°F – 790°F) having the greatest influence on resistance.

Recommendation
Use unleaded or low lead gasoline. Cleaning of spark plug is also helpful.

Figure 7.13(d)

Figure 7.13 Spark plug diagnostics

7.3.5 Spark plug diagnostics

Examination of the spark plugs is a good way of assessing engine and associated systems condition. Figure 7.13 is a useful guide as provided by NGK spark plugs.

7.3.6 Ignition waveform analysis

There are two main ignition waveforms.

- **Primary trace** picked up from the coil negative terminal.
- **Secondary trace** picked up from the main HT lead (or plug led for DIS).

However, it is possible to examine these waveforms in a number of ways. In particular changing the trigger, time base and voltage settings of the scope allows detailed examination of specific parts of the waveforms. Some further appropriate waveforms are also shown such as module signals and sensor outputs.

The following figures, together with appropriate notes, show the level of detailed diagnosis possible:

- ignition primary showing the dwell in ms (Figure 7.14);
- ignition primary showing the dwell in degrees (Figure 7.15);
- DIS primary (Figure 7.16);

- ignition secondary explained (Figure 7.17);
- ignition secondary parade (Figure 7.18);
- DIS secondary (Figure 7.19);
- spark voltages (Figure 7.20);
- spark line analysis (Figure 7.21);
- module signal (Figure 7.22);
- twin spark ignition system (Figure 7.23).

Figure 7.15 Waveform showing dwell in degrees

Figure 7.14 Waveform showing dwell in ms

Figure 7.16 Waveform showing primary DIS

Engine running at idle speed and at operating temperature. Burn time is from the firing line (15.6kV) to the oscillation after the line at 1.6kV. Look for this line to be broadly horizontal (constant voltage).

Figure 7.17 Waveform showing ignition secondary, single cylinder

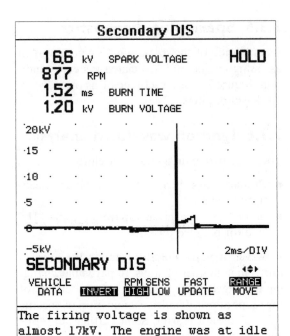

The firing voltage is shown as almost 17kV. The engine was at idle speed.

Figure 7.19 Waveform showing secondary DIS

Corvette Chevrolet V8 engine at idle speed and at normal operating temperature. Ignition peaks are displayed in firing order.

Figure 7.18 Waveform showing ignition secondary parade

Engine running at idle speed and at operating temperature. Ignition peaks (voltage to start the spark) are displayed in firing order.

Figure 7.20 Waveform showing ignition secondary parade

This trace shows the spark line or in other words the time for which the spark is burning. This trace shows that the burn lasts 1.7ms and is smooth - a sign of a good burn

Figure 7.21 Waveform showing secondary DIS spark line

Engine running at idle speed and at operating temperature. The dwell is indicated by the width of the positive pulse.

Figure 7.22 Waveform showing signal to an ignition module (trigger unit)

With a twin spark system, check that both spark plugs fire at the same time, the scope is used to display both primary ignition signals.

Figure 7.23 Waveform showing ignition primary, twin spark

7.4 Emissions

7.4.1 Introduction

The following table lists the four main exhaust emissions which are hazardous to health, together with a short description of each.

Substance	Description
Carbon monoxide (CO)	This gas is very dangerous even in low concentrations. It has no smell or taste and is colourless. When inhaled it combines in the body with the red blood cells preventing them from carrying oxygen. If absorbed by the body it can be fatal in a very short time
Nitrogen oxides (NOx)	Oxides of nitrogen are colourless and odourless when they leave the engine but as soon as they reach the atmosphere and mix with more oxygen, nitrogen oxides are formed. They are reddish brown and have an acrid and pungent smell. These gasses damage the body's respiratory system when inhaled. When combined with water vapour nitric acid can be formed which is very damaging to the windpipe and lungs. Nitrogen oxides are also a contributing factor to acid rain

Hydrocarbons (HC)	A number of different hydrocarbons are emitted from an engine and are part or unburnt fuel. When they mix with the atmosphere they can help to form smog. It is also believed that hydrocarbons may be carcinogenic
Particulate matter (PM)	This heading in the main covers lead and carbon. Lead was traditionally added to petrol to slow its burning rate to reduce detonation. It is detrimental to health and is thought to cause brain damage especially in children. Lead will eventually be phased out as all new engines now run on unleaded fuel. Particles of soot or carbon are more of a problem on diesel fuelled vehicles and these now have limits set by legislation

The following table describes two further sources of emissions from a vehicle.

Source	Comments
Fuel evaporation from the tank and system	Fuel evaporation causes hydrocarbons to be produced. The effect is greater as temperature increases. A charcoal canister is the preferred method for reducing this problem. The fuel tank is usually run at a pressure just under atmospheric by a connection to the intake manifold drawing the vapour through the charcoal canister. This must be controlled by the management system, however, as even a 1% concentration of fuel vapour would shift the lambda value by 20%. This is done by using a 'purge valve', which under some conditions is closed (full load and idle for example) and can be progressively opened under other conditions. The system monitors the effect by use of the lambda sensor signal
Crankcase fumes (blow by)	Hydrocarbons become concentrated in the crankcase mostly due to pressure blowing past the piston rings. These gases must be conducted back into the combustion process. This is usually via the air intake system. This is described as positive crankcase ventilation

7.4.2 Exhaust gas recirculation (EGR)

This technique is used primarily to reduce peak combustion temperatures and hence the production of nitrogen oxides (NOx). EGR can be either internal due to valve overlap, or external via a simple arrangement of pipes and a valve (Figure 7.24 shows an example) connecting the exhaust manifold back to the inlet manifold. A proportion of exhaust gas is simply returned to the inlet side of the engine.

This process is controlled electronically as determined by a ROM in the ECU. This ensures that driveability is not effected and also that the rate of EGR is controlled. If the rate is too high, then the production of hydrocarbons increases.

One drawback of EGR systems is that they can become restricted by exhaust residue over a period of time thus changing the actual percentage of recirculation. However, valves are now available that reduce this particular problem.

7.4.3 Catalytic converters

Stringent regulations in most parts of the world have made the use of a catalytic converter almost indispensable. The three-way catalyst (TWC) is used to great effect by most manufacturers. It is a very simple device and looks similar to a standard exhaust box. Note that in order to operate correctly, however, the engine must be run at or very near to stoichiometry. This is to ensure that the right 'ingredients' are available for the catalyst to perform its function.

Figure 7.25 shows some new metallic substrates for use inside a catalytic converter. There are many types of hydrocarbons but the example illustrates the main reaction. Note that the reactions rely on some CO being produced by the engine in order to reduce the NOx. This is one of the reasons that manufacturers have been forced to run the engine at stoichiometry. The legislation has tended to stifle the development of lean burn techniques. The fine details of the emission regulations can in fact have a very marked effect on the type of reduction techniques used. The main reactions in the 'cat' are as follows:

Figure 7.24 EGR valve

Figure 7.25 Catalytic converter metallic substrates

- $2CO + O_2 \rightarrow 2CO_2$
- $2C_2H_6 + 2CO \rightarrow 4CO_2 + 6H_2O$
- $2NO + 2CO \rightarrow N_2 + 2CO_2$

Noble metals are used for the catalysts; platinum promotes the oxidation of HC and CO, and rhodium helps the reduction of NOx. The whole three-way catalytic converter only contains about three to four grams of the precious metals.

The ideal operating temperature range is from about 400 to 800°C. A serious problem to counter is the delay in the catalyst reaching this temperature. This is known as catalyst light off time. Various methods have been used to reduce this time as significant emissions are produced before light off occurs. Electrical heating is one solution, as is a form of burner which involves lighting fuel inside the converter. Another possibility is positioning the converter as part of the exhaust manifold and down pipe assembly. This greatly reduces light off time but gas flow problems, vibration and excessive temperature variations can be problems that reduce the potential life of the unit.

Catalytic converters can be damaged in two ways. The first is by the use of leaded fuel which causes lead compounds to be deposited on the active surfaces thus reducing effective area. The second is engine misfire which can cause the catalytic converter to overheat due to burning inside the unit. BMW, for example, use a system on some vehicles where a sensor monitors output of the ignition HT system and will not allow fuel to be injected if the spark is not present.

For a catalytic converter to operate at its optimum conversion rate to oxidise CO and HC whilst reducing NOx, a narrow band within 0.5% of lambda value 1 is essential. Lambda sensors in use at present tend to operate within about 3% of the lambda mean value. When a catalytic converter is in prime condition this is not a problem due to storage capacity within the converter for CO and O_2. Damaged converters, however, cannot store sufficient quantity of these gases and hence become less efficient. The damage as suggested earlier in this section can be due to overheating or by 'poisoning' due to lead or even silicon. If the control can be kept within 0.5% of lambda the converter will continue to be effective even if damaged to some extent. Sensors are becoming available which can work to this tolerance. A second sensor fitted after the converter can be used to ensure ideal operation.

7.5 Diagnostics – emissions

7.5.1 Testing procedure

If the reported fault is incorrect exhaust emissions the following procedure should be utilised.

1. Hand and eye checks – look for the obvious such as blocked filters.
2. Run the vehicle up to temperature by road testing – note any unusual conditions.
3. Connect revcounter.
4. Connect exhaust analyser.
5. Using the throttle pedal, hold the engine speed at about 3000 rev/min for 30 seconds.

6. Allow the engine to idle and check idle speed – continue if OK or investigate further.
7. Take gas readings when stable (usually after just a few seconds).
8. Compare with manufacturer's recommended settings.
9. Adjust as required and then go back to step 5 *or* investigate the engine management system further.

Figure 7.26 is typical of the emissions data available.

7.5.2 Emissions fault diagnosis table

Symptom	Possible cause
EGR valve sticking	Buildup of carbon
	Electrical fault
High CO and high HC	Rich mixture
	Blocked air filter
	Damaged catalytic converter
	Engine management system fault
Low CO and high HC	Misfire
	Fouled plug(s)
	Weak mixture
Low CO and low or normal HC	Exhaust leak
	Fouled injector

7.6 Fuel injection

7.6.1 Introduction

The ideal air fuel ratio is about 14.7:1. This is the theoretical amount of air required to completely burn the fuel. It is given a 'lambda (λ)' value of 1.

$$\lambda = \text{actual air quantity} \div \text{theoretical air quantity}$$

Air fuel ratio is altered during the following operating conditions of an engine to improve its performance, driveability, consumption and emissions:

- **cold starting** richer mixture is needed to compensate for fuel condensation and improve driveability;
- **load or acceleration** richer to improve performance;
- **cruise or light loads** weaker for economy;
- **overrun** very weak (if any) fuel, to improve emissions and economy.

The more accurately the air fuel ratio is controlled to cater for external conditions, then the better the overall operation of the engine.

The major advantage, therefore, of a fuel injection system is accurate control of the fuel quantity injected into the engine. The basic principle of fuel injection is that if petrol is supplied to an injector (electrically controlled valve), at a constant differential pressure, then the amount of fuel injected will be directly proportional to the injector open time.

Most systems are now electronically controlled even if containing some mechanical metering components. This allows the operation of the injection system to be very closely matched to the requirements of the engine. This matching process is carried out during development on test beds and dynamometers, as well as development in the car. The ideal operating data for a large number of engine operating conditions is stored in a ROM in the ECU. Close control of fuel quantity injected allows the optimum setting for mixture strength when all operating factors are taken into account.

Further advantages of electronic fuel injection control are that overrun cut off can easily be implemented, fuel can be cut at the engines rev

Mazda 626 2.0i GX 16 valve — 1996–1997

Adjustment Data (Fuel)

DESCRIPTION	SETTING	UNITS
Carburettor/injection make	Mazda	
Carburettor/injection type	MPi	
Fuel pump pressure	5.10 ± 0.70	bar
Injection pressure	1.50	bar
Idle speed	700 ± 50	rev/min
Raised idle speed	Not applicable	rev/min
CO at idle speed	0.50 maximum	%
carbon dioxide at idle speed	14.50/16.00	%
HC at idle speed	100	ppm
Oxygen at idle speed	0.10/0.50	%

Figure 7.26 Typical emissions data (Autologic CD)

Figure 7.27 LH-Jetronic fuel injection

Figure 7.28 Petrol injection systems.

limit and information on fuel used can be supplied to a trip computer. Figure 7.27 shows a typical fuel injection system layout for LH-Jetronic.

7.6.2 Injection systems

Fuel injection systems can be classified into two main categories, single point injection and multipoint injection. Figure 7.28 shows these techniques together with a third known as continuous injection (K/KE Jetronic). Depending on the sophistication of the system, idle speed and idle mixture adjustment can be either mechanically or electronically controlled.

Figure 7.29 shows a block diagram of inputs and outputs common to most fuel injection systems. Note that the two most important input sensors to the system are speed and load. The basic fuelling requirement is determined from these inputs in a similar way to the determination of ignition timing.

Figure 7.29 Fuel injection system block diagram

An engine's fuelling requirements are stored as part of a ROM chip in the ECU. When the ECU has determined the 'look up value' of the fuel required (injector open time), corrections to this figure can be added for battery voltage, temperature, throttle change or position and fuel cut off. Figure 7.30 shows an injection system ECU.

Idle speed and fast idle are also generally controlled by the ECU and a suitable actuator. It is also possible to have a form of closed loop control with electronic fuel injection. This involves a lambda sensor to monitor exhaust gas oxygen content. This allows very accurate control of the mixture strength, as the oxygen content of the exhaust is proportional to the air fuel ratio. The signal from the lambda sensor is used to adjust the injector open time.

7.6.3 Fuel injection components

Many of the sensors and actuators associated with fuel injection are covered in Chapter 5. Figure 7.31 shows those associated with the LH-Jetronic injection system. Starting at the top left and working clockwise the components are as follows.

Figure 7.30 Engine management ECU

Air flow meter

The type shown is a hot-wire meter. This allows direct measurement of air mass as temperature compensation is built in. The air quantity helps to determine the fuel required.

Electronic control unit (ECU)

This is also referred to as the electronic control module (ECM). The circuitry to react to the sensor signals by controlling the actuators is in the ECU. The data is stored in ROM.

Fuel pump

Pressurised fuel is supplied to the injectors. Most pumps work on the centrifugal roller principle. The pump ensures a constant supply of fuel to the fuel rail. The volume in the rail acts as a swamp to prevent pressure fluctuations as the injectors operate. The pump must be able to maintain a pressure of about 3 bar.

Fuel filter

The fuel supplied to the injectors must be free from any contamination or else the injector nozzle will be damaged or blocked.

Lambda sensor

The quantity of oxygen in the exhaust, when accurately measured, ensures that the fuel air mixture is kept within the lambda window (0.97 to 1.03).

Temperature sensor

A simple thermistor is used to determine the engine coolant temperature.

Fuel injectors

These are simple solenoid operated valves designed to operate very quickly and produce a finely atomised spray pattern.

Figure 7.31 Fuel injection components

Idle or fast idle control actuator

The rotary actuator is shown here. It is used to provide extra air for cold fast idle conditions as well as controlling idle speed. It is supplied with a variable duty cycle square wave.

Fuel pressure regulator

This device is to ensure a constant differential pressure across the injectors. It is a mechanical device and has a connection to the inlet manifold.

Throttle position switch

This is used to supply information as the whether the throttle is at idle, full load or somewhere in between.

7.6.4 Fuel mixture calculation

The quantity of fuel to be injected is determined primarily by the quantity of air drawn into the engine. This is dependent on two factors:

● engine speed (rev/min);
● engine load (inlet manifold pressure).

This speed load characteristic is held in the ECU memory in ROM lookup tables.

A sensor connected to the manifold by a pipe senses manifold absolute pressure. The sensor is fed with a stabilised 5 V supply and transmits an output voltage according to the pressure. The sensor is fitted away from the manifold and hence a pipe is required to connect it. The output signal varies between about 0.25 V at 0.17 bar to about 4.75 V at 1.05 bar. The density of air varies with temperature such that the information from the MAP sensor on air quantity will be incorrect over wide temperature variations. An air temperature sensor is used to inform the ECU of the inlet air temperature such that the the quantity of fuel injected may be corrected. As the temperature of air decreases its density increases and hence the quantity of fuel injected must also be increased. The other method of sensing engine load is direct measurement of air intake quantity using a hot-wire meter or a flap type air flow meter.

In order to operate the injectors the ECU needs to know, in addition to air pressure, the engine speed to determine the injection quantity. The same flywheel sensor used by the ignition system provides this information. All four injectors operate simultaneously once per engine revolution, injecting half of the required fuel. This

helps to ensure balanced combustion. The start of injection varies according to ignition timing.

A basic open period for the injectors is determined by using the ROM information relating to manifold pressure and engine speed. Two corrections are then made, one relative to air temperature and another depending on whether the engine is idling, at full or partial load.

The ECU then carries out another group of corrections, if applicable:

● after start enrichment;
● operational enrichment;
● acceleration enrichment;
● weakening on deceleration;
● cut off on overrun;
● reinstatement of injection after cut off;
● correction for battery voltage variation.

Under starting conditions the injection period is calculated differently. This is determined mostly from a set figure varied as a function of temperature.

The coolant temperature sensor is a thermistor and is used to provide a signal to the ECU relating to engine coolant temperature. The ECU can then calculate any corrections to fuel injection and ignition timing. The operation of this sensor is the same as the air temperature sensor.

The throttle potentiometer is fixed on the throttle butterfly spindle and informs the ECU of throttle position and rate of change of throttle position. The sensor provides information on acceleration, deceleration and whether the throttle is in the full load or idle position. It comprises a variable resistance and a fixed resistance. As is common with many sensors a fixed supply of 5 V is provided and the return signal will vary approximately between 0 and 5 V. The voltage increases as the throttle is opened.

7.7 Diagnostics – fuel injection systems

7.7.1 Testing procedure

Warning
Caution/Achtung/Attention – burning fuel can seriously damage your health!

The following procedure is generic and with a little adaptation can be applied to any fuel injection system. Refer to manufacturer's recommendations if in any doubt. It is assumed that the ignition system is operating correctly. Most tests are carried out while cranking the engine.

1. Check battery state of charge (at least 70%).
2. Hand and eye checks (all fuel and electrical connections secure and clean).
3. Check diagnostic fault codes if available.
4. Check fuel pressure supplied to rail (multi-point systems it will be about 2.5 bar but check specifications). If the pressure is *not* correct jump to stage 10.
5. Is injector operation OK – Continue if *not* (suitable spray pattern or dwell reading across injector supply).
6. Check supply circuits from main relay (battery volts minimum).
7. Continuity of injector wiring (0 to 0.2 Ω and note that many injectors are connected in parallel).
8. Sensor readings and continuity of wiring (0 to 0.2 Ω for the wiring sensors will vary with type).
9. If no fuel is being injected and all tests so far are OK (suspect ECU).
10. Fuel supply – from stage 4.
11. Supply voltage to pump (within 0.5 V battery – pump fault if supply is OK).
12. Check pump relay and circuit (note in most cases the ECU closes the relay but this may be bypassed on cranking).
13. Ensure that all connections (electrical and fuel) are remade correctly – return to test 5 if necessary.

7.7.2 Fuel injection fault diagnosis table

Symptom	Possible fault
Engine rotates but does not start	No fuel in the tank!
	Air filter dirty or blocked
	Fuel pump not running
	No fuel being injected
Difficult to start when cold	Air filter dirty or blocked
	Fuel system wiring fault
	Enrichment device not working
	Coolant temperature sensor short circuit
Difficult to start when hot	Air filter dirty or blocked
	Fuel system wiring fault
	Coolant temperature sensor open circuit
Engine starts but then stops immediately	Fuel system contamination
	Fuel pump or circuit fault (relay)
	Intake system air leak
Erratic idle	Air filter blocked
	Inlet system air leak
	Incorrect CO setting
	Idle air control valve not operating
	Fuel injectors not spraying correctly
Misfire through all speeds	Fuel filter blocked
	Fuel pump delivery low
	Fuel tank ventilation system blocked
Engine stalls	Idle speed incorrect
	CO setting incorrect
	Fuel filter blocked
	Air filter blocked
	Intake air leak
	Idle control system not working
Lack of power	Fuel filter blocked
	Air filter blocked
	Low fuel pump delivery
	Fuel injectors blocked
Backfires	Fuel system fault (air flow sensor on some cars)
	Ignition timing

7.8 Diesel injection

7.8.1 Introduction

The basic principle of the four stroke diesel engine is very similar to the petrol system. The main difference is that the mixture formation takes place in the cylinder combustion chamber as the fuel is injected under very high pressure. The timing and quantity of the fuel injected is important from the usual issues of performance, economy and emissions.

Fuel is metered into the combustion chamber by way of a high pressure pump connected to injectors via heavy duty pipes. When the fuel is injected it mixes with the air in the cylinder and will self ignite at about 800°C. The mixture formation in the cylinder is influenced by the following factors.

The timing of a diesel fuel injection pump to an engine is usually done using start of delivery as the reference mark. The actual start of injection, in other words when fuel starts to leave the injector, is slightly later than start of delivery, as this is influenced by the compression ratio of the engine, the compressibility of the fuel and the length of the delivery pipes. This timing has a great effect on the production of carbon particles (soot), if too early, and increases the hydrocarbon emissions, if too late.

The duration of the injection is expressed in degrees of crankshaft rotation in milliseconds. This clearly influences fuel quantity but the rate of discharge is also important. This rate is not constant due to the mechanical characteristics of the injection pump.

Pressure of injection will affect the quantity of fuel but the most important issue here is the effect on atomisation. At higher pressures the fuel will atomise into smaller droplets with a corresponding improvement in the burn quality. Indirect injection systems use pressures up to about 350 bar and direct injection systems can be up to about 1000 bar. Emissions of soot are greatly reduced by higher pressure injection.

The direction of injection must match very closely the swirl and combustion chamber design. Deviations of only 2° from the ideal can greatly increase particulate emissions.

Diesel engines do not in general use a throttle butterfly as the throttle acts directly on the injection pump to control fuel quantity. At low speeds in particular the very high excess air factor ensures complete burning and very low emissions. Diesel engines operate where possible with an excess air factor even at high speeds.

Figure 7.32 shows a typical diesel fuel injection system. Detailed operation of the components is beyond the scope of this book. The principles and problems are the issues under consideration, in particular the way electronics can be employed to solve some of the problems.

7.8.2 Electronic control of diesel injection

The advent of electronic control over the diesel injection pump has allowed many advances over the purely mechanical system. The production of high pressure and injection is, however, still mechanical with all current systems. The following advantages are apparent over the non-electronic control system:

- more precise control of fuel quantity injected;
- better control of start of injection;
- idle speed control;
- control of exhaust gas recirculation;
- drive by wire system (potentiometer on throttle pedal);
- an anti-surge function;
- output to data acquisition systems, etc.;
- temperature compensation;
- cruise control.

Figure 7.33 shows a distributor type injection pump used with electronic control together with the ECU and injectors. Because fuel must be injected at high pressure the hydraulic head, pressure pump and drive elements are still used. An electromagnetic moving iron actuator adjusts the position of the control collar, which in turn controls the delivery stroke and therefore the injected quantity of fuel. Fuel pressure is applied to a roller ring and this controls the start of injection. A solenoid operated valve controls the supply to the roller ring. These actuators together allow control of start of injection and injection quantity.

1 Fuel tank, 2 Fuel line, 3 Fuel filter,
4 Distributor type fuel injection pump,
5 Pressure line, 6 Injection nozzle,
7 Fuel return line

Figure 7.32 Fuel injection system with distributor type pump

Figure 7.33 Distributor type injection pump with electronic control

Ideal values for fuel quantity and timing are stored in memory maps in the ECU. The injected fuel quantity is calculated from the accelerator position and the engine speed. Start of injection is determined from the following:

- fuel quantity;
- engine speed;
- engine temperature;
- air pressure.

The ECU is able to compare start of injection with actual delivery from a signal produced by the needle motion sensor in the injector.

Control of exhaust gas recirculation is a simple solenoid valve. This is controlled as a function of engine speed, temperature and injected quantity. The ECU is also in control of the stop solenoid and glow plugs via a suitable relay.

7.8.3 Diesel exhaust emissions

Exhaust emissions from diesel engines have been reduced considerably by changes in the design of combustion chambers and injection techniques. More accurate control of start of injection and spill timing has allowed further improvements to be made. Electronic control has also made a significant contribution. A number of further techniques can be employed to control emissions.

Overall the emissions from diesel combustion are far lower than emission from petrol combustion. The CO, HC and NOx emissions are lower mainly due to the higher compression ratio and excess air factor. The higher compression ratio improves the thermal efficiency and thus lowers the fuel consumption. The excess air factor ensures more complete burning of the fuel.

The main problem area is that of particulate emissions. These particle chains of carbon molecules can also contain hydrocarbons, aldehydes mostly. The dirt effect of this emission is a pollution problem but the possible carcinogenic effect of this soot gives cause for concern. The diameter of these particles is only a few ten thousandths of a millimetre. This means they float in the air and can be inhaled.

In much the same way as with petrol engines EGR is employed primarily to reduce NOx emissions by reducing the reaction temperature in the combustion chamber. However if the percentage of EGR is too high, increased hydrocarbons and soot are produced. This is appropriate to turbocharged engines such that if the air is passed through an intercooler, as well as improvements in volumetric efficiency, lower

temperature will again reduce the production of NOx. The intercooler is fitted in the same are as the cooling system radiator.

7.8.4 Catalytic converter – diesel

On a diesel engine a catalyst can be used to reduce the emission of hydrocarbons but will have less effect on nitrogen oxides. This is because diesels are always run with excess air to ensure better and more efficient burning of the fuel. A normal catalyst therefore will not strip the oxygen off the NO_x to oxidise the hydrocarbons because the excess oxygen will be used. Special NO_x converters are becoming available.

7.8.5 Filters

To reduce the emission of particulate matter (soot), filters can be used. These can vary from a fine grid design made from a ceramic material to centrifugal filters and water trap techniques. The problem to overcome is that the filters can get blocked, which adversely affects the overall performance. Several techniques are employed including centrifugal filters.

7.9 Diagnostics – diesel injection systems

7.9.1 Test equipment

Note: You should always refer to the manufacturer's instructions appropriate to the equipment you are using.

Smoke meter (Figure 7.34)

This is an essential device in the UK and other countries where the level of smoke in the exhaust forms part of the annual test. Most devices use infrared light to 'count' the number of soot

Figure 7.34 Smoke meter

particles in the exhaust sample. This particulate matter (PM) is highly suspected of being carcinogenic.

Injector tester (Figure 7.35)

The pressure required to 'crack' (lift the nozzle) on an injector can be tested.

7.9.2 Diesel injection fault diagnosis table

Symptom	Possible fault
Engine rotates but does not start	No fuel in the tank! Cam belt broken Fuel pump drive broken Open circuit supply to stop solenoid Fuel filter blocked
Excessive smoke	Refer to the next section
Lack of power	Timing incorrect Governor set too low Injector nozzles worn Injector operating pressure incorrect
Difficult to start	Timing incorrect Glow plugs not working
Fuel smell in the car	Fuel lines leaking Leak off pipes broken
Diesel knock (particularly when cold)	Timing incorrect Glow plug hold on for idle circuit not working
Engine oil contaminated with fuel	Piston broke (like me after a good holiday!) Worn piston rings Excessive fuel injected

Figure 7.35 Diesel injector tester

7.9.3 Diesel engine smoke

Diesel fuel is a hydrocarbon fuel. When it is burned in the cylinder it will produce carbon dioxide and water. There are, however, many circumstances under which the fuel may not be completely burned and one of the results is smoke. Despite the fact that diesel engines are designed to run under all conditions with an excess of air, problems still occur. Very often these smoke problems are easily avoided by proper maintenance and servicing of the engine and its fuel system. The emission of smoke is usually due to a shortage of air (oxygen). If insufficient air is available for complete combustion then unburnt fuel will be exhausted as tiny particles of fuel (smoke).

The identification of the colour of diesel smoke and under what conditions it occurs can be helpful in diagnosing what caused it in the first place. Poor quality fuel reduces engine performance, increases smoke and reduces engine life. There are three colours of smoke; white, blue and black. All smoke diagnosis tests must be carried out with the engine at normal operating temperature.

White or grey smoke

White smoke is vaporised unburnt fuel and is caused by there being sufficient heat in the cylinder to vaporise it but not enough remaining heat to burn it. All diesel engines generate white smoke when starting from cold and it is not detrimental to the engine in any way – it is a diesel characteristic. Possible causes of white smoke are listed below.

- **Faulty cold starting equipment** Cold engines suffer from a delay in the combustion process. A cold start unit is fitted to advance the injection timing to counteract this delay. This means that white smoke could be a cold start unit problem.
- **Restrictions in the air supply** a partially blocked air cleaner will restrict the air supply; an easy cause to rectify but often overlooked. Incidentally, a blocked air cleaner element at light load in the workshop becomes a black smoke problem when the engine is under load. In both cases there will not be sufficient air entering the cylinder for the piston to compress and generate full heat for combustion.
- **Cold running** check the cooling system thermostat to see if the correct rated thermostat is fitted.

- **Incorrect fuel injection pump timing** if fuel is injected late (retarded timing) it may be vaporised but not burned.
- **Poor compressions** poor compressions may lead to leakage during the compression stroke and inevitably less heat would be generated.
- **Leaking cylinder head gasket** if coolant were leaking into the combustion area, the result would be less temperature in the cylinder causing white smoke. Steam may also be generated if the leak is sufficient. All internal combustion engines have water as a by-products from burning fuel – you will have noticed your own car exhaust, especially on a cold morning.

Blue smoke

Blue smoke is almost certainly a lubricating oil burning problem. Possible causes of blue smoke are listed:

- incorrect grade of lubricating oil;
- worn or damaged valve stem oil seals, valve guides or stems where lubricating oil is getting into the combustion chamber;
- worn or sticking piston rings;
- worn cylinder bores.

Black smoke

Black smoke is partly burned fuel. Possible causes are listed below.

- **Restriction in air intake system** a blocked air cleaner element will not let enough air in to burn all the fuel.
- **Incorrect valve clearances** excessive valve clearances will cause the valves not to fully open and to close sooner. This is another form of insufficient air supply.
- **Poor compressions** air required for combustion may leak from the cylinder.
- **Defective or incorrect injectors** check the injector to see if the spray is fully atomised and solid fuel is not being injected.
- **Incorrect fuel injection pump timing** this is less likely because the timing would need to be advanced to the point where additional engine noise would be evident.
- **Low boost pressure** if a turbocharger is fitted and is not supplying enough air for the fuel injected this is another form of air starvation.

7.9.4 Glow plug circuit

Figure 7.36 shows a typical glow plug circuit controlled by an ECU. Most timer circuits put

Figure 7.36 Glow plug circuit

the glow plugs on for a few seconds prior to cranking. A warning light may be used to indicate the 'ready' condition to the driver. Take care to note the type of glow plugs used; most are 12 V and connected in parallel but some are connected in series (4 × 3 V plugs) To check the operation of most 12 V glow plug circuits, use the following steps.

1. Hand and eye checks.
2. Battery condition – at least 70%.
3. Engine must be cold – it may be possible to simulate this by disconnecting the temperature sensor.
4. Voltage supplied to plugs when ignition is switched on (spring loaded position in some cases) – 10 to 12 V.
5. Warning light operation – should go out after a few seconds.
6. Voltage supplied to plugs while cranking – 9 to 11 V.
7. Voltage supplied to plugs after engine has started – 0 V or if silent idle system is used 5 to 6 V for several minutes.
8. Same tests with engine at running temperature – glow plugs may not be energised or only for the starting phase.

7.9.5 Diesel systems

It is recommended that when the injection pump or the injectors are diagnosed as being at fault, reconditioned units should be fitted. Other than basic settings of timing, idle speed and governor speed, major overhaul is often required. Figure 7.37 shows a general diagnosis pattern for diesel systems produced by 'Autologic'.

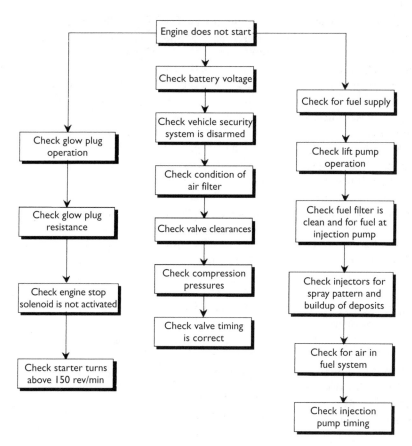

Figure 7.37 General diagnosis pattern

7.10 Combined injection and fuel control

7.10.1 Introduction

As the requirement for lower and lower emissions continues together with the need for better performance, other areas of engine control are constantly being investigated. This is becoming even more important as the possibility of carbon dioxide emissions being included in the regulations increases. Some of the current and potential areas for further control of engine operation are included in this section. Most of the common areas of 'control' have been covered under either Ignition (Section 7.2) or Fuel injection (Section 7.6). The main areas of control are as follows:

- ignition timing;
- dwell angle;
- fuel quantity;
- idle speed.

Further areas of engine control may include:

- EGR;
- canister purge;
- valve timing;
- inlet manifold length;
- closed loop lambda control.

It is not possible for an engine to operate at its best volumetric efficiency with fixed manifolds. This is because the length of the inlet tract determines the velocity of the intake air and in particular the propagation of the pressure waves set up by the pumping action of the cylinders. These standing waves can be used to improve the ram effect of the charge as it enters the cylinder but only if they coincide with the opening of the inlet valves. The length of the inlet tract has an effect on the frequency of these waves.

With the widespread use of twin cam engines, one cam for the inlet valves and one for the exhaust valves, it is possible to vary the valve overlap while the engine is running. Honda has a system that improves the power and torque range by opening both of the inlet valves only at higher speed.

A BMW system uses oil pressure controlled by valves to turn the cam with respect to its drive gear. This alters the cam phasing or relative position. The position of the cams is determined from a suitable map held in ROM in the control unit.

7.10.2 Closed loop lambda control

Current regulations have almost made closed loop control of air fuel mixture in conjunction with a three way catalytic converter mandatory. It is under discussion that a lambda value of one may become compulsory for all operating conditions, but this is yet to be agreed.

Lambda control is closed loop feedback system in that the signal from a lambda sensor in the exhaust can directly affect the fuel quantity injected. The lambda sensor is described in more detail in Chapter 5.

A graph to show the effect of lambda control in conjunction with a catalytic converter is shown in Figure 7.38. The principle of operation is as follows; the lambda sensor produces a voltage which is proportional to the oxygen content of the exhaust which is in turn proportional to the air fuel ratio. At the ideal setting this voltage is about 450 mV. If the voltage received by the ECU is below this value (weak mixture) the quantity of fuel injected is increased slightly. If

the signal voltage is above the threshold (rich mixture) the fuel quantity is reduced. This alteration in air fuel ratio must not be too sudden as it could cause the engine to buck. To prevent this the ECU contains an integrator, which changes the mixture over a period of time.

A delay also exists between the mixture formation in the manifold and the measurement of the exhaust gas oxygen. This is due to the engine's working cycle and the speed of the inlet mixture, the time for the exhaust to reach the sensor and the sensor's response time. This is sometimes known as dead time and can be as much as one second at idle speed but only a few hundred milliseconds at higher engine speeds.

Due to the dead time the mixture cannot be controlled to an exact value of lambda equals one. If the integrator is adjusted to allow for engine speed then it is possible to keep the mixture in the lambda window (0.97 to 1.03), which is the region in which the TWC is at its most efficient.

7.10.3 Engine management operation

The combination of ignition and injection control has several advantages. The information

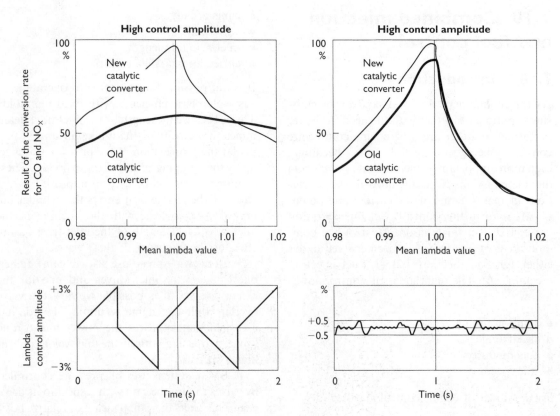

Figure 7.38 Catalytic convertor conversion rate – effect of lambda control.

received from various sensors is used for computing both fuelling and ignition requirements. Perhaps more importantly ignition and injection are closely linked. The influence they have on each other can be easily taken into account to ensure that the engine is working at its optimum, under all operating conditions. Figure 7.39 shows the layout and components of a common system.

Overall this type of system is less complicated than separate fuel and ignition systems and in many cases the ECU is able to work in an emergency mode by substituting missing information from sensors with pre-programmed values. This will allow limited but continued operation in the event of certain system failures.

The ignition system is integrated and is operated without a high tension (HT) distributor. The ignition process is controlled digitally by the ECU. The data for the ideal characteristics are stored in ROM from information gathered during both prototyping and development of the engine. The main parameters for ignition advance are engine speed and load but greater accuracy can be achieved by taking further parameters into account such as engine temperature. This provides both optimum output and close control of anti-pollution levels. Performance and pollution level control means that the actual ignition point must be in many cases a trade off between the two.

The injection system is multipoint and, as is the case for all fuel systems, the amount of fuel delivered is primarily determined by the amount of air 'drawn' into the engine. The method for measuring this data is indirect in the case of this system as a pressure sensor is used to determine the air quantity.

Electromagnetic injectors control fuel supply into the engine. The injector open period is determined by the ECU. This will obtain very accurate control of the air fuel mixture under all operating conditions of the engine. The data for this is stored in ROM in the same way as for the ignition.

The main source of reference for the ignition system is from the crankshaft position sensor.

Figure 7.39 Engine management – early Motronic

This is a magnetic inductive pick up sensor positioned next to a flywheel ring containing 58 teeth. Each tooth takes up a 6° angle of the flywheel with one 12° gap positioned 114° before top dead centre (BTDC) for number 1 cylinder. The signal produced by the flywheel sensor is essentially a sine wave with a cycle missing corresponding to the gap in the teeth of the reluctor plate. The information provided to the ECU is engine speed from the frequency of the signal and engine position from the number of pulses before or after the missed pulses.

The basic ignition advance angle is obtained from a memorised cartographic map. This is held in a ROM chip within the ECU. The parameters for this are:

- **engine rev/min** given by the flywheel sensor;
- **inlet air pressure** given by the MAP sensor.

The above two parameters (speed and load) give the basic setting but to ensure optimum advance angle the timing is corrected by:

- coolant temperature
- air temperature
- throttle butterfly position

The ignition is set to a predetermined advance during the starting phase. Figure 7.40 shows a typical advance, fuelling and other maps used by the Motronic system. This data is held in ROM. For full ignition control, the ECU has to first determine the basic timing for three different conditions.

- Under idling conditions ignition timing is often moved very quickly by the ECU in order to control idle speed. When timing is advanced engine speed will increase within certain limits.
- Full load conditions require careful control of ignition timing to prevent combustion knock. When a full load signal is sensed by the ECU (high manifold pressure) the ignition advance angle is reduced.
- Partial throttle is the main area of control and, as already stated, the basic timing is set initially by a programme as a function of engine speed and manifold pressure.

Corrections are the added according to:

- operational strategy
- knock protection
- phase correction

The ECU will also control ignition timing variation during overrun fuel cut off and reinstate-

Figure 7.40 Motronic control maps (samples)

ment and also to ensure anti-jerk control. When starting the ignition timing plan is replaced by a specific starting strategy. Phase correction is when the ECU adjusts the timing to take into account the time taken for the HT pulse to reach the spark plugs. To ensure good driveability the ECU can limit the variations between the two ignition systems to a maximum value, which varies according to engine speed and the basic injection period.

An anti jerk function operates when the basic injection period is less than 2.5 mS and the engine speed is between 720 and 3200 rev/min. This function operates to correct the programmed ignition timing in relation to the instantaneous engine speed and a set filtered speed. This is done to stabilise the engine rotational characteristics as much as possible.

In order to maintain constant energy HT the dwell period must increase in line with engine speed. So that the ignition primary current reaches its maximum at the point of ignition the ECU controls the dwell by use of another memory map, which takes battery voltage into account.

Fuel is collected from the tank by a pump either immersed in it or outside, but near the tank. The immersed type is quieter in operation and has better cooling and no internal leaks. The fuel is directed forwards to the fuel rail or manifold, via a paper filter.

Fuel pressure is maintained at about 2.5 bar above manifold pressure by a regulator mounted on the fuel rail. Excess fuel is returned to the tank. The fuel is usually picked up via a swirl pot in the tank to prevent aeration of the fuel. Each of the four inlet manifold tracts has its own injector.

The fuel pump is a high pressure type and is a two stage device: a low pressure stage created by a turbine drawing fuel from the tank; and a high pressure stage created by a gear pump delivering fuel to the filter. It is powered by a 12 V supply from the fuel pump relay, which is controlled by the ECU as a safety measure.

The rotation of the turbine draws fuel in via the inlet. The fuel passes through the turbine and enters the pump housing where it is pressurised by rotation of the pump and the reduction of the volume in the gear chambers. This pressure opens a residual valve and fuel passes to the filter. When the pump stops, pressure is maintained by this valve, which prevents the fuel returning. If, due to a faulty regulator or a blockage in the line, fuel pressure rises above 7 bar an over pressure valve will open releasing fuel back to the tank. Figure 7.41 shows this type of pump.

The fuel filter is placed between the fuel pump and the fuel rail. It is fitted one way only to ensure that the outlet screen traps any paper particles from the filter element. The filter will stop contamination down to between 8 and 10

Figure 7.41 Roller cell fuel pump

microns. Replacement varies between manufacturers but 80 000 km (50 000 miles) is often recommended.

The fuel rail, in addition to providing a uniform supply to the injectors, acts as an accumulator. Depending on the size of the fuel rail some systems also use an extra accumulator. The volume of the fuel rail is large enough to act as a pressure fluctuation damper ensuring that all injectors are supplied with fuel at a constant pressure.

Multipoint systems use one injector for each cylinder although very high performance vehicles may use two. The injectors are connected to the fuel rail by a rubber seal. The injector is an electrically operated valve manufactured to a very high precision. The injector comprises a body and needle attached to a magnetic core. When the winding in the injector housing is energised the core or armature is attracted and the valve opens compressing a return spring. The fuel is delivered in a fine spray to wait behind the closed inlet valve until the induction stroke begins. Providing the pressure across the injector remains constant the quantity of fuel admitted is related to the open period, which in turn is determined by the time the electromagnetic circuit is energised.

The purpose of the fuel pressure regulator is to maintain differential pressure across the injectors at a predetermined constant. This means the regulator must adjust the fuel pressure in response to changes in manifold pressure. It is made of two compressed cases containing a diaphragm, a spring and a valve.

The calibration of the regulator valve is determined by the spring tension. Changes in manifold pressure vary the basic setting. When the fuel pressure is sufficient to move the diaphragm, the valve opens and allows fuel to return to the tank. The decrease in pressure in the manifold, also acting on the diaphragm at say idle speed, will allow the valve to open more easily, hence maintaining a constant differential pressure between the fuel rail and the inlet manifold. This is a constant across the injectors and hence the quantity of fuel injected is determined only by the open time of the injectors. The differential pressure is maintained at about 2.5 bar.

The air supply circuit will vary considerably between manufacturers but an individual manifold from a collector housing, into which the air is fed via a simple butterfly, essentially supplies each cylinder. The air is supplied from a suitable filter. A supplementary air circuit is utilised during the warm up period after a cold start and to control idle speed.

7.11 Diagnostics – combined injection and fuel control systems

7.11.1 Testing procedure

Warning
Caution/Achtung/Attention – burning fuel can seriously damage your health!

Warning
Caution/Achtung/Attention – high voltages can seriously damage your health!

The following procedure is very generic but with a little adaptation can be applied to any system.

Refer to manufacturer's recommendations if in any doubt.

1. Check battery state of charge (at least 70%).
2. Hand and eye checks (all fuel and electrical connections secure and clean).
3. Check for spark at plug lead (if poor or no spark jump to stage 15).
4. Check fuel pressure supplied to rail (for multipoint systems it will be about 2.5 bar but check specifications). If the pressure is *not* correct jump to stage 10.
5. Is injector operation OK? Continue if *not* (suitable spray pattern or dwell reading across injector supply).
6. Check supply circuits from main relay (battery volts minimum).
7. Continuity of injector wiring (0 to 0.2 Ω and note that many injectors are connected in parallel).
8. Sensor readings (Figure 7.42) and continuity of wiring (0 to 0.2 Ω for the wiring sensors will vary with type).
9. If no fuel is being injected and all tests so far are OK (suspect ECU).
10. Fuel supply – from stage 4.
11. Supply voltage to pump (within 0.5 V battery – pump fault if supply is OK).
12. Check pump relay and circuit (note in most cases the ECU closes the relay but this may be bypassed on cranking).
13. Ensure that all connections (electrical and fuel are remade correctly).
14. Ignition section (if appropriate).
15. Check supply to ignition coil (within 0.5 V of battery).

Figure 7.42 Air flow meter under test

16. Spark from coil via known good HT lead (jumps about 10 mm, but do not try more).
17. If good spark then check HT system for tracking and open circuits. Check plug condition (leads should be a maximum resistance of about 30 k Ω/m and per lead). Stop here in this part and continue other sections.
18. If no spark or it will only jump a short distance continue with this procedure (colour of spark is not relevant).
19. Check continuity of coil windings (primary 0.5 to 3 Ω, secondary several k Ω.
20. Supply and earth to 'module' (12 V minimum supply, earth drop 0.5 V maximum).
21. Supply to pulse generator if appropriate (10 to 12 V).
22. Output of pulse generator (inductive about 1 V AC when cranking, Hall type switches 0 V to 8 V DC).
23. Continuity of LT wires (0 to 0.1 Ω).
24. Suspect ECU but only if all of the above tests are satisfactory.

7.11.2 Combined injection and fuel control fault diagnosis table

Symptom	Possible fault
Engine will not start	Engine and battery earth connections
	Fuel filter and fuel pump
	Air intake system for leaks
	Fuses/fuel pump/system relays
	Fuel injection system wiring and connections
	Coolant temperature sensor
	Auxiliary air valve/idle speed control valve
	Fuel pressure regulator and delivery rate
	ECU and connector
	Limp home function – if fitted
Engine difficult to start when cold	Engine and battery earth connections
	Fuel injection system wiring and connections
	Fuses/fuel pump/system relays
	Fuel filter and fuel pump
	Air intake system for leaks
	Coolant temperature sensor
	Auxiliary air valve/idle speed control valve
	Fuel pressure regulator and delivery rate
	ECU and connector
	Limp home function – if fitted
Engine difficult to start when warm	Engine and battery earth connections
	Fuses/fuel pump/system relays
	Fuel filter and fuel pump
	Air intake system for leaks
	Coolant temperature sensor
	Fuel injection system wiring and connections
	Air mass meter
	Fuel pressure regulator and delivery rate
	Air sensor filter
	ECU and connector
	Knock control – if fitted
Engine starts then stops	Engine and battery earth connections
	Fuel filter and fuel pump
	Air intake system for leaks
	Fuses/fuel pump/system relays
	Idle speed and CO content
	Throttle potentiometer
	Coolant temperature sensor
	Fuel injection system wiring and connections
	ECU and connector
	Limp home function – if fitted
Erratic idling speed	Engine and battery earth connections
	Air intake system for leaks
	Auxiliary air valve/idle speed control valve
	Idle speed and CO content
	Fuel injection system wiring and connections
	Coolant temperature sensor
	Knock control – if fitted
	Air mass meter
	Fuel pressure regulator and delivery rate
	ECU and connector
	Limp home function – if fitted
Incorrect idle speed	Air intake system for leaks
	Vacuum hoses for leaks
	Auxiliary air valve/idle speed control valve
	Idle speed and CO content
	Coolant temperature sensor
Misfire at idle speed	Engine and battery earth connections
	Air intake system for leaks
	Fuel injection system wiring and connections
	Coolant temperature sensor
	Fuel pressure regulator and delivery rate
	Air mass meter
	Fuses/fuel pump/system relays
Misfire at constant speed	Air flow sensor
Hesitation when accelerating	Engine and battery earth connections
	Air intake system for leaks
	Fuel injection system wiring and connections
	Vacuum hoses for leaks
	Coolant temperature sensor
	Fuel pressure regulator and delivery rate
	Air mass meter
	ECU and connector
	Limp home function – if fitted
Hesitation at constant speed	Engine and battery earth connections
	Throttle linkage
	Vacuum hoses for leaks
	Auxiliary air valve/idle speed control valve
	Fuel lines for blockage, fuel filter and fuel pump
	Injector valves

ECU and connector
Limp home function – if fitted

Hesitation on overrun	Air intake system for leaks
	Fuel injection system wiring and connections
	Coolant temperature sensor
	Throttle potentiometer
	Fuses/fuel pump/system relays
	Air sensor filter
	Injector valves
	Air mass meter
Knock during acceleration	Knock control – if fitted
	Fuel injection system wiring and connections
	Air mass meter
	ECU and connector
Poor engine response	Engine and battery earth connections
	Air intake system for leaks
	Fuel injection system wiring and connections
	Throttle linkage
	Coolant temperature sensor
	Fuel pressure regulator and delivery rate
	Air mass meter
	ECU and connector
	Limp home function – if fitted
Excessive fuel consumption	Engine and battery earth connections
	Idle speed and CO content
	Throttle potentiometer
	Throttle valve/housing/sticking/initial position
	Fuel pressure regulator and delivery rate
	Coolant temperature sensor
	Air mass meter
	Limp home function – if fitted
CO level too high	Limp home function – if fitted
	ECU and connector
	Emission control and EGR valve – if fitted
	Fuel injection system wiring and connections
	Air intake system for leaks
	Coolant temperature sensor
	Fuel pressure regulator and delivery rate
CO level too low	Engine and battery earth connections
	Air intake system for leaks
	Idle speed and CO content
	Coolant temperature sensor
	Fuel injection system wiring and connections
	Injector valves
	ECU and connector
	Limp home function – if fitted
	Air mass meter
	Fuel pressure regulator and delivery rate
Poor performance	Engine and battery earth connections
	Air intake system for leaks
	Throttle valve/housing/sticking/initial position
	Fuel injection system wiring and connections
	Coolant temperature sensor
	Fuel pressure regulator/fuel pressure and delivery rate
	Air mass meter

ECU and connector
Limp home function – if fitted

7.11.3 ECU auto-diagnostic function

Most ECUs are equipped to advise the driver of a fault in the system and to aid the repairer in detection of the problem. The detected fault is first notified to the driver by a dashboard warning light. A code giving the details is held in RAM within the ECU. The repairer as an aid to fault finding can read this fault code.

Each fault detected is memorised as a numerical code and can only be erased by a voluntary action. Often if the fault is not detected again for 50 starts of the engine the ECU erases the code automatically. Only serious faults will light the lamp but minor faults are still recorded in memory. The faults are memorised in the order of occurrence. Certain major faults will cause the ECU to switch over to an emergency mode. In this mode the ECU substitutes alternative values in place of the faulty signal. This is called a 'limp home facility'.

Faults can be read as two digit numbers from the flashing warning light by shorting the diagnostic wire to earth for more than 2.5 seconds but less than 10 seconds. Earthing this wire for more than 10 seconds will erase the fault memory as does removing the ECU constant battery supply. Earthing a wire to read fault codes should only be carried out in accordance with the manufacturer's recommendations. The same coded signals can be more easily read on many after sales service testers. On some systems it is not possible to read the fault codes without a code reader. Figure 7.43 shows the serial connector on one vehicle.

7.11.4 On board diagnostics (OBD)

Figure 7.44 shows the Bosch Motronic M5 with the OBD2 system. On-board diagnostics are becoming essential for the longer term operation of a system for it to produce a clean exhaust. Many countries now require a very comprehensive diagnosis of all components in the system which affect the exhaust. Any fault detected will be indicated to the driver by a warning light. OBD2 is intended to standardise the many varying methods used by different manufacturers. EOBD is the European version; however, it is

Figure 7.43 Serial link diagnostic connector

also thought that an extension to total vehicle diagnostics through a common interface is possible in the near future.

Digital electronics allow both sensors and actuators to be monitored. Allocating values to all operating states of the sensors and actuators does this. If a deviation from these figures is detected this is stored in memory and can be output in the workshop to assist with faultfinding.

Monitoring of the ignition system is very important as misfiring not only produces more emissions of hydrocarbons but the unburned fuel enters the catalytic converter and burns there. This can cause higher than normal temperatures and may damage the catalytic converter.

An accurate crankshaft speed sensor is used to monitor ignition and combustion in the cylinders. Misfiring alters the torque of the crankshaft for an instant, which causes irregular rotation. This allows a misfire to be recognised instantly.

A number of further sensors are required for the OBD2 functions. Another lambda sensor after the catalytic converter monitors its operation. An intake pressure sensor and a valve are needed to control the activated charcoal filter to reduce and monitor evaporative emissions from the fuel tank. A differential pressure sensor also monitors the fuel tank permeability. Besides the driver's fault lamp a considerable increase in the electronics is required in the control unit in order to operate this system. A better built in monitoring system will have a better effect in reducing vehicle emissions than tighter MOT type controls.

The diagnostic socket used by systems conforming to OBD2 standards should have the following pin configuration.

1. manufacturer's discretion
2. bus + line, SAE J1850
3. manufacturer's discretion
4. chassis ground
5. signal ground
6. manufacturer's discretion
7. K Line, ISO 9141
8. manufacturer's discretion
9. manufacturer's discretion
10. bus - line, SAE J1850
11. manufacturer's discretion
12. manufacturer's discretion
13. manufacturer's discretion
14. manufacturer's discretion
15. L line, ISO 9141
16. vehicle battery positive

It is hoped that with future standards and goals set it will be beneficial for vehicle manufacturers to begin implementation of at least the common connector in the near term. Many diagnostic system manufacturers would welcome this move.

7.11.5 Fuel pump testing

Typical high pressure fuel pump characteristics are:

- **delivery** 120 litres per hour (1 litre in 30 s) at 3 bar;
- **resistance** 0.8 Ω (static);
- **voltage** 12 V (Figure 7.45 shows the relay supply under test);
- **current** 10.5 A.

An ideal test for a fuel pump is its delivery. Using a suitable measuring receptacle, bypass

Figure 7.44 Motronic M5 with OBD II. Bosch Press Photo

Secondary air pump

Secondary air valve

Lambda sensor

Lambda sensor

Car body acceleration sensor

Phase sensor

Ignition coil

Temperature sensor

Pressure adjuster

Fuel pressure controller

Knock sensor

Engine rev/min sensor

Electric fuel pump

Injection valve

Fuel filter

Exhaust return valve

Differential pressure sensor

Intake pipe pressure sensor

Air temp. sensor

Idle running adjustor

Activated charcoal container

Tank airbleed valve

Isolating valve

Air mass flow meter

Diagnostic interface

Diagnostic lamp

Figure 7.45 Supply voltage test

the pump relay and check the quantity of fuel delivered in a set time (refer to manufacturer's specifications). A reduced amount would indicate either a fuel blockage, a reduced electrical supply to the pump or an inefficient pump.

7.11.6 Injector testing

Injectors typically have the characteristics as listed:

- **supply voltage** 12 V;
- **resistance** 16 Ω;

- **static output** 150 cc per minute at 3 bar.

Resistance checks (with the supply disconnected) are an ideal start to testing injectors. Further tests with the fuel pressurised by the pump and each injector in turn held in a suitable receptacle, include:

- **spray pattern** usually a nice cone shape with good atomisation;
- **delivery** set quantity over a set time;
- **leakage** any more than two drops a minute is considered excessive (zero is desirable).

Figure 7.46 Waveform showing supply to injector – saturated switch driver

Figure 7.47 Waveform showing supply to injector – pulse width modulated

7.11.7 Injection duration signals

Two typical injector signals as would be shown on an oscilloscope during a test procedure are shown in Figures 7.46 and 7.47. These will vary depending on the particular system but in principle are the same. The most important parts of the traces are the open time or dwell, current limiting phase and the back emf produced when the injector is switched off. The traces showing variations in the dwell are to represent how the quantity of fuel injected is varied. The difference in how the dwell is varied is due to the method of injector switching. If a simple on/off technique is used then the trace will be as shown in Figure 7.46. If current limiting is used then the trace will be slightly different, as shown by Figure 7.47.

These traces are very useful for diagnosing

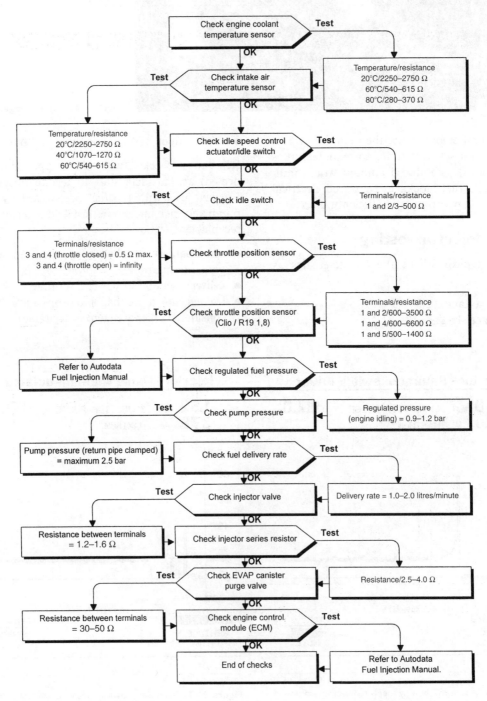

Figure 7.48 Bosch Mono-Jetronic (single point injection). Autodata

VOLKSWAGEN

Autodata

Models covered	■ Golf/Vento 1.4	1992-
	■ Golf/Vento 1.8	1992-
Engine code		ABD, AAM, ABS
Injection system		Bosch Mono-Motronic
Fault finding		Trouble shooter 5

Fuel injection system layout and components

- **A** Electronic control unit
- **B** Injector
- **C** Throttle body
- **D** Idle speed stepper motor
- **E** Throttle valve potentiometer
- **F** Fuel pump (in tank)
- **G** Inlet manifold heater
- **H** Coolant temperature sensor
- **H** Fuel pump relay (relay plate)
- **J** Diagnostic socket (below heater controls)

Figure 7.49 Fuel injection system layout and components. Autodata book example page

BMW 3 Series 1.6 316i E36 auto.   **1991–1993**

Figure 7.50 'Autologic' circuit from CD

faults. It is possible to see how the trace changes under the engine operating conditions, for example:

- does the trace width extend under acceleration?
- does the trace cut off on overrun?
- does the trace width reduce as the engine warms up?

7.12 Engine management and faultfinding information

7.12.1 Diagnostic charts

'Autodata' supply diagnostic charts specific to particular management systems. Figure 7.48 is a

Mazda 626 2.0i GX 16 valve   1993–1998

Fuel and Ignition Diagnostics

Air Mass Meter
position   in the intake tubing
condition
ignition on / meter plug disconnected
connection 5 / green / red v+
                          from   4.8   to   5.2   volts
connection 3 / black / orange v–
condition
ignition on / meter plug disconnected
connection 2 / brown / blue v+
                          from   4   to   6   volts
connection 3 / black / orange v–
condition
ignition on / meter plug connected / engine off
connection 1 / white / blue v+
                          from   0   to   0.3   volts
connection 3 / black / orange v–
condition
meter plug connected / engine running at idle
connection 1 / white / blue v+
                          from   0.4   to   1   volts
connection 3 / black / orange v–

Figure 7.51 'Autologic' testing data

typical example. Note that some boxes refer you to a further publication, an example page of which is reproduced as Figure 7.49.

7.12.2 Circuit diagrams

'Autologic' allow circuit diagrams to be printed out from their 'Workshop manual CD'. Figure 7.50 is an example of this.

7.12.3 Component testing data

Figure 7.51 is a printout from the 'Autologic' CD, showing what data is available for testing a specific component.

8

Chassis system electronics

8.1 Anti-lock brakes

8.1.1 Introduction

The reason for the development of anti-lock brakes (ABS) is very simple. Under braking conditions if one or more of the vehicle wheels locks (begins to skid) then this has a number of consequences:

- braking distance increases;
- steering control is lost;
- tyre wear is abnormal;

The obvious consequence is that an accident is far more likely to occur. The maximum deceleration of a vehicle is achieved when maximum energy conversion is taking place in the brake system. This is the conversion of kinetic energy to heat energy at the discs and brake drums. The potential for this conversion process between a tyre skidding, even on a dry road, is far less. A good driver can pump the brakes on and off to prevent locking but electronic control can achieve even better results.

ABS is becoming more common on lower price vehicles, which should be a contribution to safety. It is important to remember, however, that for normal use, the system is not intended to allow faster driving and shorter braking distances. It should be viewed as operating in an emergency only. Figure 8.1 shows how ABS can help to maintain steering control even under very heavy braking conditions.

8.1.2 Requirements of ABS

A good way of considering the operation of a complicated system is to ask: 'What must the system be able to do?' In other words, 'what are the requirements?' These can be considered for ABS under the following headings:

Fail safe system	In the event of the ABS system failing then conventional brakes must still operate to their full potential. In addition a warning must be given to the driver. This is normally in the form of a simple warning light
Manoeuvrability must be maintained	Good steering and road holding must continue when the ABS system is operating. This is arguably the key issue as being able to swerve round a hazard whilst still braking hard is often the best course of action
Immediate response must be available	Even over a short distance the system must react such as to make use of the

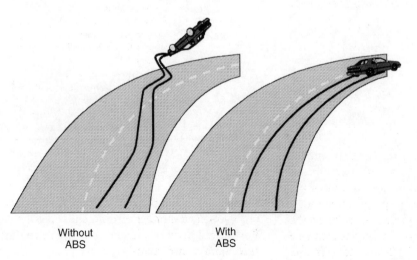

Without ABS

With ABS

Figure 8.1 Advantages of ABS

best grip on the road. The response must be appropriate whether the driver applies the brakes gently or slams them on hard

Operational influences	Normal driving and manoeuvring should produce no reaction on the brake pedal. The stability and steering must be retained under all road conditions. The system must also adapt to braking hysteresis when the brakes are applied, released and then re-applied. Even if the wheels on one side are on dry tarmac and the other side on ice, the yaw (rotation about the vertical axis of the vehicle) of the vehicle must be kept to a minimum and only increase slowly to allow the driver to compensate
Controlled wheels	In its basic form at least one wheel on each side of the vehicle should be controlled on a separate circuit. It is now general for all four wheels to be controlled on passenger vehicles
Speed range of operation	The system must operate under all speed conditions down to walking pace. At this very slow speed even when the wheels lock the vehicle will come to rest very quickly. If the wheels did not lock then in theory the vehicle would never stop!
Other operating conditions	The system must be able to recognise aquaplaning and react accordingly. It must also still operate on an uneven road surface. The one area still not perfected is braking from slow speed on snow. The ABS will actually increase stopping distance in snow but steering will be maintained. This is considered to be a suitable trade off

A number of different types of anti-lock brake systems are in use, but all try to achieve the requirements as set out above.

8.1.3 General system description

As with other systems ABS can be considered as a central control unit with a series of inputs and outputs. An ABS system is represented by the closed loop system block diagram shown in Figure 8.2. The most important of the inputs are the wheel speed sensors and the main output is some form of brake system pressure control.

The task of the control unit is to compare signals from each wheel sensor to measure the acceleration or deceleration of an individual wheel. From this data and pre programmed look up tables, brake pressure to one or more of the wheels can be regulated. Brake pressure can be reduced, held constant or allowed to increase.

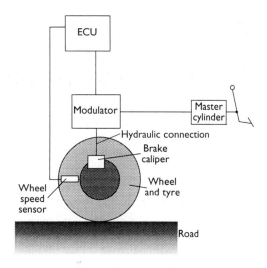

Figure 8.2 ABS block diagram

The maximum pressure is determined by the driver's pressure on the brake pedal.

From the wheel speed sensors the ECU calculates the following.

Vehicle reference speed	Determined from the combination of two diagonal wheel sensor signals. After the start of braking the ECU uses this value as its reference
Wheel acceleration or deceleration	This is a live measurement that is constantly changing
Brake slip	Although this cannot be measured directly a value can be calculated from the vehicle reference speed. This figure is then used to determine when/if ABS should take control of the brake pressure
Vehicle deceleration	During brake pressure control the ECU uses the vehicle reference speed as the starting point and decreases it in a linear manner. The rate of decrease is determined by the evaluation of all signals received from the wheel sensors Driven and non-driven wheels on the vehicle must be treated in different ways as they behave differently when braking A logical combination of wheel deceleration/acceleration and slip are used as the controlled variable. The actual strategy used for ABS control varies with the operating conditions

8.1.4 ABS components

There are a few variations between manufacturers involving a number of different components. For the majority of systems, however, there are three main components.

Wheel speed sensors

Most of these devices are simple inductance sensors and work in conjunction with a toothed wheel. They consist of a permanent magnet and a soft iron rod around which is wound a coil of wire. As the toothed wheel rotates the changes in inductance of the magnetic circuit generates a signal; the frequency and voltage of which are proportional to wheel speed. The frequency is the signal used by the ECU. The coil resistance is in the order of 800 to 1000 Ω. Coaxial cable is used to prevent interference affecting the signal. Some systems now use 'Hall effect' sensors.

Electronic control unit

The function of the ECU is to take in information from the wheel sensors and calculate the best course of action for the hydraulic modulator. The heart of a modern ECU consists of two microprocessors such as the Motorola 68HC11, which run the same programme independently of each other. This ensures greater security against any fault which could adversely affect braking performance, because the operation of each processor should be identical. If a fault is detected, the ABS disconnects itself and operates a warning light. Both processors have nonvolatile memory into which fault codes can be written for later service and diagnostic access. The ECU also has suitable input signal process-ing stages and output or driver stages for actuator control.

The ECU performs a self-test after the ignition is switched on. A failure will result in disconnection of the system. The following list forms the self test procedure:

- current supply;
- exterior and interior interfaces;
- transmission of data;
- communication between the two microprocessors;
- operation of valves and relays;
- operation of fault memory control;
- reading and writing functions of the internal memory:

All this takes about 300 mS!

Hydraulic modulator

The hydraulic modulator as shown in Figure 8.3 has three operating positions:

- **pressure build up** brake line open to the pump.
- **pressure holding** brake line closed;
- **pressure release** brake line open to the reservoir;

The valves are controlled by electrical solenoids, which have a low inductance so they react very quickly. The motor only runs when ABS is activated. Figure 8.4 shows an ABS hydraulic modulator with integrated ECU.

Figure 8.3 ABS hydraulic modulator operating positions

Figure 8.4 ABS modulator and ECU.

```
ABS wheel speed sensor
 94.3  Hz  FREQUENCY           HOLD
 1.08  V   PEAK-PEAK
 48.6  %   DUTY CYCLE ⇕
 5.40  ms  PULSE WIDTH ⇕
·1500mV
·1000
 500
  0
 -500
 -1000mV                      5ms/DIV
GENERAL SENSORS              ◄⇕►
VOLT AND    CONTINUITY       RANGE
TIME        OHM OPEN CLOSE   MOVE
```

The signal is only about 1V peak to peak because the wheel is rotating slowly

Figure 8.5 Waveform showing ABS wheel speed sensor

8.2 Diagnostics – anti-lock brakes

8.2.1 Systematic testing procedure

Note: ABS problems may require specialist attention – but don't be afraid to check the basics. An important note, however, is that some systems require special equipment to reinitialise the ECU if it has been disconnected (BMW for example).

If the reported fault is the ABS warning light staying on proceed as follows.

1. Hand and eye tests – fluid levels, connection security, etc.
2. Battery condition.
3. Fuses/supplies to ECU.
4. Operation of the normal brakes.
5. Check wheel sensor operation – clean regular sine wave output proportional to wheel speed (a scope is the best method, see Figure 8.5).
6. Check wire continuity from sensors to ECU – signal should be the same at the ECU.
7. Check continuity of wires to modulator assembly – 0 Ω.
8. Check resistance of modulator valve solenoids – equal values.
9. Check resistance of pump motor – 0.3 to 0.5 Ω (or run the motor if possible).
10. Check operation of the stop lamp switch – separate switch for ABS in some cases.
11. Reset fault memory in ECU – disconnect ABS fuse for 10 seconds.

8.2.2 Anti-lock brakes fault diagnosis table

Symptom	Possible cause
ABS not working and/or warning light on	Wheel sensor or associated wiring open circuit/high resistance
	Wheel sensor air gap incorrect
	Power supply/earth to ECU low or not present
	Connections to modulator open circuit
	No supply/earth connection to pump motor
	Modulator windings open circuit or high resistance
Warning light comes on intermittently	Wheel sensor air gap incorrect
	Wheel sensor air gap contaminated
	Loose wire connection

8.2.3 Bleeding anti-lock brakes

Special procedures may be required to bleed the hydraulic system when ABS is fitted. Refer to appropriate data for the particular vehicle. 'Autologic' data is reproduced as an example in Figure 8.6.

Mercedes Benz C220 2.2 Sport D   1993–1998

ABS diagnostics

Removal/bleeding the system

Speed sensor
- The sensors are protected by tubes which are handed left and right for the vehicle
- Remove safety harness from nearest block connector
- Remove rear road wheel for access to sensor if needed
- Remove brake caliper
- Remove sensor retaining bolt(s) and remove sensor and shims if fitted
- Lightly lubricate sensor sleeve and push in sensor as far as it will go, do not rotate wheel
- Refit sensor retaining bolt and tighten to correct torque
- Check air gap and adjust if needed
- Reconnect harness

Hydraulic control unit
- Disconnect battery
- Remove fluid regulator
- Remove relay cover if fitted
- Remove earth lead
- Remove assistance cable from the centrifugal regulator
- Fit absorbent cloth underneath hydraulic control unit
- Undo hydraulic pipe(s)
- Disconnect retaining nuts/bolts/bracket/mountings
- Remove hydraulic control unit
- Refit in reverse order
- Tighten mounting nuts/bolts to correct torque
- Tighten hydraulic pipes to correct torque
- Bleed system-see bleed instructions

Electronic control unit
- Disconnect battery
- Remove battery, if needed and tray
- Remove seat / trim or mountings for access
- Remove wiring multi-plug/block
- Remove ECU securing screws/bolts or strap
- Remove ECU
- Refit in reverse order

G or acceleration sensor
- This operation only applies to four wheel drive models
- Disconnect electrical connections
- Drill out mounting bolts
- Remove mounting bolts/nuts and remove unit
- Fit unit with arrow pointing in direction of vehicle movement

Bleeding the brakes
- Do not switch on ignition before bleeding the system as this could cause air bubbles to form in the hydraulic unit
- Bleed system without the aid of the servo, on a level surface and without the wheels suspended
- If the hydraulic control unit is fitted with bleed screw(s), bleed these first in the conventional manner. Bleed screw first then second bleed screw, (if fitted with two bleed screws)
- Cars fitted with delay valve must be bled before the remainder of the system
- To bleed delay valve release screw (below bleed screw) one turn
- Pump pedal 10 times and hold pressure
- Open bleed screw and close before pressure is completely lost
- For cars with diagonally split systems bleed each system in turn starting with right rear, left front, left rear right front
- For cars with front/rear split systems bleed rear first then front
- Fill fluid reservoir
- Check operation of warning lights
- Low speed road tests and check ABS operation

Figure 8.6 'Autologic' data re ABS bleeding, etc.

8.3   Traction control

8.3.1   Introduction

The steerability of a vehicle is not only lost when the wheels lock up on braking; the same effect arises if the wheels spin when driving off under severe acceleration. Electronic traction control has been developed as a supplement to ABS. This control system prevents the wheels from spinning when moving off or when accelerating sharply while on the move. In this way, an individual wheel which is spinning is braked in a controlled manner. If both or all of the wheels are spinning, the drive torque is reduced by means of an engine control function. Traction control has become known as ASR or TCR.

Traction control is not normally available as an independent system, but in combination with ABS. This is because many of the components required are the same as for the ABS. Traction control only requires a change in logic control in

Figure 8.7 Traction control integrated with ABS and other systems

the ECU and a few extra control elements such as control of the throttle. Figure 8.7 shows a block diagram of a traction control system. Note the links with ABS and the engine control system.

Traction control will intervene to:

● maintain stability;
● reduction of yawing moment reactions;
● provide optimum propulsion at all speeds;
● reduce driver workload.

An automatic control system can intervene in many cases more quickly and precisely than the driver of the vehicle. This allows stability to be maintained at a time when the driver might not have been able to cope with the situation. Figure 8.8 shows an ABS and traction control modulator, complete with an ECU.

8.3.2 Control functions

Control of tractive force can be by a number of methods.

Throttle control	This can be via an actuator, which can move the throttle cable or, if the vehicle employs a drive by wire accelerator, then control will be in conjunction with the engine management ECU. This throttle control will be independent of the driver's throttle pedal position. This method alone is relatively slow to control engine torque
Ignition control	If ignition is retarded the engine torque can be reduced by up to 50% in a very short space of time. The timing is adjusted by a set ramp from the ignition map value
Braking effect	If the spinning wheel is restricted by brake pressure the reduction in torque at the affected wheel is very fast. Maximum brake pressure is not used to ensure that passenger comfort is maintained

8.3.3 System operation

The description that follows is for a vehicle with an electronic accelerator (drive by wire). A

Figure 8.8 ABS and traction control modulator and ECU

simple sensor determines the position of the accelerator and, taking into account other variables such as engine temperature and speed for example, the throttle is set at the optimum position by a servomotor. When accelerating the increase in engine torque leads to an increase in driving torque at the wheels. To achieve optimum acceleration the maximum possible driving torque must be transferred to the road. If driving torque exceeds that which can be transferred then wheel slip will occur on at least at one wheel. The result of this is that the vehicle becomes unstable.

When wheel spin is detected the throttle position and ignition timing are adjusted but the best results are gained when the brakes are applied to the spinning wheel. This not only prevents the wheel from spinning but acts to provide a limited slip differential action. This is particularly good when on a road with varying braking force coefficients. When the brakes are applied a valve in the hydraulic modulator assembly moves over to allow traction control operation. This allows pressure from the pump to be applied to the brakes on the offending wheel. The valves, in the same way as with ABS, can provide pressure buildup, pressure hold and pressure reduction. This all takes place without the driver touching the brake pedal. The summary of this is that the braking force must be applied to the slipping wheel so as to equalise the combined braking coefficient for each driving wheel.

8.4 Diagnostics – traction control

8.4.1 Systematic testing

Note: Traction control (TCR or TCS or ASC) is usually linked with the ABS and problems may require specialist attention – but don't be afraid to check the basics. As with ABS, note that some systems require special equipment to reinitialise the ECU if it has been disconnected (BMW for example).

If the reported fault is the traction control system not working proceed as follows.

1. Hand and eye tests – fluid levels, connection security such as in Figure 8.9, etc.
2. Battery condition.
3. Check fault codes if possible (Figure 8.10).
4. Fuses/supplies to ECU.

Figure 8.9 Check security of all connectors such as the one shown here

5. Traction control switch operation – 0 V drop across or 0 Ω.
6. Normal operation of the throttle.
7. Check wheel sensor operation (same sensors as for ABS) – clean regular sine wave output proportional to wheel speed (a scope is the best method).
8. Check wire continuity from sensors to ECU – signal should be the same at the ECU.
9. Check continuity of wires to modulator assembly – 0 Ω.

8.4.2 Traction control fault diagnosis table

Symptom	Possible cause
Traction control inoperative	Wheel sensor or associated wiring open circuit/high resistance
	Wheel sensor air gap incorrect
	Power supply/earth to ECU low or not present
	Switch open circuit
	ABS system fault
	Throttle actuator inoperative or open circuit connections
	Communication link between ECUs open circuit
	ECU needs to be initialised

Figure 8.10 Diagnostic system tester

8.5 Cruise control

8.5.1 Introduction

Cruise control is the ideal example of a closed loop control system as shown in Figure 8.11. The purpose of cruise control is to allow the driver to set the vehicle speed and let the system maintain it automatically. The system reacts to the measured speed of the vehicle and adjusts the throttle accordingly. The reaction time is important so that the vehicle's speed does not feel as if it is surging up and down.

Other facilities are included such as allowing the speed to be gradually increased or decreased at the touch of a button. Most systems also remember the last set speed and will resume this again at the touch of a button.

To summarise and to add further refinements, the following is the list of functional requirements for a good cruise control system:

- hold the vehicle speed at the selected value;
- hold the speed with minimum surging;
- allow the vehicle to change speed;
- relinquish control immediately the brakes are applied;
- store the last set speed;
- contain built in safety features.

8.5.2 System description

The main switch switches on the cruise control; this in turn is ignition controlled. Most systems do not retain the speed setting in memory when the main switch has been turned off. Operating the 'set' switch programs the memory but this will normally work only if conditions similar to the following are met:

- vehicle speed is greater than 40 km/h;
- vehicle speed is less than 12 km/h;
- change of speed is less than 8 km/h/s;
- automatics must be in 'drive';
- brakes or clutch are not being operated;
- engine speed is stable.

Once the system is set, the speed is maintained to within about 3–4 km/h until it is deactivated by pressing the brake or clutch pedal, pressing the 'resume' switch or turning off the main control

Figure 8.11 Cruise control – closed control loop

switch. The last 'set' speed is retained in memory except when the main switch is turned off.

If the cruise control system is required again then either the 'set' button will hold the vehicle at its current speed or the 'resume' button will accelerate the vehicle to the previous 'set' speed. When cruising at a set speed, the driver can press and hold the 'set' button to accelerate the vehicle until the desired speed is reached when the button is released. If the driver accelerates from the set speed, to overtake for example, then, when the throttle is released, the vehicle will slow down until it reaches the last set position.

8.5.3 Components

The main components of a typical cruise control system are as follows.

Actuator	A number of methods are used to control the throttle position. Vehicles fitted with drive by wire systems allow the cruise control to operate the same actuator. A motor can be used to control the throttle cable or in many cases a vacuum operated diaphragm is used which is controlled by three simple valves. This technique is shown in Figure 8.12. When the speed needs to be increased valve 'x' is opened allowing low pressure from the inlet manifold to one side of the diaphragm. The atmospheric pressure on the other side will move the diaphragm and hence the throttle. To move the other way valve 'x' is closed and valve 'y' is opened allowing atmospheric pressure to enter the chamber. The spring moves the diaphragm back. If both valves are closed then the throttle position is held. Valve 'x' is normally closed and valve 'y' normally open; thus in the event of electrical failure cruise will not remain engaged and the
	manifold vacuum will not be disturbed. Valve 'z' provides extra safety and is controlled by the brake and clutch pedals
Main switch and warning lamp	This is a simple on/off switch located in easy reach of the driver on the dashboard. The warning lamp can be part of this switch or part of the main instrument display as long as it is in the driver's field of vision
'Set' and 'Resume' switches	These are fitted either on the steering wheel or on a stalk from the steering column. When part of the steering wheel slip rings are needed to transfer the connection. The 'set' button programmes the speed into memory and can also be used to increase the vehicle and memory speed. The 'resume' button allows the vehicle to reach its last set speed or to temporarily deactivates the control
Brake switch	This switch is very important, as braking would be dangerous if the cruise control system was trying to maintain the vehicle speed. This switch is normally of superior quality and is fitted in place or as a supplement to the brake light switch activated by the brake pedal. Adjustment of this switch is important
Clutch or automatic gearbox switch	The clutch switch is fitted in a similar manner to the brake switch. It deactivates the cruise system to prevent the engine speed increasing if the clutch is pressed. The automatic gearbox switch will only allow the cruise to be engaged when it is in the 'drive' position. This is again to prevent the engine overspeeding if the cruise tried to accelerate to a high road speed with the gear selector in position '1' or '2'. The gearbox will still change gear if accelerating back up to a set speed as long as it 'knows' top gear is available
Speed sensor	This will often be the same sensor that is used for the speedometer. If not several types are available, the most common producing a pulsed signal the frequency of which is proportional to the vehicle speed
Headway sensor (Figure 8.13)	Only on the very latest and top of the range systems, this device uses radar or light to sense the distance from the vehicle in front

To vent
To inlet manifold via check valve
Vent valve y
Safety valve z
Control windings
Vacuum valve x
Diaphragm
Throttle linkage

Figure 8.12 Vacuum operated cruise control actuator

8.6 Diagnostics – cruise control

8.6.1 Systematic testing

If the cruise control system will not operate then considering the ECU as a black box, the following procedure should be followed.

Figure 8.13 Headway sensor and control electronics

1. Hand and eye checks (don't forget the simplest things – as in Figure 8.14!).
2. Battery condition.
3. Disconnect ECU plug, refer to the circuit diagram or trace each circuit in turn.
4. Check the ignition supply voltage to the ECU – battery voltage.
5. Check the earth wire – 0 Ω to a known good earth.
6. Measure the signal/resistance of each input in turn (sensor or switch).
7. If incorrect then check *at* the sensor or switch.
8. Measure the resistance of the actuator windings (all types have windings of some kind).
9. Check actuator operation by supplying direct feed if appropriate.
10. The system can be 'road tested' on a secure wheel-free ramp as long as the wheels are not hanging too low.

8.6.2 Cruise control fault diagnosis table

Symptom	Possible fault
Cruise control will not set	Brake switch sticking on Safety valve/circuit fault Diaphragm holed Actuating motor open circuit or seized Steering wheel slip ring open circuit Supply/earth/fuse open circuit General wiring fault
Surging or uneven speed	Actuator cable out of adjustment ECU fault Engine/engine management fault

8.7 Air bags and belt tensioners

8.7.1 Introduction

Seat belt, seat belt tensioner and an air bag are at present the most effective restraint system in the event of a serious accident. At speeds in excess of 40 km/h the seat belt alone is no longer adequate. The method becoming most popular for an air bag system is that of building most of the required components into one unit. This reduces the amount of wiring and connections, thus improving reliability. An important aspect is that some form of system monitoring must be built in, as the operation cannot be tested – it only ever works once.

The sequence of events in the case of a

Figure 8.14 Battery earth connection – so easy to forget the obvious

frontal impact at about 35 km/h, as shown in Figure 8.15, is as follows.

1. Driver in normal seating position prior to impact.
2. About 15 ms after the impact the vehicle is strongly decelerated and the threshold for triggering the air bag is reached. The igniter ignites the fuel tablets in the inflater.
3. After about 30 ms the air bag unfolds and the driver will have moved forwards as the vehicle's crumple zones collapse. The seat belt will have locked or been tensioned depending on the system.
4. At 40 ms after impact the air bag will be fully inflated and the driver's momentum will be absorbed by the air bag.
5. About 120 ms after impact the driver will be moved back into the seat and the air bag will have almost deflated through the side vents allowing driver visibility.

Passenger air bag events are similar to the above description. A number of arrangements are used with the mounting of all components in the steering wheel centre becoming the most popular. None-the-less the basic principle of operation is the same.

8.7.2 Components and circuit

The main components of a basic air bag system are as follows:

- driver and passenger air bags;
- warning light;
- passenger seat switches;
- pyrotechnic inflater;
- igniter;
- crash sensor(s);
- ECU.

The air bag is made of a nylon fabric with a coating on the inside. Prior to inflation the air bag is folded up under suitable padding which has specially designed break lines built in. Holes are provided in the side of the air bag to allow rapid deflation after deployment. The driver's air has a volume of about 60 litres and the passenger air bag about 160 litres. Figure 8.16 shows a steering wheel with an air bag fitted in the centre.

A warning light is used as part of the system monitoring circuit. This gives an indication of a potential malfunction and is an important part of the circuit. Some manufacturers use two bulbs for added reliability.

Consideration is being given to the use of a seat switch on the passenger side to prevent deployment when not occupied. This may be more appropriate to side-impact air bags.

Figure 8.15 Air bag deployment

The pyrotechnic inflater and the igniter can be considered together. The inflater in the case of the driver is located in the centre of the steering wheel. It contains a number of fuel tablets in a combustion chamber. The igniter consists of charged capacitors, which produce the ignition spark. The fuel tablets burn very rapidly and produce a given quantity of nitrogen gas at a given pressure. This gas is forced into the air bag through a filter and the bag inflates breaking through the padding in the wheel centre. After deployment a small amount of sodium hydroxide will be present in the air bag and vehicle interior. Personal protection equipment must be used when removing the old system and cleaning the vehicle interior.

The crash sensor can take a number of forms; these can be described as mechanical or electronic. The mechanical system works by a spring holding a roller in a set position until an impact above a predetermined limit provides enough force to overcome the spring and the roller moves, triggering a micro switch. The switch is normally open with a resistor in parallel to allow the system to be monitored. Two switches similar to this may be used to ensure that the bag is deployed only in the case of sufficient frontal impact. Note the air bag is not deployed in the event of a roll over. The other main type of crash sensor can be described as an accelerometer. This will sense deceleration, which is negative acceleration.

The final component to be considered is the ECU or diagnostic control unit. When a mechanical type crash sensor is used, in theory no electronic unit would be required. A simple circuit could be used to deploy the air bag when the sensor switch operated. However, it is the system monitoring or diagnostic part of the ECU which is most important. If a failure is detected in any part of the circuit then the warning light will be operated. Up to five or more faults can be stored in the ECU memory, which can be accessed by blink code or serial fault readers. Conventional testing of the system with a multimeter and jump wires is not to be recommended as it might cause the air bag to deploy!

A block diagram of an air bag circuit is shown in Figure 8.17. Note the 'safing' circuit, which is a crash sensor that prevents deployment in the event of a faulty main sensor. A digital based system using electronic sensors has about 10 ms at a vehicle speed of 50 km/h to decide if the supplementary restraint systems (SRS) should be activated. In this time about 10 000 computing operations are necessary. Data for the development of these algorithms is based on computer simulations but digital systems can also remember the events during a crash allowing real data to be collected.

8.7.3 Seat belt tensioners

Taking the 'slack' out of a seat belt in the event of an impact is a good contribution to vehicle passenger safety. The decision to take this action is the same as for the air bag. The two main types are:

- spring tension;
- pyrotechnic.

The mechanism used by one type of seat belt tensioner is shown in Figure 8.18. When the explosive charge is fired, the cable pulls a lever on the seat belt reel, which in turn tightens the belt. The unit must be replaced once deployed. This feature is sometimes described as anti-submarining. Figure 8.19 shows a full seat belt, air bag system and other safety features employed by Renault.

Figure 8.16 Supplementary restraint system (SRS) – an air bag is incorporated in this steering wheel

Figure 8.17 Air bag block diagram showing the 'safing circuit'

Figure 8.18 Seat belt tensioners

8.8 Diagnostics – air bags and belt tensioners

8.8.1 Systematic testing

Warning
Careless or incorrect diagnostic work could deploy the air bag causing serious injury. Leave well alone if in any doubt.

The only reported fault for air bags should be that the warning light is staying on! If an air bag has been deployed then all the major components should be replaced. Some basic tests that can be carried out are as follows.

1. Hand and eye checks.
2. Disconnect the SRS fuse or the battery earth lead – prevent risk of accidental deployment of air bags or belt tensioners (wait for at least 10 minutes to allow the igniter capacitors to discharge).
3. Check general security of connections.
4. Pay particular attention to slip ring connections on the steering wheel if appropriate.
5. Refit fuse, switch ignition on – note warning light operation.
6. Access fault codes with appropriate scanner.

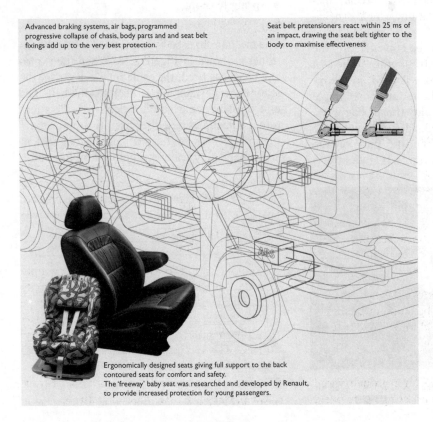

Advanced braking systems, air bags, programmed progressive collapse of chasis, body parts and and seat belt fixings add up to the very best protection.

Seat belt pretensioners react within 25 ms of an impact, drawing the seat belt tighter to the body to maximise effectiveness

Ergonomically designed seats giving full support to the back contoured seats for comfort and safety.
The 'freeway' baby seat was researched and developed by Renault, to provide increased protection for young passengers.

Figure 8.19 Some of the safety features employed by Renault

8.8.2 Air bags and belt tensioners fault diagnosis table

Symptom	Possible cause
Warning light on	Wiring fault
	Fuse blown on removed
	ECU fault
	Crash sensor fault
	Igniter fault

8.8.3 Deactivation and activation procedures

Air bag simulators are required to carry out diagnosis and testing of the air bag system. For the frontal air bag(s) this tool is a 2.5 Ω resistor, used to simulate an air bag module connection to the system. Do not short-circuit the air bag module connections with a jumper wire. If a jumper wire is used to short-circuit the air bag module connections, a lamp fault code will be displayed and a diagnostic trouble code logged by the air bag control module.

Ford recommend the following procedure for the air bag system fitted to the Ford Focus (Figure 8.20).

Deactivation procedure

1. Disconnect the battery ground cable.
2. Wait one minute for the backup power supply in the Air Bag Control Module to deplete its stored energy.

Figure 8.20 Ford Focus

3. Remove the driver air bag module from the vehicle.
4. Connect the air bag simulator to the sub-harness in place of the driver air bag module at the top of the steering column.
5. Remove the passenger air bag module.
6. Connect the air bag simulator to the harness in place of the passenger air bag module.
7. Disconnect the driver five-way under seat connector.
8. Connect the air bag simulator to driver five-way under seat floor harness in place of the seat belt pretensioner and side air bag.
9. Disconnect the passenger five-way under seat connector.
10. Connect the air bag simulator to the passenger five-way under seat floor harness in place of the seat belt pretensioner and side air bag.
11. Reconnect the battery ground cable.

Reactivation procedure

1. Disconnect the battery ground cable.
2. Wait one minute for the backup power supply in the Air Bag Control Module to deplete its stored energy.
3. Remove the driver air bag simulator from the sub-harness at the top of the steering column.
4. Reconnect and install the driver air bag module.
5. Remove the passenger air bag simulator from the passenger air bag module harness.

6. Reconnect and install the passenger air bag module.
7. Remove the air bag simulator from the driver five-way under seat connector.
8. Reconnect the driver five-way under seat connector.
9. Remove the air bag simulator from the passenger five-way under seat connector.
10. Reconnect the passenger five-way under seat connector.
11. Reconnect the battery ground cable.
12. Prove out the system, repeat the self test and clear the fault codes.

Note: This section is included as general guidance; however, do not assume it is relevant to all vehicles.

9

Conclusions and the World Wide Web

9.1 Introduction

9.1.1 Summary

If like me you continue to be fascinated by the technology of the automobile, then you will also be interested in the future technology. The following graph (Figure 9.1) is an illustration of how technology has developed and how it will perhaps continue to do so. To keep up to date you will have to keep learning. But remember the way in which you apply your knowledge is just as important at the knowledge itself.

9.1.2 The future of diagnostics

But what will the pace of technology change mean for the diagnostic technician? The follow-ing graph (Figure 9.2) illustrates the developments of diagnostic test equipment. On-board diagnostics will continue to develop but there will always be a need for the highly skilled diagnostic technician. Due to the cost and complexity of some of the equipment even today, only the large main dealers can afford it. If you continue to keep up to date with the technology, learn how to use good quality but basic test equipment and apply the diagnostic processes highlighted in this book. You will not be short of work!

Figure 9.1 Technological development

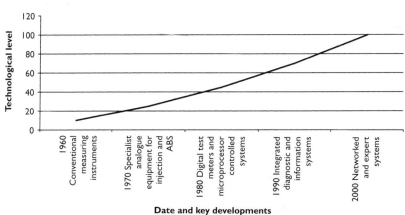

Figure 9.2 Diagnostic equipment development

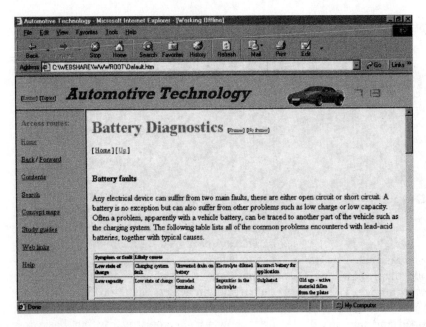

Figure 9.3 Screen shot from the 'Automotive Technology' web site

9.2 Useful web contacts

9.2.1 Introduction

If you have access to a computer and modem then you are no doubt already interested in the Internet and the World Wide Web (WWW). In this short section I have highlighted some of the resources available to you on the net or on disk.

All the major vehicle manufacturers have web pages as do most of the parts suppliers. There are user groups, forums for discussion and many other sources of information, or let's admit it – just good fun. So go ahead and surf the net. I would be most pleased to meet you at my home site where you will find up to date information about my books, new technologies and links to just about everywhere. Just point your browser to:

http://www.automotive-technology.co.uk

Figure 9.3 shows a page from the site at the above address. All the links to sites in the next section can be accessed from here as well as many more. It will also be kept up to date as I find more interesting places to visit. Please let me know if you have any suggestions for useful links – I am mostly interested in sites that provide good technical information, not just advertising material!

tom_denton@compuserve.com

9.2.2 Web site addresses

Here are some site addresses that I have found useful and interesting. I can't guarantee that the addresses will stay current so check my web site for updates.

Vehicle manufacturers

http://www.alfaromeo.com/	Alfa Romeo
http://www.audi.com/	Audi
http://www.bmw.com/	BMW
http://www.citroen.com/eng/	Citroen
http://www.dm.co.kr/	Daewoo
http://www.ferrari.it/	Ferrari
http://www.fiat.com/	Fiat
http://www.ford.com/	Ford
http://www.honda.com/	Honda
http://www.jaguarcars.com/	Jaguar
http://www.lamborghini.com/	Lamborghini

http://www.landrover.com/	Landrover
http://www.lotuscars.com/	Lotus
http://www.mazda.com/	Mazda
http://www.mercedes-benz.com/	Mercedes Benz
http://www.mitsubishi-motors.co.jp/	Mitsubishi
http://www.nissan.com/	Nissan
http://www.peugeot.com/	Peugeot
http://www.porsche.com/	Porsche
http://www.renault.com/	Renault
http://www.rover.co.uk/	Rover Cars
http://www.seat.com/	Seat
http://www.subaru.com/	Subaru
http://www.suzuki.com/	Suzuki
http://www.toyota.com/	Toyota
http://www.vauxhall.co.uk/	Vauxhall
http://www.volkswagen.com	Volkswagen
http://www.volvo.com/	Volvo

Automotive and engineering societies

http://www.iee.org.uk/	Institute of Electrical Engineers (IEE)
http://www.imeche.org.uk/	Institute of Mechanical Engineers (ImechE)
http://www.sae.org/	Society of Automotive Engineers (SAE)

Publishers and media

http://www.arnoldpublishers.co.uk/	Arnold Publishers
http://www.autodata.ltd.uk/autoweb4/english/	Autodata Reference Books
http://www.autologicuk.com	Autologic Reference and CDs
http://www.macmillan-press.co.uk/	Macmillan Press
http://www.sae.org/automag/	Automotive International Magazine

Equipment suppliers

http://www.fluke.com/	Fluke instruments
http://www.snapon.com/	Snap-on Tools
http://www.genrad.com/	Diagnostics and Equipment
http://www.golucas.com/	LucasVarity

9.2.3 Searching the WWW

My favourite search engine is 'Yahoo!' at *http://www.yahoo.com/*. This is because a lot of work has already been done for you and it is easy to use. The following is a short extract from guidance given by Yahoo! on using their search site:

> Yahoo!, like the Web itself, is too large to be explored entirely link by link. However, with over half a million sites divided into more than 25 000 categories, Yahoo! is both browseable and searchable. Use these two features and you will almost always find something to match your interests.
>
> You can browse Yahoo! by simply clicking on the various categories listed on each page. Search Yahoo! by entering a word (or a few words) into the search box that appears on every page in the directory. Combine the two strategies and you can 'browse and then search' or 'search and then browse.' Of course, a key question remains . . .
>
> If you put quotation marks around your search terms, you'll get search results that only contain that exact phrasing. If you leave off the quotation marks, you'll get results that contain any of the words that you typed in.
>
> If you know exactly what you're looking for or even have a general idea, try using Yahoo! search. Specify a keyword or set of keywords, and Yahoo! will search its entire database to find listings that match the keywords you provide.

After you have specified keyword(s) inside the query box and clicked on the search button, Yahoo will search through the five areas of its database for keyword matches. The five areas are:

- Yahoo! Categories;
- Yahoo! Web Sites;
- Web Pages;
- News Stories;
- Yahoo! Net Events.

The first page returned to you will be a list of matching Yahoo Categories followed by a list of matching Yahoo Sites. If no matching Yahoo Categories and Sites are found, Yahoo will automatically perform a Web-wide, full-text document search using the 'Inktomi' search engine.

You are able to navigate through matches from Yahoo! Categories and Yahoo! Sites, Web Sites, Yahoo! News and Yahoo! Net Events by clicking on the links in the bar at the top and bottom of the page.

9.3 Programs and information to download

9.3.1 Introduction

Many web sites will have information you can download. This is in addition to the information on the normal web pages. In some cases the information is in the form of a '.pdf' (portable document format) file. To read this you will need

'Acrobat Reader', which is available free from http://www.adobe.com/acrobat/ or on many 'magazine' CDs.

9.3.2 Automotive technology – electronics

From the 'Help File':

Click on the key button in the toolbar to open the 'Controls' window if it is not already visible. Now click on the key button in this window to start the engine. You can also right click the screen and choose to start the engine from there. Don't forget to check that the car is not in gear – or else it won't start!

Next choose from the 'Run' menu the electronic system you would like to operate or work with. I suggest 'Engine Management' is the best place to start.

In common with all of the other simulation windows you will use, you can set or control the operating inputs to the system. For engine management control, these are engine speed, engine load, temperature and so on. The system will react and control the outputs in just the same way as a real vehicle. Be warned the unregistered version runs out of fuel!

Available as shareware; Figure 9.4 is a screenshot from the program. An automotive diagnostics program is also available to download.

Figure 9.4 Screen shot from the simulation program

Index